Continuum Studie
Research in Educa

Series editor: Richard Anarews

Teaching and Learning Science

Related titles:

Richard Andrews: *Teaching and Learning English*
Martin Blocksidge (ed.): *Teaching Literature*
Manjula Datta: *Bilinguality and Literacy*
John Eggleston (ed.): *Teaching and Learning Design and Technology*
Andrew Goodwyn (ed.): *English in the Digital Age*
Helen Nicholson (ed.): *Teaching Drama 11–18*

Teaching and Learning Science

Judith Bennett

continuum
LONDON • NEW YORK

Continuum

The Tower Building   15 East 26th Street
11 York Road   New York
London, SE1 7NX   NY 10010

www.continuumbooks.com

First published 2003
Reprinted 2005

British Library Cataloguing-in-Publication Data
A catalogue record for this book is available from the British Library.

ISBN   0-8264-6527-7 (hardback)
       0-8264-7745-3 (paperback)

Typeset by YHT Ltd, London
Printed and bound in Great Britain by Antony Rowe Ltd, Chippenham, Wiltshire

Contents

Acknowledgements

First, I would like to thank my friends and colleagues for their encouragement and support, and also for their comments on draft chapters. In particular, I would like to thank Richard Andrews, Bob Campbell, John Holman, Declan Kennedy, Robin Millar, Marissa Rollnick and David Waddington.

Second, I would like to thank Anthony Haynes and his colleagues at Continuum for their support and advice.

Third, I would like to thank the teachers, most of whom are former students of the MA in Science Education programme at the University of York, whose work is included in this book as examples of small-scale studies.

Finally, I would like to thank Mike Bennett, who gave me helpful comments from the perspective of someone outside the field of science education and whose eagle eye proved invaluable at the proof-reading stage.

I would like to dedicate this book to the two people to whom I owe most for my interest in science education: my mother, Morfydd, a teacher, and my father, David, a research chemist.

Series Editor's Introduction

The function and role of the series

The need for the series

Internationally, the gap between research, policy and practice in public life has become a matter of concern. When professional practice – in nursing, education, local governance and other fields – is uninformed by research, it tends to reinvent itself in the light of a range of (often conflicting) principles. Research uninformed by practical considerations tends to be ignored by practitioners, however good it is academically. Similarly, the axis between policy and research needs to be a working one if each is to inform the other. Research is important to the professions, just as it is in industry and the economy: we have seen in the last fifteen years especially that companies which do not invest in research tend to become service agents for those companies that are at the cutting edge of practice. The new work order (see Gee *et al.*, 1996) makes research a necessity.

There is increasing interest in teaching as an evidence-based profession, though it is not always clear what an 'evidence-based profession' is. In the mid-1990s, in England, the Teacher Training Agency (TTA) was promoting a close link between research and the application of research in practice – for example, in the classroom. It also laid particular emphasis on teachers as researchers, seeming at the time to exclude university-based researchers from the picture. It quickly became evident, however, that research-based teaching was generally impracticable and often a diversion from the core business of teaching and learning. Furthermore, there was policy confusion as to whether the main thrust of the initiative was to encourage teachers to be researchers, or to encourage teachers to use research to improve their performance in the classroom. It is the second of these aims that gained in momentum during the late 1990s and the first part of the present century.

Teachers as users of research brought about a subtly different term: 'evidence-based practice' in an evidence-based profession. The analogy with developments in nursing education and practice were clear. David Hargreaves made the analogy in a keynote TTA lecture, speculating as to why the teaching profession was not more like the nursing and medical professions in its use of research. The analogy was inexact, but the message was clear enough: let researchers undertake education research, and let teachers apply it. With scarce resources and an increasing influence from the Department for Education and Employment (DfEE) in the formation and implementation of teachers' professional development following the 1988 paper *Teachers: Meeting the Challenge of Change*, the TTA's own position on evidence-based practice was limited and more focused. In 1999–2000 the agency initiated a series of conferences entitled 'Challenging teachers' thinking about research and evidence-based practice'. The DfEE's own paper *Professional Development* (2000) sets out for discussion the place of research within teachers' professional development, including the announcement of best practice research scholarships for serving teachers:

> We are keen to support teachers using and carrying out research, which is a valuable way to build knowledge and understanding about raising standards of teaching and learning. Research can have advantages for the individual teacher; for their school; and for other schools in sharing lessons learned. We believe that research can be a particularly valuable activity for experienced teachers. (p. 25)

Part of the function of the present series is to provide ready access to the evidence base for busy teachers, teacher-researchers, parents and governors in order to help them improve teaching which, in turn, will improve learning and raise standards. But it is worth discussing here what the evidence base is for teaching a school subject, and how it might be applied to the acts of teaching and learning.

Evidence is inert. It needs not so much application as *transformation* in order to make learning happen in the classroom. That transformation requires the teacher to weigh up the available evidence, devise pedagogical approaches to be included in an overall teaching programme for a year, term, week or unit of work and then to put those approaches into action. Evidence can inform both the planning and the actual delivery. Imagine yourself in the middle of teaching a class about differences between spoken standard English and a number of dialects. You can draw on the evidence to help you plan and teach the lesson, but you will also need to depend on the evidence in order to improvise, adapt and meet particular learning needs *during* the course of the lesson.

The gaps between policy, research and practice

In February 2000, in a possibly unprecedented gesture, the British Secretary of State for Education addressed a community of education researchers about the importance of its research for the development of government policy (DfEE, 2000). The basic message was that research, policy and practice needed to be in closer relation to each other in order to maximize the benefits of each. During the 1980s and 1990s, the gap between research and policy was chasm-like. Politicians and other policy-makers tended to choose research evidence to support their own prejudices about education policy. A clear case was the affirmation of the value of homework by successive governments in the face of research which suggested homework had little or no effect on the performance of pupils. Similarly, the gap between research and practice was often unbridged. One problem facing the education sector as a whole is that research moves to a different rhythm from policy or practice. Longitudinal research may take ten or fifteen years to gestate; policy moves in four-year cycles, according to governments and elections; practice is often interested in a short-term fix.

The creation of a National Education Research Forum in late 1999 goes some way to informing policy with research. Its function is very much to inform policy rather than to inform practice, and its remit is much larger than a focus on schooling. But its creation, along with the emergence of series such as the present one and websites which aim to mediate between research and practice can only improve the relationship between research, policy and practice. A virtuous triangle is slowly taking shape.[1]

The focus on subjects, at early years, primary/elementary and secondary/high school levels

The series is built around subjects. At the time of going to press, there are titles on English, Mathematics, Science, Design and Technology, Modern Foreign Languages and Economics and Business Studies either published or in the pipeline. Further titles will be added in due course. All but one of these subjects applies to primary/ elementary and secondary/high school levels; one of the aims of the series is to ensure that research in the teaching and learning of school subjects is not confined by phase, but is applicable from the early years through to the end of compulsory education.

The focus on subjects is a pragmatic one. Although there is considerable pressure to move away from an essentially nineteenth-century conception of the curriculum as divided into disciplines and subjects, the current National Curriculum in England and Wales, and curricula elsewhere in the world, are still largely designed on the basis of subjects. The research we have drawn on in the making of the present series therefore derives from the core discipline, the school subject and the teaching of the school subject in each case. Where other research is contributory to practice, we have not stopped at including it (for example the work of the social psychologist Vygotsky in relation to the teaching of English) so that each book is an interpretation by the author(s) of the significance of research to teaching and learning within the subject. With some subjects, the research literature is vast and the authors have made what they take to be appropriate selections for the busy teacher or parent; with other subjects, there is less material to draw on and the tendency has been to use what research there is, often carried out by the author or authors themselves.

We take it that research into the development of learning in a subject at primary school level will be of interest to secondary school teachers, and vice-versa. The books will also provide a bridge between phases of education, seeing the development of learning as a continuous activity.

The international range

The series is international in scope. It aims not only to draw on research undertaken in a range of countries across the world in order to get at the best evidence possible; it will also apply to different systems across the world because of its attempt to get at the bedrock of good teaching and learning. References to particular education systems are kept to a minimum, and are only used when it is necessary to illuminate the context of the research. Where possible, comparative research is referred to.

Such an international perspective is important for a number of reasons: first, because research is sometimes carried out internationally; second, because globalization in learning is raising questions about the basis of new approaches to learning; third, because different perspectives can enhance the overall sense of what works best in different contexts. The series is committed to such diversity, both in drawing on research across the world and in serving the needs of learners and teachers across the world.

The time frame for the research

In general, the series looks at research from the 1960s to the present. Some of the most significant research in some subjects was undertaken in the 1960s. In the 1990s, the advent of the Internet and the World Wide Web has meant that the research toolkit has been increased. It is now possible to undertake literature reviews online and via resources in formats such as CD-ROM, as well as via the conventional print formats of journals and books. The books cannot claim to be comprehensive; at the same time each is an attempt to represent the best of research in particular fields for the illumination of teaching and learning.

The nature of applied research in education

Applied research, as a term, needs some explication. It can mean both research into the application of 'blue-skies' research, theory or ideas in the real-world contexts of the classroom or other site of education and learning; and it can also mean research that arises from such contexts. It sometimes includes action research because of the close connection to real-world contexts. It is distinctly different from desk-based research, 'blue-skies' research or research into the history, policy or socio-economics of education as a discipline. There is further exploration of different kinds of research in the next section. Here I want to set out why applied research cannot be fully disconnected from other kinds of research, and to demonstrate the unity and inter-connectedness of research approaches in education.

Research has to be 'academic' in the sense of the *disinterested* pursuit of truth (to the extent that truth is an absolute). If the research does not attempt to be as objective as it can be (within the paradigm within which it adopts – which may be a subjective one), it cannot be taken seriously.

Second, research – like practice – has to be informed by theory. There is little point in undertaking action research or empirical research without a clear sense of its underlying assumptions and ideologies. Theory, too, needs to be examined to ensure that it supports or challenges practice and convention. The crucial point in the present response is that a research cycle may require full treatment of each of the following phases of research:

- definition of the problem or research question; or positing of a hypothesis;
- review of the theory underpinning the field or fields in which the empirical research is to be undertaken;
- devising of an appropriate methodology to solve the problem, answer the research question or test the hypothesis;
- empirical work with qualitative and/or quantitative outcomes;
- analysis and discussion of results;
- conclusion; and implications for practice and further research.

The stages of conventional research, outlined above, might be undertaken as part of a three-year full-time or five- to six-year part-time research degree; or they might form the basis of an action research cycle (at its simplest, 'plan–do–review'). Although the cycle as a whole is important, research is not invalidated if it undertakes one or more stages or elements of the cycle. For example, research which undertook to cover the first two stages in a thorough examination of the literature on a particular topic could be very useful research; similarly, research which aimed to test an existing theory (or even replicate an earlier study in a new context) – the fourth, fifth and sixth stages as outlined above – might also be very useful research.

It is a mistake to think that research must be immediately applicable. If we think of the most influential research of the last thirty years – Barnes *et al.*'s work on talk in classrooms in the late 1960s for example – we would note in this case that its impact might not be felt fully until fifteen years later (in the introduction of compulsory testing of oral competence in English (in England and Wales) in 1986).

In short, a large cycle over a number of years can be as important (it is often more so) than a short action research cycle over a year or two. We do need further research into how teachers actually change and improve their practice before we can make too many assumptions about the practical value of research.

Different kinds of research

Different kinds of research can be identified. They are:

1. theoretical, historical and strategic research;
2. applied research (including evaluation, consultancy);
3. research for and about learning;
4. scholarship.

These categories are not perfect; categories rarely are. Nor are they exclusive.

Theoretical, historical and strategic research

These kinds of research, along with strategic research, do not have immediate practical application. Their importance is undiminished in the light of a gradual shift towards the impact of research and the presence of 'users' on Research Assessment Exercise panels.2 In the 1990s, there was a gradual widening of the definition of research to include artefacts and other patentable inventions.

The following definition of research is both catholic and precise:

> 'Research' for the purpose of the research assessment exercise is to be understood as original investigation undertaken in order to gain knowledge and understanding. It includes work of direct relevance to the needs of commerce and industry, as well as to the public and voluntary sectors; scholarship; the invention and generation of ideas, images, performances and artefacts including design, where these lead to new or substantially improved insights; and the use of existing knowledge in experimental development to produce new or substantially improved materials, devices, products and processes, including design and construction. It excludes routine testing and analysis of materials, components and processes, e.g. for the maintenance of national standards, as distinct from the development of new analytical techniques. It also excludes the development of teaching materials that do not embody original research. (HEFCE, 1998)

Applied research, including evaluation and consultancy

Much research may be of an applied kind. That is to say, it might include:

- research arising from classroom and school needs;
- research undertaken in schools, universities and other workplaces;
- research which takes existing knowledge and applies or tests it in different contexts;
- research through knowledge and technology transfer;

- collaborations with industry, other services (e.g. health), arts organizations and other bodies concerned with improving learning and the economy in the region and beyond;
- evaluation;
- consultancies that include a research dimension; and
- the writing of textbooks and other works designed to improve learning, as long as these textbooks are underpinned by research and there is evidence of such research.

The common factor in these approaches is that they are all designed to improve learning in the different fields in which they operate, and thus to inform teaching, training and other forms of education.

Research for and about learning and teaching

Research into the processes of learning is often interdisciplinary. It might include:

- fundamental enquiry into learning processes;
- research into a region's educational needs;
- the creation of a base of applied research to underpin professional practice;
- the establishment of evidence for the provision of specific pedagogic materials;
- the development of distance-learning techniques, materials and modes of delivery; and
- examination of cases of cutting-edge learning.

Research *for* learning means research designed to improve the quality of learning; in some quarters, it is referred to as 'research and development' ('R&D'). It is a well-known and well-used approach in the making of new products. The writing of school textbooks and other forms of publication for the learning market, whether in print or electronic form, qualifies as research for learning if there is evidence of research underpinning it. Such research is valuable in that it works towards the creation of a new product or teaching programme.

Research *about* learning is more conventional within academic research cultures. It is represented in a long-standing tradition with the cognitive sciences, education, sociology and other disciplines. Education research does and should cover learning in informal and formal settings. Research for learning should be grounded in research about learning.

Scholarship

Scholarship can be defined as follows: 'scholarship [is] defined as the creation, development and maintenance of the intellectual infrastructure of subjects and disciplines, in forms such as dictionaries, scholarly editions, catalogues and contributions to major research databases' (HEFCE, 1998). But there is more to scholarship than this. As well as supporting and maintaining the intellectual infrastructure of subjects and disciplines, scholarship is a practice and an attitude of mind. It concerns the desire for quality, accuracy and clarity in all aspects of learning; the testing of hunches and hypotheses against rigorous evidence; the identification of different kinds of evidence for different purposes (e.g. for the justification of the arts in the curriculum). It also reflects a quest for excellence in design of the written word and other forms of communication in the presentation of knowledge.

Teacher research

One aspect of the move to put research into the hands of its subjects or respondents has been the rise of practitioner research. Much of the inspiration for this kind of research has come from the work of Donald Schön on the reflective practitioner (e.g. Schön, 1987) in the 1980s. Practitioner research puts the practitioner centre stage and in its purest form the research is directed, undertaken and evaluated by the practitioners themselves. In less pure forms, it is facilitated by outside researchers who nevertheless make sure that the needs and ideas of the practitioners are central to the progress of the research. Teacher research or 'teachers as researchers' is one particular manifestation of this movement. Key books are those by Webb (1990) and Webb and Vulliamy (1992).

The advantages of teacher research are that it is usually close to the concerns of the classroom, its empirical work is carried out in the classroom and the benefits of the research can be seen most immediately in the classroom. Most often it takes the form of action research, with the aim of improving practice. When the research is of a rigorous nature, it includes devices such as pre-test (a gauging of the state of play before an experiment is undertaken), the experimental period (in which, for example, a new method of teaching a particular aspect of a subject is tried) and post-test (a gauging of the state of play at the end of the experimental period). Sometimes more scientifically based approaches, like the use of a control group to compare the effects on an experimental group, are used. Disadvantages include the fact that unless such checks and balances are observed, the experiments are likely to become curriculum development rather than research, with no clear means of evaluating their value or impact. Furthermore, changes can take place without a sense of what the state of play was beforehand, or how far the changes have had an effect. Grass-roots projects like the National Writing Project and National Oracy Project in England and Wales in the late 1980s were of this nature: they tended to embrace a large number of practitioners and to be pursued with much enthusiasm; but at the end of the day, the community as a whole was none the wiser about the effect or impact of the innovations.

In the second half of the 1990s, the TTA in England and Wales initiated two programmes that gave more scope for teachers to undertake research themselves rather than be the users or subjects of it. The Teacher Research Grant Scheme and the School-Based Research Consortia enabled a large number of teachers and four consortia to undertake research. Much of it is cited in this series, and all of it has been consulted. Not all this kind of research has led to masters or doctoral work in universities, but a larger number of teachers have undertaken dissertations and theses across the world to answer research questions and test hypotheses about aspects of education. Again, we have made every effort to track down and represent research of this kind. One of the criticisms made by the TTA in the late 1990s was that much of this latter academic research was neither applicable nor was applied to the classroom. This criticism may have arisen from a misunderstanding about the scope, variety and nature of education research, discussed in the section on the nature of applied research above.

The applicability of academic research work to teaching

This section deals with the link between masters and doctoral research, as conducted by students in universities, and its applicability to teaching. The section takes question-and-answer format.3 The first point to make is about the nature of dissemination. Dissemination does not only take place at the end of a project. In many projects (action research, research and development) dissemination takes place along the way, for example in networks that are set up, databases of contacts, seminars, conferences and in-service education. Many of these seminars and conferences include teachers (e.g. subject professional conferences).

What arrangements would encourage busy education departments, teacher-researchers and their colleagues to collaborate in the dissemination of good quality projects likely to be of interest and use to classroom teachers? What would make teachers enthusiastic about drawing their work to the attention of colleagues?

Good dissemination is partly a result of the way a research project is set up. Two examples will prove the point: one from the University of Hull and one from Middlesex University.

Between 1991 and 1993 an action research project was undertaken by the University of Hull's (then) School of Education to improve the quality of argument in ten primary and ten secondary schools in the region. Teachers collaborated with university lecturers to set up mini-projects in each of the schools. These not only galvanized interest among other teachers in each of the schools, but made for considerable exchange between the participating schools. Much dissemination (probably reaching at least two hundred teachers in the region) took place *during* the project. Conventional *post hoc* dissemination in the form of articles and presentations by teachers took place after the project.

In early 1998, Middlesex University, through the TTA's inservice education and training (INSET) competition, won funding in collaboration with the London Boroughs of Enfield and Barnet to run INSET courses from September 1998. Alongside the INSET courses themselves, four MPhil/PhD studentships were awarded for teachers to undertake longer-term evaluations of in-service curricular development. At the time (September 1998) several applicants wished to focus their research on the literacy hour. This research informed INSET activity and was of interest to teachers in the region, as well as providing summative evidence for a wider community.

In conclusion, the research projects of relevance to teachers must a) be engaging, b) be disseminated during the course of the research as well as after it, c) be seen to benefit schools during the research as well as after it, and d) involve as large a number of teachers in the activity of the project as possible. Diffidence about research is not felt if there is involvement in it.

How can we encourage more pedagogic research with a focus on both *teaching and learning?*

Research into learning often has implications for teaching; and it is difficult in disciplined research to have two foci. Indeed such bifocal research may not be able to sustain its quality. Inevitably, any research into teaching must take into account the quality and amount of learning that takes place as a result of the teaching. Research into *learning* is again a pressing need. Having said that, research with a focus on *teaching* needs to be encouraged.

Would it be beneficial to build a requirement for accessible summaries into teacher research programmes? Given the difficulties involved in this process, what training or support would be needed by education researchers?

The ability to summarize is an important skill; so is the ability to write accessibly. Not all teachers or teacher researchers (or academics for that matter) have such abilities. We do not see such a requirement to be problematical, however, nor to need much attention. Teacher researchers must simply be required to provide accessible summaries of their work, whether these are conventional abstracts (often no longer than 300 words) or longer summaries of their research. Their supervisors and the funding agency must ensure that such summaries are forthcoming and are well written.

Where higher degree study by teachers is publicly funded, should teachers be required to consider from the start how their work might involve colleagues and be made accessible to other teachers?

Making a researcher consider from the start how their work might involve colleagues and be made accessible to other teachers is undesirable for a number of reasons. First, it might skew the research. Second, it will put the emphasis on dissemination and audience rather than on the research itself. Part of the nature of research is that the writer must have his or her focus on the material gathered or the question examined, not on what he or she might say. This is why writing up research is not necessarily like writing a book; a thesis must be true to its material, whereas a book must speak to its audience. There is a significant difference in the two genres, which is why the translation of thesis into book is not always as easy as it might seem. Third, what is important 'from the start' is the framing of a clear research question, the definition of a problem or the positing of a testable hypothesis.

In summary, as far as teacher research and the use of findings in MA and PhD work go, there are at least the following main points which need to be addressed:

- further research on how teachers develop and improve their practice;
- exploration and exposition of the links between theory and practice;
- an understanding that dissemination is not always most effective 'after the event';
- an appreciation of the stages of a research project, and of the value of work that is not immediately convertible into practice;
- further exploration of the links between teaching and learning.

Research is not the same as evaluation

It is helpful to distinguish between research and evaluation for the purposes of the present series. Research is the critical pursuit of truth or new knowledge through enquiry; or, to use a now obsolete but nevertheless telling definition from the eighteenth century, research in music is the seeking out of patterns of harmony which, once discovered, can be applied in the piece to be played afterwards. In other words, research is about discovery of new patterns, new explanations for data – or the testing of existing theories against new data – which can inform practice.

Evaluation is different. One can evaluate something without researching it or using research techniques. But formal evaluation of education initiatives often requires the use of research approaches to determine the exact nature of the developments that have taken place or the value and worth of those developments. Evaluation almost always assumes critical detachment and the disinterested weighing up of strengths and weaknesses. It should always be sensitive to the particular aims of a project and should try to weigh the aims against the methods and results, judging the appropriateness of the methods and the validity and effect (or likely effect) of the results. It can be formative or summative: formative when it works alongside the project it is evaluating, contributing to its development in a critical, dispassionate way; and summative when it is asked to identify at the end of a project the particular strengths and weaknesses of the approach.

Evaluation can use any of the techniques and methods that research uses in order to gather and analyse data. For example, an evaluation of the strengths and weaknesses of the TTA's School-Based Research Consortia could use formal questionnaires, semi-structured interviews and case studies of individual teachers' development to assess the impact of the consortia. Research methods that provide quantitative data (largely numerical) or qualitative data (largely verbal) could be used.

Essentially, the difference between research and evaluation comes down to a difference in function: the function of research is to discover new knowledge via a testing of hypothesis, the answering of a research question or the solving of a problem – or indeed the creation of a hypothesis, the asking of a question or the formulating or exploring of a problem. The function of evaluation is simply to evaluate an existing phenomenon.

How to access, read and interpret research

The series provides a digest of the best and most relevant research in the teaching and learning of school subjects. Each of the authors aims to mediate between the plethora of research in the field and the needs of the busy teacher, headteacher, adviser, parent or governor who wants to know how best to improve practice in teaching in order to improve standards in learning. In other words, much of the work of seeking out research and interpreting it is done for you by the authors of the individual books in the series.

At the same time, the series is intended to help you to access and interpret research more generally. Research is continuing all the time; it is impossible for a book series, however comprehensive, to cover all research or to present the very latest research in a particular field. The publisher and authors of individual titles will be happy to hear from readers who feel that a particular piece of research is missing from the account, or about new research that extends our understanding of the field.

In order to help you access, read and interpret research the following guidelines might help:

- How clear is the research question or problem or hypothesis?
- If there is more than one question or problem, can you identify a main question or problem as opposed to subsidiary ones? Does the researcher make the distinction clear?
- Is any review of the literature included? How comprehensive is it? How critical is it of past research? Does it, for instance, merely cite previous literature to make a new space for itself? Or does it build on existing research?
- Determine the size of the sample used in the research. Is this a case study of a particular child or a series of interviews with, say, ten pupils, or a survey of tens or hundreds of pupils? The generalizability of the research will depend on its scale and range.
- Is the sample a fair reflection of the population that is being

researched? For example, if all the 12- to 13-year-old pupils in a particular town are being researched (there might be 600 of them), what is the size of the sample?

- Are the methods used appropriate for the study?
- Is the data gathered appropriate for an answering of the question, testing of the hypothesis or solving of the problem?
- What conclusions, if any, are drawn? Are they reasonable?
- Is the researcher making recommendations based on sound results, or are implications for practice drawn out? Is the researcher aware of the limitations of the study?
- Is there a clear sense of what further research needs to be undertaken?

Equipped with questions like these, and guided by the authors of the books in the series, you will be better prepared to make sense of research findings and apply them to the improvement of your practice for the benefit of the students you teach. The bibliographies at the end of each book (or of individual chapters) will provide you with the means of exploring the field more extensively, according to your own particular interests and needs.

Richard Andrews

Notes

1   The creation of this Evidence-Informed Policy and Practice Initiative (EPPI) in 2000, based at the Institute of Education, has been a significant step forward. Six review groups, including one on English based at The University of York, were set up initially to conduct systematic reviews in the field.

2   The Research Assessment Exercise, conducted by the Higher Education Funding Council For England, was undertaken at four or five-year intervals between 1986 and 2001 and may or may not take place in the middle of the first decade of the century. Its aim is to gauge the quality of research produced by research institutions around the UK in order to attribute funding in subsequent years. Critics of the exercise have suggested that, despite attempts to make it recognize the value of applied research and the applicability of research, its overall effect has been to force departments of education in universities to concentrate on producing high quality research rather than working at the interface of research and practice.

3   This section is based on a submission by the author to the TTA in 1998.

Introduction

Starting points

Two particular events provided the starting points for this book. The first of these was a very mundane one – the fitting of additional bookshelves in my office! The second was visiting my student teachers in the schools where they were undertaking their teaching placement as part of their initial teacher training course. Though on the surface these events were very different in nature, they were linked, as both raised questions in my mind about educational research and its impact on classroom practice.

The additional bookshelves in my office were needed to cope with my ever-expanding collection of books on research in science education. Certainly the last ten years or so have seen a huge increase in the number of books on this topic. However, the books are just one of the indicators of a dramatic increase in the amount of research activity going on in science education. For there are not just more books, there are more edited collections of papers, there are new journals, there are more frequent issues of journals and there are more conferences taking place with accompanying compendia of conference proceedings. As I started to rearrange my books, my initial thoughts were about how good it was that so many people were actively engaged in research in science education in such a wide range of areas. There is work on pupils, on teachers, on learning, on responses to science, on assessment, on the structure of the curriculum, on practical work, on gender, on evaluation of curriculum initiatives, on teacher training … indeed, there must be few areas of activity in science education which have not been the focus of research at some stage. By the time I had got to the end of sorting out my books, I found myself wondering if the sheer quantity of literature on science education research created something of a problem. *Faced with evidence of all this research activity in science education, how might someone comparatively new to the area begin to make sense of it all?*

This question was very much in my mind when I was visiting my student teachers in their schools. These visits are occasions I almost always enjoy, and I am frequently impressed by the creativity, the enthusiasm and the quality of reflection on the developing teaching skills demonstrated by many of the student teachers with whom I work. As is always the case when I make my visits, I observed a range of lessons in terms of content, approach and style of classroom management. Unsurprisingly, some of the students met with more success than others in the particular lessons I observed, yet almost all, I felt, were likely to go on to make competent teachers. This made me wonder *what impact would educational research, particularly research in science education, have had on what these teachers would be doing in their lessons in five years' time?*

It is certainly possible to identify several ways in which educational research *might* have an impact on lessons. One way might be through the use made by beginning teachers of the ideas about educational research they encountered in their teacher training courses. These ideas are likely to include, for example, theories about how children learn and studies on children's difficulties with certain key ideas in science. To what extent beginning teachers draw on this knowledge (or even remember it!) has not been investigated on a systematic basis, but it seems likely that some beginning teachers at least would find such knowledge helpful in informing and making sense of some of their experiences in the classroom. A second way in which educational research might have an impact in lessons is through teachers reading reports of research in publications such as educational journals, professional journals and educational sections of newspapers. Third, teachers might engage in professional development activities, either in the form of short courses or through further study for a diploma or higher degree. Finally, teachers may make use of curriculum materials which have drawn on research evidence.

A key word in the preceding paragraph is *might*. For most teachers, the only time they are ever likely to encounter ideas about educational research in any kind of systematic way is during their initial teacher training courses. Paradoxically, at this particular stage in becoming a teacher, most time and energy is devoted to more pragmatic concerns over lesson planning and classroom management. Beyond this point, for both beginning teachers and their more experienced colleagues, there are few formal links in place to draw together educational research and educational practice. Where research does influence practice is often down to chance and to decisions made by individual teachers to pursue particular interests. However, most teachers reach a stage in their teaching where the questions they start to ask about their practice move beyond the pragmatic. For science teachers, these might include questions about why pupils find particular topics so difficult, about the nature of practical work, about the most effective ways of assessing pupils' knowledge and abilities in science, or questions about why so many pupils appear to become increasingly alienated by science as they progress through their secondary education. These are all questions where research in science education can offer insights and suggestions for classroom practice.

About this book

This book has two main aims. The first is to draw together research findings in a number of areas of importance in science education, using examples of both large-scale and small-scale studies to illustrate these findings. The second aim is to show how these findings offer insights into events in lessons and offer ways of enhancing classroom practice. This book has been written with two groups of people in mind. In the first group are people who want to *know about research* in science education: the main areas in which work has been undertaken, key questions which have been asked, issues which need to be considered, the sort of work which has been done and the main findings. In the second group are people who want to build on this knowledge to *engage in research* themselves. This book will provide an entry into the research literature in a number of areas of science education.

There are a number of challenges associated with producing a book of this nature. One is making decisions about which areas of work should and should not be included. In reaching decisions, I have been guided primarily by what seem to me (though others might disagree!) to be areas of interest shared by classroom practitioners and others working in science education.

A second challenge concerns the quantity of literature on research in science education. It may well be that the literature is so extensive because school science is not generally perceived as a 'success story'. Whatever the reason, no single book could do justice to all the work which has been undertaken. The guiding principles for including studies in this book are that they address aspects of issues and questions which have emerged as being important in science teaching in a number of countries, that they contribute to a growing knowledge base in the area, that they carry messages which are important for future policy development or point to action which could be implemented viably into normal classrooms. Although the emphasis is on recent research studies, these have been set in the context of earlier work where this has been significant and influential.

The structure of the book

Chapter 1 looks at science education in the context of the bigger picture – a picture which includes matters to do with the purpose of educational research and the evolution of school science over the past twenty years or so into its current form in the curriculum.

The next two chapters consider children's learning in science. Chapter 2 looks at constructivist research, exploring children's intuitive ideas about scientific phenomena and the impact they have on developing scientific understanding. Chapter 3 considers how children's understanding of science ideas links to their cognitive development. These two areas of work constitute the two largest research programmes in science education.

Issues to do with curriculum content and approaches form the focus of Chapters 4 to 7. Chapter 4 looks at what is very often perceived to be an essential feature of school science, practical work. Chapter 5 focuses on a significant feature of school science over the last decade or so: the development of scientific ideas through the contexts and applications of science, and its implications for teaching approaches adopted in science lessons. The huge developments in information and communications technology (ICT) over the last twenty years or so have opened up many possibilities for its applications in science teaching, and this forms the focus of Chapter 6. In Chapter 7, the role of language in science education is considered in terms of both how the role language can play in helping develop scientific understanding, as well as the potential barriers to learning posed by the vocabulary and terminology of science.

How pupils feel about the science they encounter in lessons is just as important as the science ideas they learn. The next two chapters therefore consider aspects of pupils' affective responses to science, with Chapter 8 looking at pupils' attitudes to science and school science, and Chapter 9 exploring a phenomenon particularly associated with science – the differential involvement of girls and boys.

An aspect of the school curriculum which has received increasing attention in the last decade is assessment of pupils' performance, and the concluding chapter of the book therefore examines the nature and purpose of assessment in school science. Finally, the Endpiece briefly pulls together some of the more general messages about research in science education which have emerged from undertaking this review.

The appendices provide brief summaries of information which will be helpful to readers wishing to know more about features of educational research, and theories and ideas about learning.

The structure of chapters in the book

Each chapter in the book is structured to provide two levels of access to the information in the text. This is based on the premise that academic books are rarely read from cover to cover, or chapters within such books read from beginning to end! To help readers gain a quick overview, each chapter contains summary boxes relating to material in the text. These are:

- *key issues and questions*, setting the scene for the discussion and forming the framework for the more detailed discussion within the chapter;

- *key research findings*, highlighting the main points to emerge from the research;
- an example of a *larger-scale study* and a *small-scale study* in the area, summarizing not just the main findings but also illustrating how research principles are put into practice through the use of particular research strategies and techniques to gather data;
- *implications for practice*, identifying areas for possible action in the classroom;
- *first stops for further reading*.

This last summary is to assist with one of the more daunting features of educational research publications – the length of the list of references! To help with decisions about what to pursue in the first instance, a limited number of references has been identified as possible 'first stops for further reading'. These references chosen will generally do one or more of the following: provide a good and accessible review of key issues in the area; report a study of particular significance; illustrate an example of a particularly appropriate research strategy or technique. The 'first stops' should also be readily accessible in an academic library.

Inevitably, in making decisions about structure and content, some degree of personal preference and selectivity has to be exercised. In summarizing what other people have written about their work, there is also the risk that what is presented does not quite reflect what was intended by the original authors. Shortcomings in the book are mine, and I would be pleased to be alerted to possible errors or omissions with a view to improving any future edition.

And finally ...

To end on a personal note, I will say very briefly why and when educational research became important to me. My background is in school science teaching and, in common with many teachers, my first two years or so in school were fairly heavily focused on pragmatic considerations related to survival! I hope that, during this time, there were occasions when I was a 'reflective practitioner' (though I am not sure the phrase was as widely used in those days as it is now). It was some time towards the end of my third year in teaching that I started to ask questions about why things were the way they were in my classes. In particular, the 'Why?' question I asked was why so few girls seemed interested in science and wanted to study it further. It was in pursuing the answers to this question that I became interested in educational research and how it might help me look, in a systematic and structured way, for answers to some of my questions. Getting involved in research added a new dimension to the way in which I thought about teaching and convinced me that educational research could be used to enhance the experiences offered to pupils in lessons. I hope that this book shows some of the ways in which this might happen.

Chapter 1

Science Education and the 'Bigger Picture'

This book is about exploring links between research and practice in science education. However, research in science education is just one part of a 'bigger picture', and an understanding of other parts of this bigger picture is very helpful in providing a framework for thinking about and making sense of research studies in science education and their findings. This chapter therefore focuses on two aspects of the bigger picture, the questions each raises and possible answers to some – but not all! – of these questions. The first of aspect of the bigger picture concerns issues to do with the purposes of educational research. The second concerns the way in which science has evolved over the last twenty years or so into its current form as a school subject.

The purposes of educational research

This section considers:

- the purposes of education research;
- current issues and concerns in educational research and research in science education.

There are probably as many definitions of educational research as there are books about research methods. Essentially, educational research involves asking questions about what and why certain features are evident in particular educational contexts – and then seeking to provide answers in a rigorous and systematic way. Educational research is also about communicating – presenting the work done in a way which enables other people to understand what has been done and how conclusions have been reached.

Why undertake educational research?

Educational research is undertaken with the aim of doing one or more of the following: increasing knowledge, improving understanding, informing decision-making and improving practice. Because educational research is very often undertaken in the hope that its findings can be used to improve a situation, it is sometimes called *applied* research. However, educational research cannot guarantee improvements. It involves an investment of time, energy and, probably, money. Like any investment, there is an element of risk, as the outcomes may not meet the hopes.

Few people would argue against engaging in an activity which aims to improve understanding and practice. Moreover, there are currently moves to make teaching an 'evidence-based' or 'evidence-informed' profession, in which much closer links are formed between research and practice through encouraging teachers to draw on research findings in their teaching. The impetus for these moves is the drive to raise standards, and research is seen as one means of providing evidence of strategies which are effective in raising standards. Yet, increasingly, educational research is being subjected to attack and criticism. From both within and outside the education research community, questions are being asked about educational research. Many of these questions centre on the *impact* of research on practice. How do people find out about what educational research has to say? How do people decide which findings are 'important'? How do they make use of these findings? Most crucially, what – if anything – does educational research have to offer educational practice?

Issues and concerns in educational research

In the UK, the mid-1990s onwards saw the publication of a number of articles, most from within the research community itself, offering critiques of educational research. Though these articles focused largely on the state of research in the UK, the questions they raised are being asked in many countries. The debate was launched at the annual Teacher Training Agency (TTA) lecture given by David Hargreaves (Hargreaves, 1996). He argued that schools would be more effective if teaching became a research-based profession, and blamed researchers for supposedly failing to make this happen. Hargreaves also accused researchers of producing 'inconclusive and contestable findings of little worth', and demanded an end to:

> ... the frankly second rate educational research which does not make a serious contribution to fundamental theory or knowledge; which is irrelevant to practice; which is uncoordinated with any preceding or follow-up research; and which clutters up academic journals which virtually nobody reads. (p. 7)

In making these scathing criticisms, Hargreaves also encouraged the educational research community to look to medical research as good model for research whose procedures supposedly allowed definite conclusions to be reached about what works and why. Although Hargreaves subsequently softened his criticisms (Hargreaves, 1999), and talked about the role of research helping to inform policy and practice, rather than providing answers, others picked up on what he had said, most notably the then Chief Inspector for Schools, Chris Woodhead, who infamously described much educational research as 'dross' in an article in *The Times* in July 1998. Woodhead also commissioned an enquiry into educational research (Tooley and Darbey, 1998). The enquiry based its findings on a review of a sample of 41 articles from four leading British journals, of which 26 were identified as 'not satisfying criteria of good practice'. These articles demonstrated shortcomings in four areas: a failure to take a detached, non-partisan approach; methodological concerns over aspects such as sampling; poor presentation by, for example, including insufficient data on sample size; and lack of focus. Perhaps unsurprisingly, the many critics of the report which emerged from the enquiry accused it of demonstrating a number of the faults it had identified in the papers it had reviewed!

A further report (Hillage *et al.*, 1998), and one which was generally more favourably received, concluded that research was often too small scale to be reliable and generalizable, not based on existing knowledge, not presented in a form which was accessible to non-academic audiences and not interpreted for audiences of policy-makers and practitioners.

A number of potentially positive outcomes have emerged from the very negative picture painted of educational research by some. The research community has 'taken stock' of what it means to do educational research, what such research has achieved, what it has not achieved, what it is reasonable to expect – and not expect – of research and how it might be improved (see, for example, Mortimore, 2000). More attention has been focused on potential users of research, the ways in which they might be involved in research and appropriate ways of communicating research findings in an accessible form to groups which would include practitioners, policy-makers, curriculum developers and textbook writers.

The issues of communication and impact are worth considering in more detail. Researchers who work in higher education institutions are very often under considerable pressure to generate publications. In the UK, for example, academics are required to submit four publications for the Research Assessment Exercise (RAE), a five-yearly peer review of research output. On the surface, such a system is of benefit – it encourages researchers to communicate their work with others. However, the outcome is linked to funding, and the highest status normally accorded to academic books and papers published in prestigious international journals, whose principal audience is other academics. With limited time and resources, researchers are often placed in the position of having to make uncomfortable choices about where to disseminate their findings and discuss research issues, with the inevitable consequence that fewer articles are written with teachers – the 'end users' of research – as the main audience. An additional problem often arises from the 'genre' or writing style associated with academic books and papers, a style which can be alienating for many audiences. Put bluntly, whereas almost all readers would understand phrases such as 'theories of the development of knowledge' or 'what teachers know about how to teach their subject', rather fewer might engage so easily with 'epistemology' or 'PCK – pedagogic content knowledge'!

The argument that research has little impact on practice is frequently made – and with some justification. If this argument is examined more closely, the 'research' to which reference is being made is often large-scale funded research, initiated and undertaken by professional researchers. However, this is not the only kind of research which is carried out. There are numerous teachers engaged in higher degree work or professional development activities which involve carrying out a research study. It is hard to imagine that the work of these practitioner researchers does not have an impact on their own practice, and possibly that of their colleagues in school and beyond.

A more controversial outcome of the criticism and debate in educational research has been the exploration of the applicability of medical research models in educational settings. Educational research mainly draws on the strategies developed in the social sciences, such as action research, case studies, surveys and, sometimes, experiments. (A brief overview of the strategies and techniques employed in educational research is provided in Appendix 1.) Experiments are used comparatively infrequently on the basis that educational settings are complex and therefore do not readily lend themselves to the controlled conditions, randomized treatments and repeat tests which characterize much scientific research. However, a strategy to which increasing attention is being given is that of randomized control trials, or 'RCTs', a technique used in medical research to establish the effectiveness of particular drugs or treatments. For those arguing that educational research needs to be improved through the introduction of aspects of scientific rigour (see, for example, Oakley, 2000), RCTs are seen as a way of strengthening research findings by enabling claims about cause and effect to be made with more confidence than has formerly been the case in educational research. A key question with RCTs concerns *when* such a strategy is appropriate, and it will be interesting to see what impact RCTs have in educational research.

Worries about RCTs have also led to exploration of the possibilities of *design experiments* in educational research. The term has its origins in the work of Brown (1992) and Collins (1993) in the USA, and draws on approaches used in technology and engineering to explore how a product, developed to solve a particular problem, performs in selected situations. This has clear parallels in educational contexts, where the 'product' being tested would be new curriculum materials. A design experiment might involve, for example, selecting teachers who teach roughly comparable groups, but who have different teaching styles. The effects of the new materials on each group would then be explored in order to yield information on the circumstances in which the materials are most likely to be successful. Design experiments appear to have the benefit of being able to encompass the complexity of educational settings and interactions whilst also enabling features of new materials to be tested systematically. As with RCTs, their impact in educational research has yet to be seen.

Issues and concerns in research in science education

The widespread concerns about educational research are echoed in recent writing about research in science education. Science as a school subject has attracted particular research interest in part because of the high status in the curriculum and in part because of the persisting worry over the high numbers of pupils opting out of studying science as soon as they have a choice. Despite the volume of research undertaken and reported, there are questions about its achievements, its future directions, its cohesive nature and its knowledge base. In their recent book *Improving Science Education: The Contribution of Research*, Millar *et al.* (2000) ask:

> Is there any sense that the field of science education research is making 'progress'? (Do newer studies build on earlier ones? Is the effort *cumulative*? Are there any areas of agreement about theoretical frameworks and terminology, or about research approaches, procedures or tools, or even about areas of work that are more or less worthwhile? And are there findings that command general assent?) (p. 1)

Jenkins (2000a), in his review *Research in science education: time for a health check?*, poses a question about the nature of the research agenda in science education:

> To what extent should the research agenda in science education seek to address the immediate or short-term concerns of legislators, policy-makers or teachers, rather than address more fundamental questions which may be of longer term significance for policy or practice? (p. 21)

The preceding discussion raises a number of questions about the role and impact of educational research and research in science education, some of which are not easy to answer. Nonetheless, as subsequent chapters will demonstrate, a number of the questions those undertaking research have asked about science education have yielded many insights into practice and resulted in a number of very practical suggestions for incorporation into science teaching.

Science education in schools today

This section considers:

- the changes which have taken place in school science over the last two decades, and some of the reasons for these changes;
- how research activity in science education is linked to changes in school science;
- current provision and future developments in school science.

The last two decades or so have seen change on an unprecedented scale in education in many countries. Changes in society have resulted in changing expectation of schools, and much of the debate in education has centred on how to provide access for all young people to an education which is both relevant and serves as a preparation for later life. The increasing impact of scientific and technological developments on everyday life has served to focus considerable attention on the role of science within the school curriculum, and it could be argued that no subject has been influenced more than science over the last twenty years by the twin aims of accessibility and relevance. Although the discussion in this section concentrates on the picture in the UK, the issues under consideration are common to many countries.

In England and Wales, it is certainly the case that few subjects could present two more contrasting pictures than those of school science twenty years ago and school science today. Today, almost all pupils follow a science programme in schools which includes aspects of biology, chemistry and physics for the whole of the period of compulsory education. This is a very different picture from that of the late 1970s, when a study (Department of Education and Science (DES), 1979) revealed a gloomy picture of school science in terms of the numbers of pupils studying science subjects beyond the point of choice (then at age 14). Approximately 20 per cent of girls and 10 per cent of boys studied no science at all beyond the age of 14. A further 60 per cent of girls and 50 per cent of boys took only one science subject, principally biology in the case of girls and physics in the case of boys. Fewer than 5 per cent of girls and 10 per cent of boys studied all three sciences. The study demonstrated that most pupils were 'voting with their feet' and opting out of science subjects at the earliest opportunity. Many other countries shared similar problems of low levels of participation in science, particularly the physical sciences. Growing dissatisfaction over science provision in schools united government bodies, employers, professional associations, teachers and others involved in science education in a call for a science curriculum which was meaningful and accessible to all pupils.

One outcome of this dissatisfaction was a period of intense introspection within the science education community, with many questions being asked about the structure, content and approach of school science. What sort of science course should be offered? Should there be a compulsory core, and, if so, what should be in it? Is it possible (or desirable) to have one science course which will meet the needs of all pupils, whether or not they intend to specialize in science? At what point might pupils begin to specialize? What form should practical work take? To what extent should the science be pure or vocational? What sorts of approaches should be taken to the teaching of science to try and broaden its appeal? How would a science curriculum address issues of equity? What would constitute appropriate and valid forms of assessing the knowledge, understanding and skills associated with science? In England and Wales, some of the answers, at least, were provided by the introduction of a National Curriculum in 1988, a curriculum which specified English, mathematics and science as the three foundation subjects to be studied through the whole of the period of compulsory education (age 5–16).

Perhaps the most important point to make about the questions in the preceding paragraph is that there are no right or wrong answers. Rather, there are good and less good answers. It is therefore not surprising that, well over a decade later, most of these questions are being revisited. A key to arriving at good, rather than less good, answers is informed decision-making, and it is here that research in science education has a contribution to make.

In order to understand current thinking in science education, it is necessary to look at what has characterized the thinking and activity of the last two decades. A brief comparison of the central features of the thinking and activity in science education in each of the last two decades serves to illustrate why these questions are being revisited, and how research might inform the debate over possible answers.

The 1980s – the decade of reaction and action

Three main strands are discernible in the thinking and activity of the 1980s. The first of these strands concerns the overall structure of the curriculum. The drive was for a science course for all pupils throughout their period of compulsory schooling which was both broad and balanced: broad in terms of its coverage of the main areas of science, and balanced both in the time devoted to each of these areas within science teaching and in the time devoted to science in the curriculum as a whole. In England and Wales, the move to broad balanced science was supported by the government (DES, 1985) and professional associations such as the Association for Science Education (ASE, 1981), and through the work of teachers in the Secondary Science Curriculum Review (SSCR, 1987).

In seeking to justify the claim for science to form a central component of the curriculum, it was necessary to give careful consideration to the purposes of school science. A number of arguments were put forward for the inclusion of science as a compulsory subject in the curriculum. Thomas and Durant (1987) usefully divided these arguments into three groups: socio-cultural arguments, democratic arguments and utilitarian arguments. Socio-cultural arguments focused on the value of studying science for its own sake: science helps people make sense of and understand the world they live in, science is exciting and interesting, and its impact on life and contribution to knowledge represents one of the major cultural achievements of the twentieth century. Democratic arguments centred on the need to educate the citizens of the future, particularly those who would go on to be key decision-makers, all of whom needed some understanding of science, the way it works and its limitations to help with decisions and choices in the many areas where science would affect their lives, such as genetic engineering, pollution and dealing with nuclear waste. Utilitarian arguments concerned matters such as the need for future scientists and the role science has to play in developing general skills, such as formulating and testing hypotheses, and presenting and interpreting data. Although questions about the structure and nature of school science provision are now being revisited, the arguments outlined above remain persuasive arguments for the inclusion of some form of science in the curriculum.

The second strand of the thinking and activity in the 1980s emerged from the curriculum development work. Much of the work was characterized by two rather different responses to the challenge of providing a science curriculum which was relevant and accessible to the majority of pupils. One response, particularly apparent in schools in the UK, was to develop materials which focused less on the content and more on the *processes* of science, such as *Science in Process* (Wray, 1987). A more widespread trend in curriculum development was to produce resources which emphasized the social and technological implications of science. In the UK, such materials include the *Science and Technology in Society* (*SATIS*) materials (ASE, 1986) and *Chemistry: the Salters Approach* (University of York Science Education Group (UYSEG), 1984–8). Elsewhere saw the development of, for example, the *PLON* materials in the Netherlands (Dutch Physics Curriculum Development Project, 1988), and *ChemCom* in the United States (American Chemical Society (ACS), 1988).

The final strand concerned the insights provided by research in science education into some of the problems school science was facing. The work of Shayer and Adey (1981) had demonstrated the very high academic demands placed on pupils by much of the science they encountered in lessons. Other studies (for example, Driver *et al.*, 1985; Osborne and Freyberg, 1985) revealed that only a very small minority of pupils seemed able to understand some of the most elementary ideas in science by the time they were 16. The work of the Assessment of Performance Unit (APU) in the 1980s raised a number of issues about the nature and assessment of practical skills (Black, 1990). A number of studies (for example, Kelly, 1986) showed that many pupils – particularly girls – were negatively disposed towards school science and science more generally. The work undertaken for all these studies is explored more fully in later chapters, but the brief overview here serves to illustrate the point that research was providing the science education community with evidence that many pupils had problems with concepts and skills they encountered in science and that they also had a poor perception of science as a subject. It could be argued that insufficient attention was given to these important messages when decisions about the structure and content of the curriculum were being made, and curriculum materials being developed.

The 1990s – the decade of reassessment and assessment

In twenty years' time, it will be interesting to read accounts of science education in the 1990s. Policy-makers probably hope that the decade will be remembered for the drive to raise standards. However, it may well be that what will come most readily to mind for others in science education will be the pace of change and the impact of assessment on practice. Certainly the decade was one characterized by increasing centralized control, increasing curriculum prescription and increasing accountability.

It is difficult to argue against a policy of raising standards. More questionable are the strategies which have been implemented in an effort to achieve higher standards. Implicit in the notion of 'raising standards' is the need to make comparisons, and comparisons have to be based on some form of reliable measurement. This search for the measurable has led to a *reductionist* curriculum, in other words, one which has involved increasingly detailed specifications of objectives in the form of knowledge and skills described in such a way that they can be measured. One has only to look at science – and practical work in particular – to see evidence of some of the problems associated with a reductionist approach. One important aim of the National Curriculum in England and Wales was to help pupils develop an understanding of scientific enquiry or the way scientists work. (This idea is explored more fully in Chapter 4.) Yet much of practical work in science lessons in the 1990s took the form of very small assessable components, mechanistically assembled in a particular order into 'investigations'. Such an approach was an oversimplified and misleading picture of much scientific enquiry.

Increasing centralized control and increasing prescription of the curriculum have also had a significant impact on curriculum development, with a noticeable reduction in activity, particularly in large-scale curriculum development for the period of compulsory schooling. By and large, the curriculum materials of the 1990s have attempted to provide a palatable means of covering and assessing the requirements of a very detailed curriculum specification. Some evidence of research findings can be seen in curriculum materials. For example, gender bias in resources has been significantly reduced, and most resources now try to demonstrate to pupils how the science that they are studying relates to everyday life. There is rather less to indicate curriculum materials are drawing on the evidence and recommendations of research into pupils' learning, for example their understanding (or misunderstanding) of scientific ideas.

The 1990s have seen research in science education continue to grow, with more work being undertaken in established areas such as assessment and practical work, and, for example, through looking at primary children's understanding of key ideas in science and the effects of investigative work. Interest has grown in new areas, such as the impact of ICT and, in particular, the role of language in helping develop understanding. Work has also continued in areas which saw significant activity in the 1980s, such as pupils' attitudes to science and gender issues in science education, though publications on these aspects have appeared less frequently than was formerly the case.

It has become increasingly evident in the 1990s that some of the aspirations of 'broad, balanced science for all' are not being realized. It is true that, in England and Wales, most pupils now obtain formal examination qualifications at the age of 16. However, there is little evidence to suggest that compelling pupils to do science has significantly altered the picture of under-involvement reported in the 1979 DES study described earlier, other than to shift the age at which this picture emerges from 14 to 16. Thus, in the 2000s, the structure and content of the science curriculum are once again under close scrutiny.

The arguments outlined earlier for the inclusion of science in the curriculum are still seen as making a good case for 'science for all'. However, there are serious question marks over the ability of one science curriculum to meet the needs of all pupils, and over the appropriateness of the majority of pupils spending up to one-fifth of their lessons studying science. Although there have been many changes to the science curriculum over the past two decades, it has essentially evolved from the specialist curriculum formerly offered to only the most able pupils, some of whom would go on to further study of science and to work in scientific fields. Can a curriculum designed along these lines provide a worthwhile and satisfying experience for the majority of pupils who are future citizens, but not future scientists? In an important document, *Beyond 2000*, Millar and Osborne (1998) suggest that the answer to this question is 'No' and they put forward a vision of a core school science curriculum in which pupils are educated *about* science rather than *for* science. In other words, the 'science for all' of the 2000s should be one which places less emphasis on the facts and theories of science, and more on how scientific knowledge is applied and how decisions are reached about what could and should be done with the knowledge. Those pupils who wish to specialize in science would study additional modules covering more traditional content. A curriculum of this form is currently being developed for trial in some schools (University of York Science Education Group (UYSEG), 2001), and it remains to be seen to what extent future versions of a National Curriculum reflect this vision.

Conclusion

This chapter has attempted to set research in science education in context by exploring some of the more general issues in educational research and examining some of the recent developments and thinking in science education.

It is clear that the science education community is in the process of trying to answer some of the 'big' questions about the sort of science which pupils should encounter in school. Research in science education cannot possibly provide all the answers, but it can – and has – contributed to the pool of information available to inform decisions. The following chapters explore this contribution in more detail.

Chapter 2

Children's Learning in Science and the Constructivist Viewpoint

Student teacher:	Now I want you to imagine you are on the bus going home, and the driver has to brake sharply because someone steps out into the road. What happens to the passengers?
Pupil 1:	Does someone die, sir?
Student teacher:	No, it's not as bad as that. What happens to the passengers when the driver brakes?
Pupil 2:	They get thrown forward.
Student teacher:	OK, yes, they get thrown forward. So why does that happen?
Pupil 2:	Well ... it's like ... it's like ... well, a force sort of pushes them.
Student teacher:	A force pushes them. Is that really what happens? Who agrees with [Pupil 2]? Put your hands up. Quite a few people, I see. Well, sorry to tell you this, but you're all wrong!
Pupil 3:	But if you were standing up, sir, you'd get pushed right down the bus.

This extract comes from the early part of a lesson on forces and motion taught by a student teacher to a class of 15-year olds. It illustrates a situation which may arise in science lessons – the ideas and explanations the teacher is hoping to develop are not those which pupils are offering intuitively from their own experiences – the pupils have constructed their own meanings. What does this mean for science teaching?

This chapter looks at:

- ideas about constructivism and pupils' learning in science;
- why people have become so interested in constructivism;
- ways in which data on pupils' understanding has been gathered;
- key findings of constructivist research;
- implications for teaching;
- current issues and debates in constructivist research.

Introduction: ideas about learning

If you were to ask science teachers what they hoped their pupils would get out of their lessons, the chances are they would probably say that they wanted their pupils to learn some scientific ideas and to enjoy what they were learning. In other words, teachers are concerned about both the *cognitive* (or thinking) and *affective* (or feeling) impact of their lessons on pupils. Later chapters in this book, particularly Chapter 8, explore matters to do with pupils' affective responses to science, but this chapter and the one that follows focus on pupils' learning in science. Teachers would probably also say that, despite their best efforts, many of their pupils struggle to understand the ideas they encounter in science lessons. It is therefore not surprising that one significant strand of research in science education has focused on pupils' learning in science.

There are several perspectives on the way in which pupils (and others) learn. Four which have been particularly influential in science education are:

- transmission of knowledge;
- discovery learning;
- developmental views of learning;
- constructivism.

Transmission of knowledge

It would be difficult to argue with the notion that science teachers know things about science that their pupils do not. The transmission view of teaching and learning sees teachers as passing over their knowledge to their pupils. This view is strongly linked to expository teaching – the teacher standing at the front 'telling' their pupils about scientific ideas. As any experienced teacher will know, transmission teaching has its uses, but also limitations: simply telling pupils something is no guarantee that they will receive the message as transmitted, nor that they will understand it. Moreover, the transmission view implies that pupils' role in the learning process is largely passive, and that a pupil's mind is what is sometimes called a 'tabula rasa' – a blank slate on to which knowledge can be written. Again, as experienced teachers know, pupils very often already have ideas about some of the things they encounter in their science lessons. These limitations have led to the development of other views of learning.

Discovery learning

Discovery learning involves presenting pupils with information in a form which requires them to discover relationships within the information, and to structure and make sense of the information and relationships. Discovery learning therefore sees pupils as having a much more active role in their learning, and supporters of the approach argued that learning was enhanced as a result. Discovery learning has been associated with science education for well over a century, with the chemist H. E. Armstrong being a strong advocate in the first decades of the twentieth century of the use of heuristic (discovery) methods in science lessons (Van Praagh, 1973). Although Armstrong's work had some influence, it was not until the 1940s and 1950s, when the psychologist Jerome Bruner (see Appendix 2) started to publish his work, that the science education community began to draw on discovery learning approaches in any significant way. Science curriculum development projects, such as the Nuffield courses of the 1960s and 1970s (e.g. Nuffield Foundation, 1966a, 1966b), were developed to challenge the traditional 'teacher-astransmitter-of-knowledge' model of teaching and to present science to pupils as a way in which they could conduct their own inquiries into the nature of things. Discovery learning in science placed a strong emphasis on practical work organized in such a way that pupils made observations, looked for patterns and came up with possible explanations for these patterns.

By the 1980s, it was becoming apparent that there were limitations to discovery learning. Questions were being asked about the appropriateness of asking pupils to 'discover' things for themselves when both teachers and pupils knew that the answers were already there in the form of currently accepted scientific theories. There was also a question mark over the nature of the understanding pupils developed – left to their own devices, to what extent do pupils 'discover' the scientifically accepted explanations of the phenomena they experience? At the most elementary level, errors in results from pupils' practical work often make the identification of patterns difficult. Finally, at a philosophical level, discovery learning was criticized on the basis of the misleading view of science it presented. This view, often called the inductivist view, suggests that scientists work by collecting unbiased data free of any ideas they might have themselves, and then arrive at explanations for what they have observed. There is now general agreement that no-one, including scientists, collects data without being influenced by what they already know.

Developmental views of learning

Much work in the psychology of education has looked at how children's abilities to obtain, process and use information (their cognitive abilities) develop as they mature. The single most influential theory of cognitive development in the twentieth century emerged from the work of Jean Piaget, and describes four stages of intellectual development through which children pass. (An outline of Piaget's work may be found in Appendix 2.) Two key learning processes are central to Piaget's work: *assimilation* (interpreting new learning experiences within existing frameworks) and *accommodation* (modifying existing thinking to take account of new learning experiences). Piaget's work has been drawn on extensively in science education, most notably in the UK in the Cognitive Acceleration through Science Education (CASE) project (see Chapter 3).

Constructivism

The notion that learning is influenced by prior experiences and ideas has led to the development of what has become the dominant view of learning in science education today: constructivism. Essentially, a constructivist view of learning holds that people construct their own meanings from what they experience, rather than acquiring knowledge from other sources. The impact and influence of this view of learning forms the focus for the remainder of this chapter.

The origins of interest in the constructivist approach

Any review of science education research literature over the last three decades would reveal that one of the most significant areas of activity has focused on pupils' understanding of scientific ideas, the area which has become to be known as *constructivism*. As Jenkins (2001) comments, ' ... it has become almost impossible to escape any reference to constructivism among the papers published in the research journals'. Jenkins goes on to suggest that 'Work drawing on constructivist perspectives is perhaps, the nearest that has emerged to a research paradigm within science education ... '. Whilst it is arguable that constructivism has evolved to produce something close to an underlying theory (i.e. a paradigm), it is undeniable that work in the area forms the largest research programme in science education.

The early beginnings of constructivist research can be found in the 1970s, with the 1980s seeing a huge upsurge in interest and activity, a trend which continued well into the 1990s. It is difficult to pinpoint exactly why this upsurge in interest occurred but, looking back, it appears that a number of factors came together at a particular point in time to create a climate in which it seemed important to explore more deeply aspects of pupils' understanding of scientific ideas.

The climate was one of reaction to the discovery learning

approaches embraced by curriculum developers in the 1960s and 1970s. By the late 1970s and early 1980s, the limitations of this approach in science lessons were becoming apparent. At this time, there was also increasing interest in the work of two different psychologists and what their ideas might mean for science teaching. One of these psychologists was George Kelly, who had developed his influential theory of 'personal constructs' in the 1950s (Kelly, 1955). Kelly argued that people make sense of their own environment by developing theories to explain the world as they experience it and then testing these theories against new experiences – they are 'proto-scientists' (Kelly, 1971), constantly constructing or reconstructing their theories about the world. Kelly's most fundamental belief was that the way in which people behave is anticipatory rather than reactive.

The second psychologist was David Ausubel, who argued very strongly against the idea of discovery learning, saying that research demonstrating its effectiveness was virtually non-existent. Ausubel's work involved a search for what he described as 'laws of meaningful classroom learning' and the outcome was his theory of 'meaningful verbal learning'. Ausubel sums up his theory in what is his most often-quoted remark: 'If I had to reduce all of educational psychology to just one principle, I would say this: the most important single factor influencing learning is what the learner already knows. Ascertain this and teach him accordingly' (1968: vi). Thus 'meaningful learning' takes place when the learner already possesses concepts to which new ideas can be related. (Appendix 2 provides more information on the work of these two psychologists.)

Although the advent of discovery learning had brought about one fundamental shift in the way pupils' learning was perceived, in one sense, it shared with the transmission model of learning a view of the pupil's mind as the blank slate on to which new knowledge could be written. The ideas of Ausubel and Kelly challenged this perception by suggesting that the knowledge and ideas pupils brought with them to lessons exerted a significant effect on the way in which they tried to make sense of new experiences in lessons.

The work of Kelly and Ausubel was of particular interest and relevance to people working in science education in suggesting that it could be informative to look at children's ideas about the phenomena they met in school science. Research in this area has become known as *constructivism*, or the *constructivist viewpoint*. Box 2.1 summarizes the key issues and questions in constructivist research.

Box 2.1: Key issues and questions

- What are the origins of constructivism and why has it become such a significant influence on research activity in science education?
- What are the main features of a constructivist model of learning?
- What research techniques can be used for gathering data on pupils' ideas about particular science topics?
- What difficulties or issues are associated with gathering data on pupils' ideas?
- What are the key findings to emerge from constructivist research?
- What messages does constructivist research have for curriculum planning and for teaching?
- What are the current areas of critical reflection and debate about the constructivist approach?

The main features of constructivism and the constructivist viewpoint

A good starting point for identifying the main features of constructivism and the constructivist viewpoint is to look at how they are described by some of the key workers in the field. The classic introduction to constructivism is in *The Pupil as Scientist?* (Driver, 1983). A more concise account may be found in Driver and Bell (1986), in which they identify the following characteristics of a constructivist view of learning:

1. Learning outcomes depend not only on the learning environment but also on the knowledge of the learner.
2. Learning involves the constructing of meaning.

Meanings constructed by students from what they see or hear may or may not be those intended. Construction of a meaning is influenced to a large extent by existing knowledge.

3. The construction of meaning is a continuous and active process.
4. Meanings, once constructed, are evaluated and can be accepted or rejected.
5. Learners have the final responsibility for their learning.
6. There are patterns in the types of meanings students construct due to shared experiences with the physical world and through natural language. (pp. 353–454)

In other words, a constructivist view of learning science takes account of the prior ideas pupils have about the natural world, either from their own observation or from everyday language, acknowledges that learning will involve developing, modifying and even rejecting existing ideas, and accepts that understanding is something learners construct for themselves. Further accounts of the constructivist view of learning may be found in Osborne and Wittrock (1985) and Scott (1987).

Three important points are worth making about constructivism. The first is that the fundamental principles of constructivism are not particularly exceptional. Rather than describing something which was very new to those involved in science education, constructivism was a way of explicitly articulating something of which people were already aware. This may be one reason for its ready acceptance and the rapid growth of work in the area. A second point is that constructivism is a way of viewing pupils' *learning*. As such, it does not say anything directly about teaching, though some of the findings of research have implications for teaching strategies which might be adopted in the classroom. The final point concerns what is meant by *understanding*. Levels of understanding cannot be measured directly, only inferred from learners' responses to questions, and it is assumed that these responses provide an indication of understanding. Thus, when constructivist research talks about misunderstandings, it is using a *model* based on these inferences.

It is also worthwhile considering briefly how the constructivist view of learning relates to other views of learning, particularly those of Jean Piaget (see Appendix 2). Piaget certainly held that children's knowledge is constructed through interactions with their environment. There are clear overlaps between Piaget's concepts of assimilation and accommodation and the notion of children making sense of new ideas in terms of their existing thinking. As such, Piaget could be considered to be a constructivist. However, Piaget's main interest was in exploring context-independent or general features of the way in which children's cognitive abilities develop, whereas constructivists are interested in looking at children's learning in specific areas (or domains). This difference in focus has led some constructivists to question Piaget's stage theory of development. For example, Novak (1978) argues that children's ability to grasp certain scientific concepts appears less dependent on the stage of intellectual development they have attained than on the framework into which they can locate the concept.

Ways of gathering data on pupils' ideas

A range of techniques has been developed and refined for gathering data which provides insights into pupils' understanding of science ideas. Reviews of the literature (Driver and Erickson, 1983; White and Gunstone, 1992) have shown that four principal techniques are employed. These are written diagnostic questions, interviews about events, interviews about instances and concept mapping.

Written diagnostic questions

Written diagnostic questions are the most widely employed technique. Most take the form of a question about a particular event, with a follow-up open question in which pupils are asked to offer an explanation for their answer. Figure 2.1 shows a typical written diagnostic question aimed at exploring secondary level pupils' ideas about conservation of mass. Written diagnostic questions share many of the advantages of written questionnaires as a research tool: they enable a lot of data to be gathered very rapidly from a large sample. The work done by the Assessment of Performance Unit (APU) (1984 onwards) and the Children's Learning in Science Project (CLISP)

(1984–5) made extensive use of written diagnostic questions. Written diagnostic questions have the disadvantage of not being able to probe responses in more detail, though it is not uncommon for studies to use follow-up interviews with a selected sub-set of pupils who have provided written answers to questions. Written diagnostic questions are also not particularly well-suited to gathering data from primary age pupils, who often find it easier to talk about ideas rather than to write about them. This has led to two different types of interview being developed to gather data.

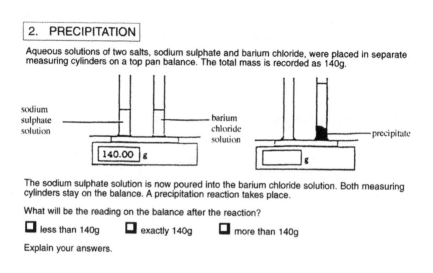

Figure 2.1 A typical written diagnostic question
Source: Ramsden (1997)

Interviews about events

An alternative to gathering written answers to questions involves interviewing pupils about particular events or phenomena. An early example of such as study was undertaken by Novick and Nussbaum (1978) to explore lower high school pupils' ability to use ideas about the particulate nature of matter to explain a variety of physical phenomena. To gather their data, they designed an interview which involved presenting pupils with three different phenomena and asking them questions about what they observed. For example, one phenomenon involved using a vacuum pump to suck air out of a flask. Pupils were asked to draw what they thought the air would look like before the pump was used and then after some air had been removed.

Interview about instances

Osborne and Gilbert (1980) developed a particular type of interview, the 'interviews-about-instances', for gathering data on particular scientific ideas. The technique is described in detail in Gilbert *et al.* (1985). In interviews about instances, pupils are presented with a series of pictures which illustrate a particular event or context (the 'instance') and then asked if the scientific idea in question applies to this. If they say 'yes', they are then asked to explain why. The technique works best when the idea being explored can be expressed in a word or short phrase, such as 'energy' or 'force'. Watts (1983) used the interview about instances technique to gather data on secondary school pupils' ideas about the concept of force. Pupils were presented with cards showing, for example, hitting a golf ball, a book sitting on a table, pushing a car to start it and sledging down a hill, and asked the question, 'Is there a force here?' The initial response to this questions was then followed with questions to explore pupils' reasons for saying there was – or was not – a force in the picture. The answers given by pupils reveal their understanding of the idea through their use of the term.

Interviews may be carried out with individuals or with small groups. However, because gathering data using interviews is more time-consuming, sample sizes tend to be small which may, in turn, raise issues about the extent to which the findings apply to other groups. The main advantage of interviews over written diagnostic questions is that they allow responses to be clarified and probed in more detail by asking follow-up questions to initial answers.

All three of the techniques above are not without their problems related to the reliability and validity of pupils' responses. For example, McClelland (1984) suggests that children may not actually have well-formed views about many of the things teachers or researchers ask them about. Rather, they adopt a strategy of 'instant invention', making up an answer on the spot to avoid an admission of ignorance. A further methodological issue concerns the administration – or the re-administration – of the same probes in longitudinal studies and studies involving pre- and post-tests. If pupils have already experienced a probe on an earlier occasion, this may well influence a later response. On the other hand, a different probe may not test the same meaning. Related to this, Wood (1998) has noted that respondents often feel they have to offer a different response if they are faced with a question a second time on the basis that their first answer was not satisfactory. To try and resolve this issue, most researchers take the view that re-administration of the initial probes is acceptable provided that initial answers have not been discussed and sufficient time has passed since they were last administered.

Concept mapping

The principle of a concept map is that it provides a visual means of showing connections and relationships between a hierarchy of ideas ranging from the very concrete to the abstract. Examples of studies using concept maps include those of Champagne *et al.* (1981); Fensham *et al.* (1981), Adamczyk *et al.* (1994) and Markham *et al.* (1994). One way in which concept maps can be used is to ask respondents to modify their maps at a number of points during a period of instruction as a means of establishing how their thinking is developing. Concept maps pose two particular problems as a research technique. First, they are not easy to construct, and respondents require training and practice in producing maps. Researchers have attempted to overcome this difficulty in part by providing ideas already written on cards and asking respondents to use these as a basis for producing a concept map by linking the ideas together. Second, there are difficulties with the interpretation of concept maps, in particular with devising appropriate ways of scoring to enable valid comparisons to be made.

What has emerged from constructivist research?

Broadly speaking, three main phases can be identified in constructivist research. The initial work in the 1970s and 1980s focused on identifying and documenting misunderstandings. This early work emphasized the patterns in the ideas held by individual learners and is now often referred to as 'personal constructivism' or sometimes 'radical constructivism' (von Glasersfeld, 1995). The early and mid-1980s saw the focus shift to what this might mean for teaching. At the same time, many more studies were being undertaken documenting the misunderstandings of a range of learners in a variety of science topics. This period could probably be described as the 'golden age' of constructivist research, when its approaches and ideas were virtually unchallenged. However, the late 1980s onwards saw the emergence of writing which was more critical of certain aspects of the work and an increasingly more theoretical debate on the nature of constructivism and the development of constructivist research. One outcome of this debate has been a more critical reflection on the messages from constructivist research as a 'mature' area of research for teaching science. The most recent writing has broadened out to locate the constructivist viewpoint within a broader view of learning which places more emphasis on the socio-cultural aspects of learning. Each of these phases is now considered in turn, and Box 2.2 provides a summary of the main research findings.

Identifying and documenting understandings

Early work on constructivism focused on secondary age pupils and explored their ideas about a number of scientific concepts, primarily in the area of physics. For example, Driver and Erickson (1983) list almost thirty studies exploring pupils' understanding of the topics of dynamics, gravity, heat, light, the particulate nature of matter, electricity and pressure. This list also gives an indication of the widespread interest in constructivism, as it includes studies undertaken in Australia, Canada, France, Israel, New Zealand, Norway, South Africa, the UK and the USA. Subsequent work has seen an expansion both in the number of topics explored and in the age ranges of the learners, with bibliographies (Carmichael *et al.*, 1990;

Box 2.2: Key research findings

- There is considerable research evidence to support the notion that children construct their own explanations for scientific phenomena, and that these explanations may differ from the accepted scientific explanations. Areas where this has been demonstrated to be the case include: photosynthesis, respiration, biological classification, evolution, matter, chemical reactions, energy, electricity, forces and motion, and heat and temperature.
- Learning involves the *reconstruction* of existing ideas not just the accumulation of new ideas.
- The ideas and explanations children construct tend to persist even after formal instruction because they make sense in terms of everyday observation and experience, whereas the accepted scientific explanations are often counter-intuitive.
- A number of proposals for teaching strategies to help pupils reach accepted scientific viewpoints have been put forward by researchers.
- There is general agreement that teaching strategies should begin by eliciting children's existing ideas and then presenting children with situations which challenge this thinking.
- There is less agreement over the ways in which accepted scientific views might be introduced.
- As yet, little firm evidence has been gathered about the effectiveness of particular teaching strategies which have been developed within the constructivist framework as compared with other strategies.

Pfundt and Duit, 2000) listing well over 2000 articles, and three books providing an overview of studies (Driver *et al.*, 1985; Osborne and Freyberg, 1985; Driver *et al.*, 1994a). Though the largest body of research has been undertaken with 9–16 year-olds, studies have been undertaken with learners at primary, secondary, tertiary levels and with teachers. Topics that have been explored include: photosynthesis, respiration, biological classification, reproduction, evolution, materials, chemical reactions, magnetism, sound and gravity. Many of the studies reported are comparatively small scale, focusing on one topic area, but there are examples of large-scale studies, such as the Children's Learning in Science Project (CLISP) (1984–5) in the UK and the Learning in Science Project in New Zealand (Osborne and Freyberg, 1985). There are also numerous examples of replication studies, involving the gathering of additional data on a previously explored topic from learners in new locations.

Several other features have emerged from constructivist research. First, there is considerable diversity in the terminology employed to describe those ideas gathered from learners which do not match with accepted scientific ideas, with researchers using terms like alternative frameworks, alternative conceptions, alternative ideas, preconceptions, misconceptions, misunderstandings, everyday science, commonsense science and children's science. Second, studies have taken a number of different forms in terms of when data has been collected: some gather data at one point only ('snapshot' studies), often before formal instruction, some involve pre- and post-tests, some involve cross-age studies (i.e. data on understanding of a particular topic has been gathered at the same time from pupils in different years), whilst a more limited number have been longitudinal studies (i.e. have tracked the development of ideas of a single cohort of students over a period of time). Finally, although there appears to be a consensus over appropriate techniques for gathering data, there is far less agreement over the implications of the finding for teaching.

It is beyond the scope of this chapter to describe the findings of even a fraction of the reported studies, so this section will concentrate on discussing some of the more general patterns and issues which have emerged from the work. Boxes 2.3 and 2.4 illustrate two examples of constructivist research studies, the former being one of the classic early studies which formed part of CLISP in the UK (Brook and Driver, 1984), and the latter a more recent small-scale practitioner study.

The research has provided overwhelming evidence that children arrive in science lessons with ideas which they have formed in making sense of the world around them. Additionally, there is ample evidence to indicate that many of these ideas differ from the accepted scientific ideas, often because scientific ideas are counter-intuitive – they do not make sense in terms of everyday observations. For example, some of the pupils in the extract at the start of the chapter have their own ideas about forces based on their sense of being

Box 2.3: An example of a larger-scale study on constructivism

Brook and Driver (1984) – a study which formed part of the Children's Learning in Science Project (CLISP)

Aim
To explore secondary level pupils' ideas and understanding of the concept of energy.

Research questions

- Do students use ideas about energy spontaneously to help them interpret phenomena?
- When students are 'cued' that energy is involved in a situation, what ideas about energy do they use?
- Do students recognize that energy can be quantified?
- Do students use the idea that energy can be conserved?

Research strategy and techniques
The study took the form of a survey of a sample of 15-year-old students, using six written diagnostic questions to gather data. The sample was representative of the population as a whole in that its composition reflected the proportion of 15-year-olds who were and were not studying physics. Approximately 300 responses to each question were analysed. Additionally, a sample of eight students was interviewed using material based on that used to gather the written responses.

Main findings
Less than one in twenty students spontaneously used ideas about energy in their answers. In a question which 'cued' students that energy was involved, many students focused on observable features: for example, half the students talked about energy being 'used up' in a clockwork toy as it wound down. Less than one in five students saw a relationship between the concepts of energy and work. Students strongly associated the notions of energy and force. Studying physics appeared to have little impact on the answers given to a number of the questions.

Box 2.4: An example of a small-scale study on constructivism (Banks, 1997)

Aim
To explore changes in students' understanding of chemical equilibrium.

Research questions
What ideas and understanding do 16- and 17-year-old students have about chemical equilibrium? How do these ideas change following instruction?

Research strategy and techniques
The research took the form of a comparative longitudinal study of two cohorts of students, one following a two-year context-based chemistry course, Salters Advanced Chemistry, and another following a more traditional course. The principal research instrument used diagnostic questions to gather written responses from students. These data were supplemented by a limited number of follow-up interviews. Data were collected from a total of 95 students in six different schools at three points during their course.

Main findings
The study showed students had a number of misunderstandings about chemical equilibrium, including the notion that equilibrium could exist in open systems. Following instruction, the majority of students demonstrated ideas consistent with scientifically accepted explanations, though a significant minority retained their original views. No significant differences in patterns of understanding or changes in these patterns emerged between the two groups.

'thrown forward' if they are on a bus which brakes sharply. Intuition does not tell them that, if they are moving at a steady speed, they will continue to do so in a straight line until a force acts on them!

The varying terminology used to describe these ideas to some extent reflects the ideological perspectives of the researchers on the nature of the data they have gathered. Some researchers (e.g. Gilbert *et al.*, 1982) feel that the terms such as 'alternative ideas', 'everyday science' and 'children's science' are more appropriate than, for example, 'misunderstandings' as they give value and recognition to the ideas children have developed about scientific phenomena, even those that conflict with accepted scientific views. Terms such as 'children's science' were certainly seen as preferable in the broader educational context of the time, with its emphasis on child-centred learning. Others (e.g. McClelland, 1984) feel such terms give too much status to children's ideas.

Along with the ever-increasing number of studies being reported, there has been discussion about what is meant by the term 'concept'. Some of this discussion has been at the philosophical level, debating the extent to which concepts are fixed or variable (see, for example, Gilbert *et al.*, 1982) and some at the more pragmatic level of which ideas in science can be termed concepts. Here there is no consensus, but the term is generally applied to a word or phrase associated with a collection of linked ideas which can be used to explain a number of different situations, such as 'force', 'energy' and 'chemical reactions'. However, the area continues to be debated with, for example, diSessa and Sherin (1998) arguing that more attention needs to be paid to describing different types of concepts in science.

From the diversity of reported studies, the following general features have emerged about children's ideas:

Ideas tend to be stable and resistant to change

Gathering data which reveals pupils have misunderstandings before formal teaching can be seen as an interesting and informative exercise. However, gathering data after formal instruction which indicates little has changed gives cause for some concern. A number of studies, such as that of Wood-Robinson (1991) on pupils' ideas about plants, have involved gathering data from pupils both before and after instruction and have shown that that the ideas held by pupils are very resistant to change.

A more limited number of studies has tracked the development of pupils' ideas over a period of time. For example, Engel-Clough *et al.* (1987) looked at how pupils' ideas about three topics – heat, pressure and evolution – changed in a two-year period. Data were gathered from two cohorts of pupils, one aged 12 at the start of the study and the other aged 14. Although there were variations from topic to topic, in the words of the authors, ' ... perhaps the most impressive feature of the data is the consistency in the use of alternative responses'. One reason for the stability of pupils' ideas is that many are perfectly adequate for dealing with their everyday experiences, and are often reinforced by everyday language. Thus, when pupils encounter new ideas in science lessons, they very often ignore some aspects of the idea and adapt it to fit their current thinking – in Piagetian terms they assimilate the ideas, rather than accommodate them. As a consequence, this hinders pupils' learning of accepted scientific ideas and explanations.

Research has also identified ways in which children's thinking develops, or *learning pathways*, within particular topics. For example, Driver (1985) describes a five-stage model proposed by Andersson (see also Andersson, 1986) for the development of pupils' under-standing about chemical change:

1. That's how it happens – pupils are unquestioning about chemical change.
2. The displacement of matter – new substances because they have been moved from one place to another, such as smoke being driven out of wood.
3. Modification – a new substance is a different form of the original substance, such as ash from a burning splint being a different form of the splint.
4. Transmutation – the original substance has been transformed into a completely new substance.
5. Chemical interaction – new substances are formed by the dissociation or recombination of atoms from the original substance.

Learning pathways are illuminating in that they help identify the stage a pupil's thinking has reached in moving towards accepted scientific understanding.

Ideas tend to be consistent across cultures and follow similar patterns of development

Replication studies and planned cross-country studies, such as those undertaken by Shipstone *et al.* (1989) on electricity, and Nussbaum (1979) and Mali and Howe (1979) on the Earth as a cosmic body, have yielded evidence on pupils' ideas across cultures. The studies suggest that, though there may be variations from individual to individual, there are common patterns in misunderstanding which appear in groups of pupils as a whole irrespective of their cultural background. Moreover, studies with a cross-age dimension (such as those above) have shown similar patterns in development of pupils' ideas.

Ideas are often 'domain-specific' and may even be conflicting

Though the evidence suggests ideas are stable over time, they appear not to be stable from one context to another. A number of studies (e.g. Watts, 1983; Guesne, 1985, Shipstone, 1985; Claxton, 1993) have shown that the ideas and explanations pupils offer are 'domain-specific' — they are limited to the context in which the pupils are operating. Moreover, pupils can hold different and conflicting ideas in two contexts which a scientist would see as drawing on the same scientific ideas. Thus, for example, pupils will describe light as 'coming from' the sun and other glowing objects to their eyes but see their eyes as active agents 'giving out' something in order to see other, non-glowing objects. Such findings have led to questions about the validity of viewing pupils' ideas as 'frameworks' — an issue which has been the focus of considerable debate in the literature. A key question here concerns the extent to which children's ideas are genuinely 'theory-like', i.e. do they have a coherent internal structure which is being used consistently in different contexts? Opinions on this differ. Supporters of the existence of coherent frameworks include McCloskey (1983) and Carey (1985). Others argue that learners' ideas are much more fragmented and context-specific. Solomon (1983) refers to 'two worlds' of knowledge — the scientific and the life-world — which have very different structures, and diSessa

(1988) describes learners as having 'knowledge in pieces' rather than coherent frameworks.

Ideas may draw on more than one scientific concept

'Electricity' is a classic example of an idea children have which incorporates a number of scientific ideas. In describing electric circuits, children will talk about a battery 'making electricity', 'electricity' going round a circuit or a bulb 'using up electricity', processes which, from a scientific perspective, involve several ideas (current, energy transfer, charge, potential difference).

Ideas are developed from observable features

Unsurprisingly, the ideas children have drawn initially on what they observe: salt 'disappears' when it dissolves in water, metals 'absorb more cold' than plastics and moving objects require a force to keep them in motion. From these observable phenomena, pupils construct explanatory theories, in the same way that learning science involves moving from what is observed to constructing explanatory theories. The difficulty here is that the intuitive theories and explanations at which pupils develop, derived often very logically from their observations, do not concur with accepted scientific theories and observations. However, some researchers (e.g. Viennot, 2001) have pointed out that there may be regular patterns in the 'commonsense' reasoning applied by pupils. In particular, her work on a number of physics topics has suggested that one trend which underpins pupils' reasoning is that of considering abstract concepts, such as a ray of light or a force, as material objects.

Ideas demonstrate linear reasoning from cause to effect

Explanations children offer for events often involve identifying a cause which brings about a series of effects over a period of time. Driver *et al.* (1985) suggest that this can cause two difficulties in learning science. First, pupils can have difficulties seeing interactions between systems. For example, pupils see a force as something which produces an effect, rather than grasping the notion of equal and opposite forces described in Newton's third law of motion. Second, pupils have difficulties with reversible processes: for example, they can grasp the fact that an input of energy may change a solid to a liquid, but are less able to appreciate what happens when a liquid turns into a solid.

Implications of constructivist research for practice

It is easier to gather data on children's ideas than it is to know with clarity what the implications are for science teaching. However, most people involved in science education are concerned to know how what has been learned about pupils' ideas can be applied to teaching. Work on constructivism has yielded insights for curriculum planning in terms of the ways in which scientific ideas might be introduced and

---

Box 2.5: Implications for practice

- An important first step in the introduction of any new topic is to elicit ideas on pupils' current understanding and ideas.
- Elicitation of ideas is particularly important in topic areas which have been demonstrated to cause difficulties for pupils because they hold ideas or patterns of ideas which differ from the accepted scientific explanations (see Box 2.2 for examples of these areas).
- Constructivist approaches to teaching should be used selectively, concentrating on the topics where research evidence has suggested pupils have most difficulty with reconstructing their ideas.
- Structured discussion tasks provide pupils with useful opportunities to explore and develop their own ideas, and also to begin to address other ideas which may conflict with their own.
- Pupils are likely to need time and a number of opportunities to explore new ideas if they are to reach a point where they are willing to accept agreed scientific ideas and explanations.

developed, and for classroom practice by pointing to both general strategies which can be employed to probe pupils' thinking and specific strategies to promote more effective learning of particular topics. Box 2.5 summarizes implications for practice.

Implications for curriculum planning

Conventionally, curriculum planning has involved bringing together groups of people with expertise in science education and asking them to make recommendations about curriculum content. Driver and Oldham (1986) see this as just one strand of curriculum development, with a second strand drawing on constructivist views of learning and the evidence which has emerged from studies on pupils' ideas in particular topics, particularly studies which have implications for the ways in which ideas might be introduced and sequenced. Leach and Scott (2000) describe an example of how this influenced a revision of the National Curriculum in England and Wales: drawing on research findings which demonstrated that young children rarely use models of matter which can explain the role of process such as decay in ecosystems, they were able to recommend that the introduction of ideas about decay was delayed until pupils were older.

Implications for classroom practice

Several researchers have proposed a range of strategies for helping bring about change in pupils' ideas. Figure 2.2 shows the model developed by the Children's Learning in Science Project team, as described by Driver and Oldham (1986). Other models include the cognitive conflict model (Nussbaum and Novick, 1982) and the generative learning model (Cosgrove and Osborne, 1985). All these models have two key phases: the first of these involves gathering information about pupils' current thinking (elicitation) and the second involves presenting pupils with some form of stimulus or new idea which challenges this thinking. The desired outcome is that pupils reformulate their ideas. Posner *et al.* (1982) have identified three characteristics a new idea needs to have to bring about a change in thinking: the idea needs to be *intelligible* (it must be understood at some level), *plausible* (it must make sense in terms of offering explanations) and *fruitful* (it must offer more than the previously held idea).

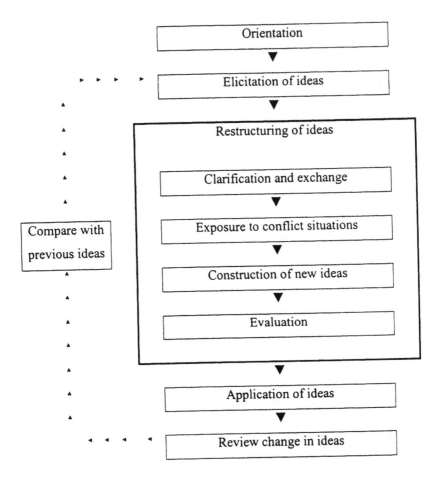

Figure 2.2 The constructivist teaching model developed by the Children's Learning in Science Project team
Source: Driver and Oldham (1986)

The simpler of the two phases is that of eliciting pupils' current ideas. Drawing on the techniques used to gather data on research studies, several strategies have been proposed. These include: pupils writing down statements and then pooling and discussing statements; card-sorting exercises; presenting pupils with descriptions of events and asking then to decide whether they are true or false; pupils producing posters on a particular idea; concept cartoons (Naylor and Keogh, 2000). The more difficult phase is responding to the outcomes of these activities. Driver *et al.* (1994a) identify five possible forms of responses, depending on the outcome of the elicitation phase. These are:

- developing existing ideas (if no misunderstandings are apparent);
- differentiating between existing ideas (where two or more scientific ideas may be seen as one by pupils, e.g. dissolving and melting);
- integrating existing ideas (where pupils may hold several ideas relating to one scientific idea);
- changing existing ideas (where pupils hold ideas which differ from the scientifically accepted ideas);
- introducing new ideas.

There is, however, a very practical problem here as, within any one class, individual pupils are likely to hold different ideas, and responding to all of these may be impractical.

Of the responses above the most difficult to bring about is that of changing existing ideas. In this context, Leach and Scott (1995) use the notion of *learning demand* – the extent of the difference between everyday and scientific ways of thinking which result in particular topics causing presenting pupils with difficulties. One approach is to introduce *discrepant events* (i.e. events which pupils cannot explain on the basis of their current ideas) in order to induce what is variously described cognitive conflict, disequilibrium (a Piagetian term) or dissonance in pupils' minds. Similar results can be achieved by setting up situations in which pupils can test their own ideas, such as predict-explain-observe strategies (White and Gunstone, 1992), or through the use of Socratic questioning: asking questions which require pupils to provide evidence to support their ideas, with a view to persuading them that there are gaps in their logic. Linked to the increasing prominence being given to the importance of language as a tool for learning (see Chapter 7), others (e.g. Champagne *et al.*, 1981) have argued that providing opportunities for peer group discussion of ideas is vital in helping promote conceptual change. More recently, Ogborn *et al.* (1996) have suggested strategies such as displaying counter-intuitive results to pupils as a basis for discussion and using stories to suggest ideas. These strategies have met with varying degrees of success and, as yet, there is no consensus over the best approach or approaches to helping children modify their ideas.

There are some examples of projects which have been designed to probe children's ideas and then to develop classroom tasks to change these ideas. One such project at the primary level is the Science Processes and Concept Exploration (SPACE) Project (King's College/University of Liverpool, 1992). However, detailed studies of the effects of particular interventions are still comparatively rare.

Areas of critical reflection and current debate in constructivist research

It is, perhaps, inevitable that, as research in the area has evolved and the focus has broadened, some people within the science education community have grown more critical of certain aspects of constructivism. In part this is because it is unlikely that any one theory is ever going to be able to provide a definitive explanation of learning in science (or in any other area) or point to a single 'best' method of instruction. A first indication that constructivism – or the 'personal constructivism' which characterized much of the early work – had passed its zenith came with the publication of the critique, *Constructive criticisms* (Millar, 1989a), with other critiques following (Matthews, 1994; Solomon, 1994; Osborne, 1996; Ogborn, 1997; Jenkins, 2000b).

By the late 1980s limitations to constructivism were beginning to surface. Some of these have been mentioned earlier, such as the debate about the extent to which 'alternative frameworks' existed. Another concern voiced in the critiques was, in Millar's words, that 'The constructivist model of learning has (invalidly) become associated with a particular model of instruction' (1989a: 588). He points out that the process of construction of new ideas takes place within the learner's own head, and is independent of the form of instruction, and therefore the constructivist model of learning does not imply any particular model of instruction. He develops this idea to suggest that science should be taught in a way which is most likely to engage the active involvement of pupils to create the circumstances in which they will want to learn. A further concern in the critiques was the failure of constructivism to take account of the social contexts and dynamics of the learning environment. One outcome of this has been a move from personal constructivism, with its emphasis on the individual, to the broader view encompassed in social constructivism.

Social constructivism

Social constructivist views in science education began to appear in the first half of the 1990s, and see scientific learning as the construction of knowledge which involves both the individual and social processes. Driver *et al.* (1994b) summarize this view:

> Learning science involves young people entering into a different way of thinking about and explaining the natural world; becoming socialised to a greater or lesser extent into the practices of the scientific community with its particular purposes, ways of seeing, and ways of supporting knowledge claims. ... Learning science involves both personal and social processes. (p. 8).

Social constructivism places less emphasis on the individual, and more on the learning context and communities of practice, with the teacher's role being one of supporting pupils by making the ideas and practices of the scientific community meaningful at the individual level (see, for example, Hodson and Hodson, 1998). Social constructivist views draw on the work of Vygotsky (see Appendix 2 for more details), who emphasized the importance of culture and language in the development of knowledge and understanding, and the studies of everyday use of mathematics and science undertaken by Lave and Wenger (1991). Social constructivist approaches also make reference to the concept of 'situated cognition', which links learning to the activities used *and* to the context in which they are used, or, in the words of Brown *et al.* (1989), 'Situations might be said to co-produce knowledge through activity' (p. 32).

The promise of the broader view of learning encompassed by social constructivism is that research into classroom interactions will help identify conditions which assist learning in science and how teachers might best achieve such conditions. Exploration of these areas opens up new avenues for constructivist research.

Conclusions

Where does constructivism stand after well over two decades of research in the area? The constructivist view of learning has developed from one of personal constructivism, with its focus on patterns in the ideas of individuals, to one which also embraces features of the learning environment and the contribution of language to learning – social constructivism. The most significant achievement of constructivist research lies in the insights it has provided into the ideas pupils hold about scientific phenomena. Another outcome of the work is the development of a range of well-tested techniques for probing understanding. For classroom teaching, a key message is that many of the ideas pupils have and the explanations they offer are not in accord with accepted scientific ideas and explanations. Constructivism has had more limited success in proposing successful strategies for bringing about change in pupils' thinking and contributed little to the understanding of why some ideas are more difficult than others. As yet, it has also yielded little on the effects of context and classroom conditions on learning. In noting these limitations, it is important to say that no single view or perspective is ever likely to provide a complete description of learning in science education. Constructivism has made a major contribution and remains *the* most significant and extensive area of research in science education to date.

Box 2.6: First stops for further reading

The classic introduction to constructivism is:
Driver, R. (1983) *The Pupil as Scientist?* Buckingham: Open University Press.

A fairly theoretical paper which covers a range of issues and is often cited in other constructivist writing is:
Driver, R. and Erickson, G. (1983) Theories-in-action: some theoretical and empirical issues in the study of students' conceptual frameworks in science. *Studies in Science Education*, 10, 37–60.

A concise overview of the constructivist model of learning may be found in:
Driver, R. and Bell, B. (1986) Students' thinking and the learning of science: a constructivist view. *School Science Review*, 67 (240), 443–56.

Three very useful compendia of studies of pupils' ideas in a range of topic areas are:
Driver, R., Guesne, E. and Tiberghien, A. (eds) (1985) *Children's Ideas in Science*. Buckingham: Open University Press.
Osborne, R. and Freyberg, P. (eds) (1985) *Learning in Science*. Auckland: Heinemann.
Driver, R., Squires, A., Rushworth, P. and Wood-Robinson, V. (eds) (1994) *Making Sense of Secondary Science: Research into Children's Ideas*. London: Routledge.

A critique of constructivist research is:
Millar, R. (1989) Constructive criticisms. *International Journal of Science Education*, 11 (5), 587–96.

Ideas about social constructivism are discussed in:
Driver, R., Asoko, H., Leach, J., Mortimer,E. and Scott, P. (1994) Constructing scientific knowledge in the classroom. *Educational Researcher*, 23 (7), 5–12.

An update of work on constructivist research may be found in:
Leach, J. and Scott, P. (2000) Children's thinking, learning, teaching and constructivism. In M. Monk and J. Osborne (eds) *Good Practice in Science Teaching: What Research has to Say*. Buckingham: Open University Press.

Though not specifically concerned with constructivism, a very useful book on the development of learning is:
Wood, D. (1998) *How Children Think and Learn* (2nd edn). Oxford: Blackwell.

Chapter 3

Cognitive Development and Children's Learning in Science

> **TEN WAYS TO THINK LIFE THROUGH**
>
> Children taught specifically to analyse events and understand probability do better in exams across a range of subjects.
>
> Children taught science reasoning tasks jumped 20 or more points on the IQ scale and doubled their success in exams.

The headline and extracts above come from the Education section of the *Independent* newspaper published in the UK in May 1991. The article was reporting the culmination of well over fifteen years of research in science education, research which suggested that it was possible to improve pupils' thinking skills, or accelerate their cognitive development, to the point where examination performance was significantly enhanced. The materials developed for use in the research programme, the Cognitive Acceleration through Science Education (CASE) materials, have had considerable impact on science provision in schools, particularly for pupils in the 11–14 age range. One feature of particular interest is that the research draws extensively on the work of Jean Piaget, who proposed one of the most influential theories of child development of the twentieth century. How has the research programme drawn on Piaget's work? What factors have contributed to the impact of research on cognitive acceleration?

This chapter looks at:

- the origins of interest in Jean Piaget's work and why it is of particular interest to those involved in science education;
- the ways in which science education researchers have drawn on Piaget's work to develop tests to assess pupils' levels of cognitive development, to analyse curriculum materials and to inform curriculum planning;
- the classroom strategies which have been proposed as a result of research into cognitive acceleration;
- implications of the work both for science teaching and for educational research more generally.

Introduction

It is undeniable that many children find it hard to get to grips with some ideas in science. As the previous chapter showed, constructivism has revealed much about what children do – or do not – understand in many areas of science, and offered some possible explanations for these understandings. As such, the constructivist research programme has been able to offer some suggestions for the introduction and sequencing of ideas in the science curriculum. However, the notion that some science ideas are more difficult than others, and what this might mean for curriculum planning, has focused the attention of some science education researchers on theories about the development of children's intellectual abilities. Not unsurprisingly, people interested in this area have turned to the work of Jean Piaget, and the work that they have undertaken forms another significant research programme in science education.

Looking back over some twenty years or so of work, it is possible to identify a number of key questions researchers have asked. The initial work in the late 1970s and early 1980s attempted to answer questions about the extent to which Piaget's theory of stage development offered any insights into why many pupils find much of science so hard. (Appendix 2 gives more details of Piaget's work.) Arising out of this came attempts to answers questions about why some ideas appeared to be more difficult than others. By the mid-1980s, the research programme was beginning to address a very crucial question: is the timescale through which a child progresses through each of Piaget's stages pre-determined, or can it be speeded up in any way? This work has led to a curriculum intervention programme, Cognitive Acceleration through Science Education (CASE). With its promise of improved exam results, not just in science but in other subjects as well, it is scarcely surprising that it has attracted considerable attention in science education in the UK and beyond, particularly in an educational climate where the agenda is very much driven by a drive to improve standards in schools. Box 3.1 summarizes the key issues and questions on research into cognitive acceleration and science education.

Box 3.1: Key issues and questions

- Why has the work of Jean Piaget on child development been of particular interest in science education?
- What impact has the work had on science curriculum development?
- What impact has Piaget's work had on research in science education?
- What are the origins of the Cognitive Acceleration through Science Education (CASE) project?
- What has the CASE project and the work that preceded it indicated about the development of pupils' learning in science?
- What are the current issues and questions emerging from CASE?
- What are the implications of CASE for science teaching?

In order to make sense of the research on cognitive acceleration, it is necessary to look in more detail at the work of Jean Piaget and consider why it has been so influential in education and in science (and mathematics) education in particular.

The work of Jean Piaget and its links with science education

Piaget's earliest work was undertaken in the 1920s and publications by Piaget and his principal co-worker, Bärbel Inhelder, appeared throughout the next four decades (e.g. Piaget, 1932; Inhelder and

Piaget, 1958; Piaget, 1961). Although English translations began to appear in the 1940s, it was not until the 1960s that Piaget's ideas on learning and their implications for teaching started to be examined in any significant way. To a very large extent, this can be attributed to the prevailing climate of thought in psychology – particularly theories of learning – in the 1940s and 1950s. At that time, psychology was trying to gain respectability as a science and, as a result, research into learning was very heavily dominated by the approaches and techniques of *behavioural psychology*. Behavioural psychologists are primarily concerned with developing general laws based on what is observable – they look at links between particular stimuli and the responses they provoke. Put simply, learning was seen to be a matter of providing a particular form of stimulus in order to generate a particular response. By the 1950s, questions were being asked about the usefulness and limitations of such approaches. There were, for example, some things that behavioural psychology seemed unable to explain: why did some animals (including humans) seem unable to learn things early in their life, yet learn them very readily once they had reached a particular stage of development? A case in point was the development of language – very young children could not be taught to talk. In seeking explanations for such observations, some psychologists became increasingly interested in mental processes – the area of *cognitive psychology*. In such a climate, Piaget's theory in which he described stages of development through which children pass, each with their associated cognitive skills, offered an attractive alternative to the behaviourist tradition. Fundamental to Piaget's theory is the notion that all children passed through invariant stages of development, and that the behaviour and thinking abilities displayed by children within each of these stages was very similar, both from child to child and from context to context. The 1960s and 1970s saw an enormous increase in interest in Piaget's work, with replication studies being carried out in many countries and an upsurge of educational initiatives aimed at applying Piaget's ideas in educational settings. Researchers who undertook this work are sometimes referred to as *neo-Piagetians*.

Piaget's stage theory of development has had a particular impact on science and mathematics education because there is considerable overlap between some of the cognitive abilities associated with each of Piaget's stage and abilities which school science and mathematics seek to develop. A brief look at some of the characteristics of thinking Piaget associated with his concrete operational and formal operational stages serves to illustrate this. According to Piaget's theory, one of the classic indicators that a child has attained *concrete operational thinking* is the ability to conserve, i.e. to realize that the quantity or amount of something does not change simply because of a change in form or spatial arrangement. For example, a child who has attained concrete operational thinking can appreciate that, when a liquid is poured from one container into another of a different shape, the quantity of liquid stays the same. In this stage, children also grasp the concept of number and become able to classify objects systematically and identify sub-categories within classifications. Children's thinking in the concrete operational stage is based on their experiences of real (i.e. concrete) objects and events. *Formal operational thinking* is characterized by the ability to deal with abstract ideas and, at this point, children become able to grasp ideas such as those involved in the setting up and testing of hypotheses, the control of variables, and ratio and proportion.

Educational implications of Piaget's work

The main focus of Piaget's work was to *describe* the way in which children's thinking developed, based on their performance in relation to a series of tasks. Piaget was much less concerned with the identification of factors which might influence this development or the speed with which it took place. However, his work clearly demonstrates that maturation (the gradual development of genetically determined characteristics) is a very important factor in the development of children's thinking abilities. Piaget (1961) also indicated that, in addition to maturation, cognitive development was influenced by the environment in which a child exists and the activities in which a child engages. He proposed three other specific factors as being of particular importance: a child's day-to-day activities and experiences, social interaction and equilibration (Appendix 2 explains this term in more detail). These other factors were those which seemed to offer particular promise for teaching, as they suggested to educational researchers that it might be possible to accelerate children's cognitive development through the provision of particular activities and experiences.

Limitations to Piaget's work

The main attractions of Piaget's theory lie in its formalization of something that people already recognize intuitively, and its emphasis on general explanations of observations in a number of different contexts. However, like any explanatory theory, it has both adherents and critics. Criticisms of Piaget's work generally centre on the extent to which it is possible to identify general stages of development, the age at which certain levels of thinking are demonstrated and on interpretation of the work with a view to making recommendations for teaching. Much work on the development of thinking in pre-school children (e.g. Donaldson, 1978) has suggested that young children are capable of more sophisticated thinking than Piaget's theory indicates, with performance on some of his tasks being depressed due to problems of language and interpretation. Novak (1978) questioned the development of general cognitive structures, citing evidence from a number of studies which indicate that individuals can operate at different Piagetian stages depending on the topic (or domain) in which they are working. In a similar vein, Brown and Desforges (1979) suggested that there was sufficient evidence from a range of studies to show that prior experience had a significant influence on levels of performance in a number of the tasks Piaget set children and from which he developed his theory. In this context, it should be noted that Piaget's theory does take account of the fact that children might perform at different levels depending on the nature of the task. However, the issue for critics was that the theory drew on a comparatively small quantity of evidence, raising serious questions about the generality of the stages of development Piaget described. Novak argued that learning was about the development of an organized framework of specific ideas arising from specific learning experiences, and Brown and Desforges suggested that research exploring the development of cognitive abilities in specific domains would be a more fruitful avenue to pursue that that of more general stages in cognitive development.

Despite the discussion and debate about the validity and implications of Piaget's work, its influence in science education is undeniable, with the last thirty years or so seeing a variety of initiatives drawing on the stage theory of development as an organizing principle for structuring the curriculum and devising teaching approaches. The 1970s saw a spate of curriculum development projects, with many focusing on the primary age range. These included the *Science Curriculum Improvement Study* (SCIS) (1970) in the USA and *Science 5–13* in the UK (Nuffield Foundation, 1972). This latter programme included a very detailed set of objectives for the science curriculum, linked very closely to Piaget's stages of development. These projects also took place at a time when discovery learning was very much in vogue and this is reflected in the activities and teaching strategies advocated. For example, the SCIS programme developed a teaching model, called the 'learning cycle approach', which structured teaching into three basic phases: exploration, invention (i.e. looking for patterns) and application.

The impact of Piaget's work on research in science education

In addition to curriculum development, Piaget's work also formed the basis for a significant research programme in science education. Much of the work in the area has been undertaken by Michael Shayer and Philip Adey in the UK, with papers arising from their work being published over a period of more than twenty-five years. This work forms the basis of the discussion in the remainder of the chapter. However, there are other examples of research, the most notable being that emerging from the SCIS programme and the efficacy of the learning cycle approach (Abraham, 1998). Here, the evidence indicated that the approach enhanced what was termed 'reasoning ability' and process skills, though it had less marked effects on performance in specific subjects.

The work of Shayer and Adey falls into three main areas:

- the development of tests to measure pupils' levels of cognitive development;
- the analysis of curriculum materials for cognitive demand;
- initiatives to accelerate cognitive development.

Box 3.2: Key research findings

- By the age of 14, pupils of average ability are unlikely to have developed the intellectual abilities to cope with abstract ideas in science.
- Much of the content of the science curriculum for 14–16-year-olds in the 1970s and 1980s was outside the intellectual grasp of substantial numbers of pupils.
- The Cognitive Acceleration through Science Education (CASE) project has yielded evidence that a specific programme of activities included in science lessons for pupils aged 11 and 12 will lead to improved performance in science, mathematics and English examinations at age 16+.
- Explanations for the effects of CASE vary as to whether the materials enhance certain specific aspects of intellectual development or more general cognitive development.
- There has been debate in the literature over the claims made for CASE and the extent of its effects on pupils' performance.

Box 3.2 summarizes the key research findings in each of these areas.

The development of tests to measure pupils' levels of cognitive development

Piaget used detailed observation and interviews over a long period of time to develop an extensive data bank from which he derived and described his stage theory of development. As such, his theory described general stages of development, but did not attempt to measure the stage any particular child had attained. Moreover, the techniques he employed for data collection made heavy demands on time. For these reasons, an important step for those wishing to use Piaget's ideas in science education was the development and validation of pencil-and-paper tests which could be used with groups of pupils to identify their stage of cognitive development. Thus a key element of the research programme was the development of what came to be called Science Reasoning Tasks (SRTs).

Early work on the development of pencil-and-paper tests was undertaken by Shayer and Wharry (1974), and the development of the SRTs themselves is described in detail by Shayer and Adey

(1981). Their aim was to develop tasks which, as far as was possible, incorporated what they identified (1981: 30) as the four essential features of a Piagetian interview:

- the use of apparatus which provided feedback following a child's suggestions and interviews;
- the ability to probe reasoning behind a child's responses;
- observation of a child's reaction to counter-arguments and proposals;
- flexibility in questioning following a child's responses.

Seven Science Reasoning Tasks were developed, each of which took the form of a structured demonstration, with pupils entering information on a worksheet at particular points. The responses on the worksheets were then used to assign pupils to one of five stages of cognitive development:

1 Pre-operational
2A Early concrete
2B Late concrete
3A Early formal
3B Late formal

The tasks were based on questions originally used by Inhelder and Piaget, and included, for example, 'the pendulum', which explored the effects of particular variables on the time of swing, and 'equilibrium in the balance', which explored the idea of inverse proportions on a balance.

Given the way in which these tasks were to be used, a vital part of their development involved establishing their reliability and, most crucially, their validity – to what extent did they provide a measure of a pupil's stage of cognitive development? The procedures which were followed are described in detail in Shayer (1979) and in Shayer and Adey (1981). To obtain measures of validity, the pencil-and-paper tests were followed up with limited pupil interviews which followed closely the protocols developed by Piaget. Pupils' performance on the tasks was also monitored from task to task. These procedures indicated good agreement between Piagetian levels allocated on written tasks and in interviews, and on levels allocated across tasks. Whilst this is clearly important, it should be noted that the SRTs do not in themselves validate Paiget's theory. It could be argued, for example, that devising tests which draw as far as possible on the methodology employed by Piaget and demonstrating that these tests allow Piagetian levels to be assessed actually says more about the reliability of Piaget's techniques than the validity of the tests.

The SRTs were used to undertake a number of large-scale surveys of pupils between the ages of nine and sixteen (see, for example, Shayer and Wylam (1978)), and indicated that only 30 per cent of 15- and 16-year-old pupils demonstrated formal operational thinking in their answers to questions on the tasks. This finding was consistent with the results of a number of studies which had replicated Piaget's methods of data collection (e.g. Wason and Johnson-Laird, 1972) and found that far fewer children than Piaget's work suggested actually demonstrated formal operational thinking by the age of 14. The Science Reasoning Tasks also indicated that formal thinking abilities concerned with spatial awareness (the ability to visualize things in three dimensions) could be identified earlier in boys than in girls.

The analysis of curriculum materials for cognitive demand

Having developed a means of assessing pupils' level of cognitive development, a logical next step was to assess the level of cognitive demand of the science courses followed by pupils. The hunch the research team wished to test out was that the level of cognitive demand of some of the ideas to which pupils were introduced in these courses was higher than the Piagetian level of thinking attained by the pupils. At the time, a number of schools in the UK had adopted the Nuffield biology, chemistry and physics courses developed for use with 15- and 16-year-old pupils. In order to assess the match between pupils' level of cognitive development and the demands of the science courses they followed, the team developed a Curriculum Analysis Taxonomy (CAT), described in detail in Shayer and Adey (1981).

The taxonomy consisted of two subdivisions, the first characterizing psychological characteristics of children's thinking (e.g.

investigation style, reasons for events) and the second characterizing responses to particular types of problem (e.g. conservation, mathematical operations, control of variables) at each of the five levels from 1 (pre-operational) to 3B (late formal), as described in the previous section. The taxonomy was then used to analyse the objectives associated with the activities in the curriculum materials in order to assign one of the levels to the objective (e.g. an activity which demonstrated that mass is conserved when salt dissolves in water was designated as level 2A). This in itself was by no means a simple task, and was made even more challenging as some of the materials examined did not have explicitly stated objectives. Thus those undertaking the analysis first had to decide on the objectives of each activity before applying the taxonomy.

Part of the process of the development of the CAT involved testing its reliability and validity in use. The reliability of the taxonomy was assessed through agreement trials – comparing the results of analyses by a panel of experienced science teachers. The validity of the taxonomy was judged by the extent to which the judgements made by panel about the level of objectives accurately predicted the success in meeting (or failure to meet) the objectives of pupils whose cognitive stages had been estimated. In other words, if the panel had judged a particular objective to be at stage 3A, pupils whose cognitive ability had been estimated as 2B should not achieve the objective, but pupils whose cognitive ability had been estimated at 3A or 3B should achieve the objective. In order to gauge the developmental stage reached by pupils, the research team administered a selection of the SRTs they had developed. The agreement trials led to modifications to the taxonomy but, overall, the research team felt that the evidence they had collected demonstrated that their taxonomy was both reliable and valid, and they went on to apply it to a selection of curriculum projects used in secondary schools. The analysis indicated that the level of demand of the materials was considerably in excess of the Piagetian stage of development which many pupils might be expected to have reached, i.e. the materials were outside the intellectual grasp of substantial numbers of pupils (Shayer, 1972; Shayer, 1974; Ingle and Shayer, 1971).

The development and use of the taxonomy raises two important issues concerning validity. In terms of the taxonomy itself, it is worth noting that judgements about its validity are closely linked to views on the validity of Piaget's stage theory of development, something which the research team have accepted as a cornerstone of their work. However, for those who question aspects of Piaget's work (e.g. the extent to which distinct and general stages do exist), the validity of the taxonomy would also be open to question. Additionally, the validity of the analysis undertaken with the taxonomy is clearly linked to the validity of the SRTs.

The mismatch in cognitive demand identified by the taxonomy analysis suggested two possible courses of action. The first concerned the modification of curriculum materials such that the content was more appropriate to the stage of development of larger numbers of pupils, and it is certainly the case that subsequent curriculum development projects took account of the findings which emerged from the use of the CAT. The second course of action concerned possible changes which might be brought about in pupils to enable them to cope with more demanding material – in other words, to see if it was possible to accelerate cognitive development. Given the exciting possibilities offered, research effort was directed at this second area.

Initiatives to accelerate cognitive development

Fundamental to initiatives to accelerate cognitive development in pupils is the notion that such development can be influenced by environmental effects such as mental stimulation, with teachers being well placed to maximize such mental stimulation. Early attempts to accelerate cognitive development tended to focus on aspects of children's ability to conserve – the most significant characteristic marking the transition from pre-operational to concrete operational thinking. These early studies, such as those on conservation of substance and weight undertaken by Smedslund (1961) and Lefrançois (1968), met with very limited success, and a review of a number of studies undertaken by Nagy and Griffiths (1982) led them to conclude that teaching strategies aimed at accelerating cognitive development had borne little fruit. In contrast, other studies being carried out in the USA and Australia and exploring aspects of developing formal operational thinking (or what was becoming known as *higher order thinking skills*) were yielding somewhat different results. For example, an intervention programme developed by Fuerstein *et al.* (1980) in the USA, the Instrumental Enrichment Programme (IEP), reported large differences in performance on Piagetian tasks between experimental and control groups.

During this period, Shayer had been working with a number of intervention strategies aimed at cognitive acceleration, the findings of which are summarized in Shayer (1987). One of these studies involved a small-scale replication of Fuerstein's IEP with secondary pupils in the UK (Shayer and Beasley, 1987). Again, promising differences were found in the performance of the control and experimental groups, though the enhanced performance of the experimental group on the Piagetian tasks was not translated into increases in achievement in school. Encouraged by the findings of this work and a number of other studies (see Adey, 1988, for more details), Shayer and Adey embarked on the development and trial of a series of activities aimed at accelerating cognitive development in secondary age pupils (Adey, 1987a, 1987b), activities which ultimately formed the basis of the Cognitive Acceleration through Science Education (CASE) programme (Adey *et al.*, 1989).

Given that a key aspect of Piaget's theory concerns the general nature of development of cognitive skills, it is worth considering why the programme was developed specifically for use in science lessons. Adey and Shayer (1993) put forward four reasons in addition to their own background in science education. First, the science education community had shown particular interest in links between teaching and learning theory. Second, there was considerable overlap in the terminology of Piaget's work and of science teaching. Third, they felt that developing materials for use in specific contexts might overcome one of the problems of subject-free intervention lessons employed in the IEP, where teachers found it difficult to relate activities aimed at promoting general thinking skills to lessons in their particular subject. Finally, at a very practical level, it was hoped that the existence of subject-specific materials would increase the chances of their being used.

The CASE activities involve presenting pupils with a problem to solve. For example, the problem presented in one activity concerns someone who claims they can always tell which of milk or tea has been poured first into a cup. Pupils have to devise a test to see if the person could indeed do this, or whether they were just guessing. In all, thirty activities, called *Thinking Science* activities (Adey *et al.*, 1989), were developed for the CASE programme, each intended to take around 70 minutes of teaching time and aimed at pupils aged 11 and 12 (the first two years of secondary education in the UK).

Adey and Shayer (1993: 193) list several features which were central to each of the CASE activities:

- the introduction, through concrete activities of the terminology of relationships and the context in which a problem will be presented (*conceptual readiness*);
- the presentation of problems which induce *cognitive conflict*);
- the encouragement of *metacognition*;
- the *bridging* of thinking strategies developed within the context of the special lessons to other areas.

As with instructional strategies proposed by the constructivists (see Chapter 2), cognitive conflict (i.e. presenting pupils with situations which challenge their current levels of thinking) is central to CASE teaching strategies. Additionally, the notion of metacognition, or encouraging pupils to reflect on their own thinking in solving the problems, is a key element of the CASE lessons.

One particularly interesting feature of the work on cognitive acceleration is that it employs a research strategy used comparatively infrequently in educational settings: the controlled experiment. The experiment involved selecting a representative sample of nine schools and 24 classes of pupils of average ability across these schools. Some of these classes contained pupils aged 11+ and some 12+. Twelve of these classes were randomly assigned as 'control' and 'experimental' groups, with the only constraint being that each school contained at least one control and one experimental class. In some instances, teachers were teaching both control and experimental classes. In 1985, teaching of the *Thinking Science* lessons began with the experimental classes, with classes experiencing one of these lessons roughly every two weeks for a period of two years. A programme of workshops was also organized for the teachers. Over the time-span of the programme, two schools withdrew, leaving ten experimental classes, four of pupils aged 11+ and six aged 12+. In total, 190 pupils comprised the experimental group, and 208 the control group. Box 3.3 summarizes the CASE experiment.

Measurements of pupils' levels of cognitive development were taken at points across the intervention. These consisted of a pre-test, a post-test immediately after the two-year intervention and a delayed post-test one year after the end of the intervention. Additional components of the data set included: the pupils' marks on a *science achievement* test agreed by the teachers participating in the experiment as a fair assessment of the objectives of the schools' science curricula and implemented at the end of the two-year intervention; the pupils' marks on each school's end-of-year science exam taken one year after the end of the intervention; and pupils' examination results for their General Certificate of Secondary Education (GCSE) taken two or three years after the intervention. The pre- and post-tests consisted of Piagetian Reasoning Tasks (PRTs), which were slight modifications of the SRTs developed in the 1970s. The modification principally involved refining the marking scale to expand the number of stages to which pupils could be allocated from the five originally used in the SRTs to a ten-point scale running from 1 (early pre-operational thinking) to 10 (mature formal operational thinking). The findings which emerged from these data up to and including the delayed post-test are discussed in detail in Adey (1989), and for the study as a whole in Adey and Shayer (1993) and Adey and Shayer (1994). The key findings are summarized below.

At the post-test point:

- pupils in experimental classes performed better than those in control classes on the PRTs;
- there were no differences in performance between groups in the science achievement test (here it is worth noting that the experimental group had spent about 20 per cent less time on their normal science lessons as a result of time spent on *Thinking Science* lessons).

At the delayed post-test point:

- there were no differences in performance between groups on the PRTs;

Box 3.3: An example of a larger-scale study on cognitive development
(Taken from Adey and Shayer, 1993 – an educational experiment with the *Thinking Science* lessons developed for the CASE project)

Aim
To see if an intervention programme would accelerate the cognitive development of secondary age pupils.

Research question
What are the effects on lower secondary level pupils' performance in tests of cognitive ability and of ability in science when the pupils experience a curriculum intervention package aimed at accelerating cognitive development?

Research strategy and techniques
The study took the form of an experiment conducted in seven schools and with 20 classes (ten control and ten experimental) of 11- and 12-year-old pupils. The experiment involved the class teachers using 30 lessons aimed at developing thinking skills to pupils in the experimental classes over a period of two years, and tracking performance during this period and at points up to three years after the intervention.

Data on cognitive levels of development were gathered at three points in the study using Piagetian Reasoning Tasks (PRTs). Data on performance in science were gathered at three points using a standard science achievement test, school examination results and public examination results (GCSEs) at 16+.

Main findings
Immediately after the intervention, the experimental classes performed better than the control classes on the PRTs, though there was little difference in the science achievement tests.

One year after the intervention, the experimental classes performed better than the control classes in science exams, though there was little difference on the PRTs.

Two or three years after the intervention, the experimental classes obtained significantly higher grades in science, mathematics and English in public examinations.

- pupils in experimental classes performed better than those in control classes in their science exams.

At the point when pupils took their GCSEs:

- pupils in experimental classes obtained significantly higher grades than those in control classes in science, mathematics and English.

Shayer and Adey termed this last set of results *far transfer effects*. Additionally, the data indicated that the gains were greater for boys than girls in science and mathematics, with the reverse being true for English, and that the gains were greatest for girls if they were 11+ at the start of the intervention, and boys if they were 12+ at the start. With schools being under ever-increasing pressure to 'deliver' good examination results and to develop policies to address boys' perceived underachievement (see Chapter 9), it is scarcely surprising that a research study which provided hard evidence of improved performance in these areas has attracted so much attention.

Current issues and questions emerging from the CASE work

There are a number of important questions and issues emerging from the CASE work. Some relate to how CASE works and its implications for science teaching: Why does it work? (Indeed, does it work?) How does it work in different contexts? Others concern the theoretical ideas on which CASE was based and, specifically, how it might relate to the work of the Russian psychologist, Lev Vygotsky. (See Appendix 2 for more details of Vygotsky's work.) A more general, but very important, issue concerns the messages the research programme has for educational research and its links to practice.

Why does CASE work?

Shayer and Adey (1993) put forward two possible hypotheses for the effects of the intervention. The first of these is that the intervention had selective effects on two aspects of intellectual development – linguistic and mathematical-scientific – each of which resulted in improved learning in that area. The second is that there was a positive effect on general cognitive structure which subsequently enhanced learning across academic disciplines. For Shayer and Adey, the evidence supporting the latter hypothesis is the more compelling. In reaching this conclusion, they draw on their evidence of the differences between girls and boys, as their findings are in keeping with the more generally reported evidence on the faster intellectual development of girls. Thus girls are better placed to benefit from the intervention at age 11 + than boys, whereas the boys benefit more at 12 +. Whatever the explanation, it seems likely that it is the practice of the skills associated with the *Thinking Science* activities which contributes to the differences established.

Does CASE work?

The evidence from the original CASE experiment is very persuasive and has certainly influenced many schools to implement the *Thinking Science* lessons into their curriculum over the last few years, making a far greater impact on classroom practice than any other research study. The explosion of interest in CASE has led to the development of CASE in-service training materials and the setting up of a network of CASE co-ordinators to run training workshops for teachers. A further outcome has been the development of other subject-based lessons aimed at developing thinking skills, for example the Cognitive Acceleration through Mathematics Education (CAME) project. CASE materials for use with younger pupils (7–11-year-olds) are also being developed.

There are two avenues which have been pursued in seeking answers to the question, *does CASE work?* Some researchers have looked back at the original experiment which demonstrated the increased levels of performance of pupils who had experienced the *Thinking Science* activities and questioned the validity of the claims. Others, of whom many are teachers in schools that have adopted CASE, have explored aspects of how it works in their particular schools. Looking first at the validity of the original CASE data, Leo and Galloway (1995) have suggested that CASE materials are more suited to certain types of motivational style than others, appealing particularly to children who have a 'mastery-oriented' learning style – they enjoy the challenge of solving a problem. For children with other motivational styles, they argue, CASE may be of far less – if any – benefit. Jones and Gott (1998) raise a number of issues to do with differences in the results of the schools involved in the experiment, suggesting that ' ... the school analysis raises more questions than it answers linked to overall differences in organisation, support and motivation ... ' (p. 762). They argue that further research is necessary before CASE can be said to work, a claim that is refuted by Shayer (1999), who suggests that data which have emerged from the more widespread use of CASE in schools confirms the findings of the original experiment.

The adoption of CASE in schools has raised a number of issues for teachers. The long-term nature of the effects means it is only comparatively recently that data has begun to emerge from a much wider pool of users but, aside from possible effects on pupils' performance, there are messages coming out about teacher confidence and the role of in-service training for teachers. Keith (1997) decided to investigate the impact of CASE in her school when, following initial high levels of enthusiasm, staff began to question the value of the intervention. Box 3.4 summarizes her study and its key findings.

Links between CASE and Vygotsky

More recent writing about CASE (e.g. Shayer, 1999; Adey, 2000) has drawn on the work of Vygotsky to offer support for the approach. Although Vygotsky was a contemporary of Piaget and also looked at child development, his work was only published outside his own country, the former Soviet Union, in the 1960s (Vygotsky, 1962). Certainly, at the time when the early work about cognitive development in science was being undertaken, little was known about Vygotsky's work. However, as it has been made available to a wider audience, Vygotsky's work has become increasingly influential in educational research.

Three themes underpin Vygotsky's theory of learning: the importance of culture, the central role of language and the means by which intellectual development takes place. As Vygotsky was

Box 3.4: An example of a small-scale study on cognitive development
(Keith, 1997)

Aim
To review the impact of the use of the CASE materials in a secondary school.

Research questions

- What views do staff have of CASE and the effects of CASE lessons on their pupils?
- What views do pupils have on CASE lessons?
- What effects does the adoption of the CASE materials have on pupils' performance in Standard Assessment Tasks (SATs) at age 14+?

Research strategy and techniques
The research took the form of a case study carried out in an 11–16 high school in the UK. Data were gathered through the use of questionnaires with students, through observation of CASE lessons and through interviews with staff. These data sources were supplemented by a statistical analysis of pupils' results in the SATs taken by pupils at age 14 before and after the implementation of CASE in the school.

Main findings
Teachers were initially broadly positive about the adoption of CASE.

Following implementation, teachers began to question its value. In part this was due to lack of confidence in using the CASE materials, despite attending in-service training sessions, and in part due to a lack of criteria against which to judge success in the short term.

Teachers' perceptions were that pupils were confused and uninterested in CASE lessons though data collected from pupils and classroom observation of CASE lessons suggested that this was not the case.

The analysis of pupils' performance in SATs indicated improvements in performance following the implementation of CASE, particularly for lower ability pupils.

interested in the ways in which intellectual development might be maximized, it is not at all surprising that his work should be of particular interest to the CASE team. In tracing the development of CASE materials, Shayer (1999) describes the materials as owing an almost equal debt to Vygotsky and Piaget. From Piaget's work came the theory which underpinned the selection of the CASE activities, and the approach of introducing and then resolving cognitive conflict. From Vygotsky's work came the theory which underpinned the inclusion of discussions in the activities to help children think about their learning (metacognition) and learn from each other.

Conclusions: what messages does CASE have for educational research?

The work of the research programme linked to CASE has been very

---

Box 3.5: Implications for practice

In many ways, the CASE materials *are* the implications for practice which have emerged from the research work. They provide concrete examples of activities which research evidence indicates should enhance pupils' cognitive development by challenging their current thinking and encouraging them to think about their learning.

The work also suggests some more general implications for practice:

- Educational research takes time and is unlikely to provide 'quick fixes' in the classroom.
- Controlled experiments, though posing a number of problems in educational research, have a role to play in testing the effectiveness of particular instructional strategies.
- The impact of research findings can be significant where they are built into curriculum materials.
- The introduction of new teaching materials and approaches needs to be well supported by training for those who will be using them.

---

influential in science lessons in the UK. It provides one example of work where the implications of research practice have been translated into very specific action for classroom practice. These implications are summarized in Box 3.5.

The principal message to emerge from the work described in this chapter has to be that educational research is unlikely to offer 'quick fixes' to problems. Whether or not one agrees with the ideas underpinning CASE and the work which preceded it, the research programme is characterized by years of thorough, detailed work and scholarly discipline. The work also demonstrates – even more sharply than the work of constructivists – that, in educational research, illuminating the problem is the easy part. The much harder task is coming up with solutions, and the researchers involved in the CASE work have had to engage in vigorous defence of their position on more than one occasion. Finally, in a climate where questions are being asked about the value of educational research and there are calls for more controlled experiments of innovation to be undertaken, the work illustrates a number of the complexities associated with educational experiments.

Box 3.6: First stops for further reading

The classic book describing the early work on linking research on cognitive development to classroom practice in science lessons is:
Shayer, M. and Adey, P. (1981) *Towards a Science of Science Teaching*. London: Heinemann.

An accessible overview of ideas about the development of intelligence and a summary of the CASE work may be found in:
Adey, P. (2000) Science teaching and the development of intelligence. In M. Monk and J. Osborne (eds) *Good Practice in Science Teaching: What Research has to Say*. Buckingham: Open University Press.

The CASE materials for use in science lessons are:
Adey, P., Shayer, M. and Yates, C. (1989) *Thinking Science: The Curriculum Materials of the CASE Project*. London: Nelson.

An overview of the work leading up to the development of the CASE materials is in:
Adey, P. (1988) Cognitive acceleration: review and prospects. *International Journal of Science Education*, 10 (2), 121–34.

A perspective from outside the CASE team, which raises issues about aspects of the work is:
Jones, M. and Gott, R. (1998) Cognitive acceleration through science education: alternative perspectives. *International Journal of Science Education*, 20 (7), 755–68.

The reply to the criticisms in the above paper is:
Shayer, M. (1999) Cognitive acceleration through science education II: its effects and scope. *International Journal of Science Education*, 21 (8), 883–902.

Chapter 4

The Role of Practical Work in School Science

In countries fortunate enough to have the resources to support pupil practical work, a question many teachers will have heard as their pupils begin a science lesson is 'Are we doing an experiment today, miss/sir?' The crestfallen looks when the answer is 'no' suggest that practical work is eagerly anticipated by most pupils and as something they expect to experience as part of their science lessons.

It is certainly true that practical work is one of the prominent features of the science curriculum in many countries, and its place in science lesson often goes unquestioned. Yet why is so much time devoted to practical work in science lessons? What sort of practical work should pupils undertake? What are the desirable skills and knowledge pupils should acquire from practical work?

This chapter looks at:

- the way in which practical work in school science has evolved;
- the purposes of practical work in the science curriculum;
- areas of debate over the purposes of practical work in the science curriculum;
- evidence gathered from research into the nature of practical work, its effects on pupils' understanding of science and ways in which practical abilities might be assessed;
- implications of research on practical work for science teaching;
- recent trends and issues in practical work.

Introduction

For many science teachers, it would be hard to imagine lessons which did not involve practical work. The prominence of practical work in the school science curricula of many countries suggests that there is a clear commitment on the part of both teachers and others involved in science education to the contribution that practical work makes to science lessons. However, such an approach to teaching science involves considerable time, effort and expense. With such an enormous investment of resources, it is important to ask the question, does the end justify the means? This is turn raises the question of what precisely *are* the ends and means of practical work in school science?

Research into practical work

Practical work in school science has been the focus of considerable research activity, as is evident from the number of books published in the last decade or so on various aspects of practical work (e.g. Hegarty-Hazel, 1990; Woolnough, 1991; Gott and Duggan, 1995; Wellington, 1998; and Leach and Paulsen, 1999). Box 4.1 summarizes the important questions and issues in practical work in school science. Broadly speaking, research on practical work in science falls into four main areas. The first of these has looked at the aims and justifications of practical work in the school science curriculum. The second has sought to establish baseline data on pupils' practical abilities. The third area has focused on the nature and effects of different types of practical activity on pupils' knowledge, skills and understanding. Finally, work has been undertaken on the assessment of practical abilities. Box 4.2 summarizes key research findings on practical work. From an original emphasis on the gathering of data on the existing practice of the time, the research agenda has to some extent shifted to exploring matters which might inform policy decisions. It is therefore worthwhile considering briefly how practical work has evolved into its current form.

Box 4.1: Key issues and questions

- What are the aims of practical work in school science lessons?
- What are the effects of practical work on pupils in terms of:
  developing their knowledge and understanding of science?
  developing their laboratory skills?
  the views and images of science they gain through engaging in practical work?
- What are the alternatives to practical work?
- What types of practical activities are appropriate for achieving particular aims?
- What role does investigative work have to play?
- What are appropriate ways of undertaking reliable and valid assessment of practical abilities?
- What are the future directions for practical work, and how do these relate to research in science education?

The evolution of practical work in school science

Practical work of some form has been part of the school science curriculum for well over a century, and its origins have been well documented (Gee and Clackson, 1992; Lock, 1988; Jenkins, 1998). In some respects, the development of practical work can be likened to a pendulum swinging between approaches which emphasize 'facts about science' and approaches which emphasize 'methods of science'. In its very early days, practical work tended to take to form of teacher demonstrations to verify facts and theories which had previously been taught. Towards the latter part of the nineteenth century, practical work was heavily influenced by the work of H. E. Armstrong, who advocated the 'heuristic' approach in which pupils were trained to find things out for themselves. It was at this time that the notion of pupils undertaking practical work for themselves became an established part of school science lessons.

When the heuristic approach fell out of favour in the early part of the twentieth century, the emphasis was again placed on illustrative, 'recipe-following', practical work, an approach which lasted for almost half a century. However, by the 1960s, the pendulum had

---

Box 4.2: Key research findings

- Pupil practical work forms a significant part of the science curriculum in a number of countries.
- Pupils generally report practical work as being enjoyable, though it is not always clear what it is about practical work that they enjoy.
- Practical work has a wide variety of aims and purposes.
- The wide variety of aims has resulted in a lack of clarity over the purposes of much practical activity in science lessons.
- Different types of practical work are needed to help achieve different aims.
- Practical work has an important function in making phenomena real for pupils.
- Practical work can help pupils gain some understanding of the way in which scientific knowledge progresses.
- Practical work can sometimes hinder rather than assist scientific understanding.
- The notion that practical work develops 'transferable skills' is open to question.
- Pupils' performance in practical tasks varies depending on the scientific ideas linked to the task.
- Pupils have difficulty with a number of aspects of investigative work in science, particularly where there is a need to control several variables, and in making judgements about the reliability of data.
- Teacher assessment has an important role in making valid assessment of the skills and abilities associated with investigative work.

---

swung once more, and the heuristic approach appeared to enjoy something of a renaissance in the curriculum projects of the 1960s and 1970s. Encapsulated by the much quoted expression, 'I hear and I forget, I see and I remember, I do and I undertand', these projects placed discovery learning through pupil practical work firmly at the centre of science teaching. Surveys undertaken at this time showed that that 11–13-year-olds spent over half their time in science lessons on practical work (Beatty and Woolnough, 1982a), and 16–19-year-olds spent around one-third of their time on practical work (Thompson, 1976). As subsequent curriculum development has retained a strong emphasis on practical work, albeit of a rather different nature, it is therefore likely that any data gathered on quantity of time currently spent on practical work would not be too dissimilar to these earlier figures.

By the late 1970s, a number of concerns were being raised about the value of discovery learning in science (see Chapter 2), and particularly about the artificial and constrained nature of much practical work. Specifically, questions were being asked about the legitimacy of encouraging pupils to 'be a scientist', whilst engaging them in activities which arrived at a pre-determined answer. Moreover, as has been seen in Chapter 3, the conceptual demand of the courses which emphasized discovery learning was proving to be well beyond the ability of average pupils. Both these factors pointed to a need for change. During this period a scheme had been developed in the USA called *Science – A Process Approach* (SAPA) (American Association for the Advancement of Science (AAAS), 1967). This approach aimed to place the emphasis in science lessons on what scientists do, rather than facts and principles of science. The 'processes and skills' or 'process science' approach to practical work, which dominated much practical work in the 1980s, had its origins in this scheme.

Much of the discussion and debate about practical work since that time has been about the nature of what scientists do, and how this might best be reflected in the activities in which pupils engage in their science lessons. One outcome of this in practical work in science lessons has been the rise of 'investigations' as an important means of developing what is often termed pupils' *procedural* understanding – their abilities to carry out the processes of scientific enquiry such as hypothesizing, observing, classifying and so on. Investigative work in science will be discussed in more detail later in this chapter.

It is clear from the discussion above that widely different views have been held about the nature and purpose of practical work in science, and one focus of discussion in the literature has been on exploring in more detail the aims of practical work and the justifications for including it in the science curriculum.

What are the purposes of practical work in science lessons?

An early study on the aims of practical work was undertaken by Kerr (1963) as part of a commission set up to enquire into the nature and purpose of practical work. The study took the form of a survey of some 700 science teachers in 150 schools. Teachers were asked to rank in order of importance a list of ten possible aims of practical work, as shown below:

1. to encourage accurate observation and careful recording;
2. to promote simple, commonsense, scientific methods of thought;
3. to develop manipulative skills;
4. to give training in problem-solving;
5. to fit the requirements of practical examinations;
6. to elucidate the theoretical work so as to aid comprehension;
7. to verify facts and principles already taught;
8. to be an integral part of the process of finding facts by investigation and arriving at principles;
9. to arouse and maintain interest in the subject;
10. to make biological, chemical and physical phenomena more real through actual experience.

Some subsequent studies have drawn on Kerr's methodology. Beatty and Woolnough (1982b) augmented Kerr's list with a further ten aims, including aspects such as to be able to comprehend and carry out instructions, to develop certain disciplined attitudes and to develop an ability to communicate. This second list of aims was also used in a much more recent study by Swain *et al.* (1998), cited in Watson (2000). Although there was some variation from study to study, and some differences amongst teachers of different subjects and age ranges, broadly speaking the findings indicated that teachers saw the most important aims of practical work as being:

- to encourage accurate observation and description;
- to make scientific phenomena more real;
- to enhance understanding of scientific ideas;
- to arouse and maintain interest (particularly in younger pupils);

- to promote a scientific method of thought.

One important aspect to note is that these findings report teachers' *views* of the aims of practical work – which may or may not reflect their actual classroom practice. For example, the high rating given to investigative work did not appear to be translated into actual use of such methods at the time when the earlier studies were undertaken.

Whilst the origins of the list of aims used in the studies is not made clear, they provide useful attempts to clarify the aims of practical work. A number of other lists of aims have been developed. For example, Woolnough and Allsop (1985) suggest that there are three fundamental aims of practical work which justify its inclusion in the school science curriculum:

- to develop practical scientific skills and techniques;
- to be a problem-solving scientist;
- to get a 'feel for phenomena'.

Hodson (1990), meanwhile, suggests that the justifications can be clustered into five main categories:

- to teach laboratory skills;
- to enhance the learning of scientific knowledge;
- to give insight into scientific method, and develop expertise in using it;
- to develop certain 'scientific attitudes' such as open-mindedness, objectivity and willingness to suspend judgement;
- to motivate pupils, by stimulating interest and enjoyment.

A number of points can be made about these lists. First, there are several different ways of summarizing the aims of practical work. Second, some of the aims are interlinked. For example, laboratory skills such as accurate observation are best acquired through observing scientific phenomena and this, in turn, is likely to enhance learning of the scientific ideas associated with the phenomena. In other words, the procedural and conceptual understanding go hand-in-hand. Finally, the expectations of practical work are *very* high indeed: not only is it expected to develop conceptual and procedural understanding, it is also intended to be a motivating influence on pupils and to help them appreciate what being a scientist involves.

Areas of debate over the purpose of practical work in the science curriculum

Whilst there might be a degree of consensus over the aims of practical work, there are also considerable areas of debate, with criticism being levelled at most, if not all, of the justifications made for the inclusion of practical work in the science curriculum. Hodson (1990: 33) describes much school practical work of the time as being 'ill-conceived, confused and unproductive' and providing 'little of real educational value'. He goes on to argue that much practical work is undertaken unthinkingly – both in the sense of practical work being an unquestioned part of science lessons and in the sense of little thought being put into the purposes of much practical activity. Further discussion of these arguments may be found in Hodson (1992; 1993).

The five justifications for the inclusion of practical work in school science described by Hodson (1990) and summarized in Table 4.2 provide a useful framework around which to structure discussion of issues and areas of debate in practical work.

Developing laboratory skills

The word 'skills' has been used in the context of practical work in a variety of different ways. Hodson (1990) distinguishes between skills which are 'science-specific', or what he terms 'craft skills', which are necessary for future scientists and technicians (e.g. using a microscope, setting up distillation apparatus), and skills which are more 'generalizable', such as reading scales. Gott and Duggan (1995) suggest that the word 'skills' has also been used, less appropriately, to describe cognitive processes (e.g. observing, classifying) which are more appropriately seen as associated with being a problem-solving scientist, and which will be discussed below in the sections on 'scientific method' and 'scientific attitudes'.

As far as the 'craft skills' go, Hodson points out that it is difficult to justify their inclusion in the science curriculum for everyone, simply on the basis that they will be needed for future scientists. Whilst there is some truth in this, it could also be argued that the curriculum in any subject must, in part at least, include aspects required by future specialists. Whatever the view here, there is a substantial body of evidence (see, for example, studies undertaken by the Assessment of Performance Unit (APU), described more fully later in this chapter) which suggests that the majority of pupils have difficulties with using standard laboratory apparatus and carrying out standard laboratory procedures even after several years of studying science.

There are also reservations about the more generalizable skills, such as 'classifying' and 'hypothesizing'. One of the arguments put forward for the inclusion of practical work in science, and more widely for the necessity of all pupils studying science, is that the skills pupils develop in practical work are transferable to wider contexts. Though little detailed research has been carried out on the extent to which skills acquired in science lessons might be transferred to other situations, a considerable body of psychological literature suggests that the notion of skills transfer is highly problematic, and unlikely to take place unless very clear links are made to pupils between one situation and another. Furthermore, as Woolnough (1991) argues, many of the abilities which pupils use to solve problems in science and elsewhere draw on their *tacit* knowledge: knowledge which has been built up over a period of time and through a range of experiences, many of which take place outside the laboratory. Such knowledge is often difficult to articulate with precision, let alone make decisions about how it can be 'transferred' to a new situation.

Enhancing the learning of scientific knowledge

Although one of the original purposes of introducing practical work was to help develop understanding, an aim which was also identified as important by teachers, there is a surprising lack of evidence to support the claim that practical work is a more effective means of developing understanding than other activities. In the USA, where pupil practical work is less central to science lessons than in a number of other countries, several studies were undertaken, mainly in the 1960s and 1970s, comparing the effectiveness of pupil practical work with teacher demonstrations. (Reviews of these studies may be found in Garrett and Roberts, 1982, and Clackson and Wright, 1992.) In keeping with the stronger tradition of experimental research in the USA, these studies tended to take the form of employing different instructional methods with groups and comparing the learning outcomes. One example of such a study (Yager *et al.*, 1969) suggested that science-specific skills were the *only* thing pupils learned better through actually doing practical work for themselves. More recent studies have provided little support for practical work as a means of enhancing learning. For example, in an evaluation of the Australian Science Education Programme (ASEP), Edwards and Power (1990) concluded that practical work had little impact on the development of understanding, though it did motivate pupils in lessons. Watson *et al.* (1995) reported similar levels of understanding of ideas about combustion in two groups of pupils, one of which had followed a course with a high proportion of practical work, and one where the practical work content had been much lower.

One problem with drawing any general conclusions from these studies is that they are open both individually and collectively to the criticisms which are often levelled at educational experiments. These include the ways in which variables are controlled within any one experiment, and the differences across studies in the instructional methods employed and the techniques used to assess pupils' learning. Nonetheless, the studies provided no conclusive evidence that pupil practical work in itself was more effective than other instructional techniques at promoting learning of science ideas. Rather, other factors appeared to be exerting a stronger influence, such as the type of practical work being undertaken, and the extent to which the teacher helped pupils see links between the practical work itself and the scientific ideas to which it related.

Other studies have also pointed to factors which inhibit learning when pupils are engaged in practical work. Much practical work places high demands on pupils: they are likely to have to read and understand instructions, use apparatus appropriately, make observations and take measurements, and make records of what they have done. All these factors may act to a greater or lesser extent to distract pupils from the main purpose of the activity. A study by Alton-Lee *et al.* (1993), in which recordings were made of pupils talking whilst they were engaged in practical work, showed that many of the conversations were about clarifying and agreeing organizational aspects of the task, rather than about the learning the task was intended to promote. Even when the focus is on the learning, the desired outcome may not be attained. Studies such as that of Driver and Bell (1986) have shown that pupils' interpretations of their observations during practical work can be influenced by the ideas they already hold about particular phenomena – ideas which may not be consistent with scientifically accepted ideas. Thus pupils sometimes see what they expect to see, rather than what they are expected to see.

Limitations to learning from practical work have also been identified by Ogborn *et al.* (1996) and Millar (1998). They question the basic assertion that observing phenomena develops understanding and point out that a particular set of observations may well not in themselves lead to understanding. As Millar suggests, pupils are highly unlikely to deduce for themselves ideas about charge transfer from observations of attraction and repulsion in charged plastic rods. This has led to the notion of practical work as a means of 'bridging' between what is observed and underlying explanations.

Gaining insights into scientific method

The claim that practical work in school science helps pupils gain insights into scientific method and develop expertise in using it has been much criticized. Part of the problem is that there are areas of disagreement on what constitutes 'scientific method'. One fairly narrow interpretation is as an umbrella term to describe a way of working which is characterized by attributes such as objectivity, systematic gathering of evidence and open-mindedness. On the one hand, the fact that these attributes are not restricted to scientific activity has resulted in claims that the abilities pupils develop through engaging in practical work are transferable to other situations and contexts. On the other hand, the non-specific nature of such attributes has also led to questions being raised about whether such a thing as 'scientific method' really exists or whether the attributes form part of systematic enquiry in general, which becomes 'scientific' when it is applied for scientific purposes.

A broader interpretation of 'scientific method' is as a description of the way in which scientific knowledge progresses. Here again, there is a lack of consensus. When discovery learning was in vogue, the message it was presenting was that scientific ideas emerged when exploration of particular instances allowed more general patterns and relationships to be identified. This is the *inductive* view of science. In the classroom, pupils struggled to grasp this message, as has been well documented (e.g. Driver, 1975; Atkinson and Delamont, 1976; Wellington, 1981). As science teachers know, pupils engaged in practical work often ask questions such as 'What's meant to have happened?' or 'What's the right answer?'. In other words, pupils see the aim of much of their practical work as confirming answers which others have already worked out, rather than arriving at answers they deduced for themselves. More fundamentally, few people now believe that the inductive view of science reflects the process in which scientists engage to advance knowledge. The prevailing view is based on that put forward by the philosopher Karl Popper (1959), in which scientific ideas and theories develop through the rigorous testing of hypotheses. This is the *hypothetico-deductive* view of science, and it is reflected in the current emphasis in school practical work on testing predictions. However, it should be noted in this context that Millar (1989b) has pointed out that school laboratories do not provide an environment for the rigorous testing of ideas, and that it is therefore misleading to claim that school practical work reflects the *hypothetico-deductive* view of science to any great extent. Moreover, current views on the nature of scientific enquiry acknowledge that decisions made by scientists about what to observe, how to interpret their data and what conclusions it suggests are more important than the application of a formalized set of rules on how to proceed.

Developing scientific attitudes

Claims that practical work in school science helps develops scientific attitudes have also been subjected to considerable criticism. As with 'scientific method', there is a diversity of views on what comprises 'scientific attitudes'. In a detailed review, Gauld and Hukins (1980) suggest that scientific attitudes fall into three main groups: (i) general attitudes towards ideas and information (such as curiosity and open-mindedness); (ii) attitudes to the evaluation of ideas and information, or 'critical-mindedness' (including attributes such as objectivity and a willingness to weigh evidence and, if necessary, change one's mind); (iii) commitment to particular beliefs (such as belief in the understandabilty of nature). Within this framework, they point out possible conflicts between aspects of the first and third groups. Again, as with 'scientific method', claims are made for the generalizability of 'scientific attitudes'.

One problem in talking about 'scientific attitude' concerns a lack of clarity over what is encompassed by the term, which raises questions about the validity of any instruments used to gather data. (Discussion of the term 'scientific attitudes' may be found in Gardner, 1975, and Gauld and Hukins, 1980.) A further problem is related to the diversity of studies undertaken and variety of instruments employed to measure attitudes, both of which make it difficult to reach any general, well-supported conclusions. Added to this is the ethical dimension – to what extent can promoting one particular set of attitudes over another be justified? Finally, as with all research into attitudes, there is the problem of the extent to which actual behaviour is linked to declared attitude. In reviewing studies on the development of scientific attitudes, Gardner and Gauld (1990: 151) conclude that, though there is evidence to suggest that teacher behaviour and the way in which teachers structure practical work can help pupils develop scientific attitudes, 'the hopes that labwork might foster students' curiosity, openness and a willingness to solve everyday problems scientifically remain hopes'.

Motivating pupils

The final justification for the inclusion of practical work is that it motivates pupils. Certainly the majority of pupils do seem to enjoy practical work in science lessons – though it is less clear what they enjoy about practical work, and there is little evidence that it has a more general effect on motivation to study science. For some pupils, at least, it is likely that their enjoyment of practical work comes from the fact that it provides them with an opportunity to talk to fellow class members – and not necessarily about the task in hand! It may also provide welcome relief from listening to teachers and from writing, a task which many pupils report as being something they particularly dislike about science lessons. Put more positively, what pupils do seem to like is the less constrained atmosphere during practical activity, and the greater control over the pace and, to a lesser extent, the nature of the activity (Gardner and Gauld, 1990). What is clear is that, underneath the umbrella term 'practical work', there are some activities which are more liked than others. Studies such as those of Kempa and Dias (1990a; 1990b) and Watson and Fairbrother (1993) have indicated that the sorts of practical activities that pupils enjoy are those where the purpose is clear, which provide them with a challenge and which give them some control over what they have to do.

What are the implications of these areas of debate for practical work?

A number of messages emerge from the preceding discussion. First, though claims for its achievements may be overstated, practical work can form a useful part of the school science curriculum. Second, merely engaging in practical work of any nature is no guarantee that learning will take place – the more crucial factor is how the teacher introduces and develops the ideas associated with the practical work. In this context, some researchers (e.g. Gunstone, 1991; Sutton, 1992) have argued very strongly that what pupils learn as a result of engaging in practical work arises from discussion of what they have done, rather than from the doing itself. Third, it is unrealistic to expect one particular form of practical work to address all, or even most, of the many different aims of practical work. Rather, different types of practical work are appropriate to help achieve different aims. The discussion also has messages about the ways in which practical work might be assessed (see later in this chapter), and a rather more general implication is that there is a need to look for alternatives to practical work.

Alternatives to practical work

Dissatisfaction with practical work has led to a number of alternative teaching strategies being proposed, though rather less research has been undertaken into their effectiveness. One strand within these alternatives involves the use of simulations and other computer-based material. Hodson (1998) puts forward a number of arguments for their use, including the potential benefits to pupils in terms of improved understanding of ideas by allowing them more time to focus on the essential features of a practical activity. Chapter 6 looks in more detail at the use of ICT in science teaching.

Other strategies which have been proposed include group discussions of phenomena where pupils' own ideas may conflict with accepted scientific ideas or where there has been controversy over the scientific explanation (Millar, 1989b; Osborne, 1997), and thought experiments (Adams, 1991). In a similar vein, a study by Solomon *et al.* (1992) has suggested that pupils gained an improved understanding of the nature of science though discussions of case studies of particular events in the history of science. What links these suggestions is their use of discussion to explore and develop understanding. To draw on another often-used quotation, 'Children solve practical tasks with their speech as well as their hands' (Vygotsky, 1978: 26). This aspect of learning is explored further in Chapter 7.

The development of investigative work in practical science

The most significant trend in practical work in the UK in the last decade or so has been the emphasis placed on investigative work. A major influence behind this trend was the extensive research carried out by the Assessment of Performance Unit (APU). The APU was set up in 1974 to explore methods of assessing and monitoring pupils' achievement. One strand of this work focused on pupils' standards of performance in practical tasks. The research spanned a period of some fifteen years and generated an extensive databank on the performance of 11-, 13- and 15-year-olds. Data were gathered from 12,000–16,000 pupils in 300–600 schools. The findings were summarized in a number of short reports (APU, 1984 onwards) and described and analysed in more detail in a series of longer reports (APU, 1988a; 1988b; 1989a; 1989b). Aspects of the work begun by the APU were continued by the Evaluation and Monitoring Unit (EMU) of the Schools Examination and Assessment Council (SEAC) (SEAC, 1991).

The APU studies used an assessment framework consisting of six categories of science performance:

1. use of graphical and symbolic representation;
2. use of apparatus and measuring instruments;
3. observation;
4. interpretation and application of (i) presented information and (ii) science concepts;
5. planning of investigations;
6. performance of investigations.

In addition to the databank on performance, the work undertaken by the APU (and, later, the EMU) made a number of other important contributions to research in science education, particularly in terms of the ways in which practical work might be assessed (see Black, 1990), and it has also exerted a significant and lasting influence on practical work in school science. By including Category 6, *'performance of investigations'*, as the culmination of other aspects tested, the APU gave out a clear signal on what it saw as the way ahead for practical work in school science: it should contain a strong element of investigative work. Moreover, the APU also signalled that the most valid route for assessing the skills and abilities needed to undertake investigative work was through teacher assessment. In England and Wales, these messages were reinforced in the Department of Education and Science (DES) publication, *Science 5–16: A Statement of Policy* (Department of Education and Science, 1985), and they subsequently became requirements of the National Curriculum for Science.

Investigative work and 'process science'

Although there has been increasing consensus over the importance of investigative work as a means of teaching pupils about a scientific approach to enquiry, there has been considerable debate over the most effective ways which might be used in the classroom to help pupils develop the abilities associated with investigative work and, at a more fundamental level, over what constitutes investigative work.

During the 1980s, much school practical work was influenced by the view that abilities associated with investigative work could be broken down into a number of discrete aspects which could be taught independently – the 'process science' view, which saw practical work as a means of developing 'transferable skills' in pupils. This approach sought to introduce pupils to basic skills such as 'observation', then move on to more complex skills, for example 'inferring' or 'hypothesizing', before finally engaging in whole investigations. For some curriculum projects, such as *Warwick Process Science* (Screen, 1986) and *Science in Process* (Wray, 1987), the emphasis on processes extended beyond practical work, with the principal aim being to teach pupils about the processes, rather than the content, of science. One justification for such an approach was that, in Screen's words, 'the most valuable aspects of a scientific education are those that remain after the facts have been forgotten' (Screen, 1986). Other curriculum materials which drew heavily on the process approach include the *Techniques for the Assessment of Practical Skills in Science* (TAPS) materials (Bryce *et al.*, 1983).

Process science has been the subject of considerable criticism (see Millar and Driver, 1987; Millar, 1989b; Wellington, 1989; Gott and Duggan, 1995). Criticisms include:

- a lack of clarity over the meaning of the terms 'process' and 'process skills';
- the extent to which it is possible to break down aspects of scientific enquiry into a hierarchy of discrete 'processes';
- the distorted and over-simplified view of science presented by such an approach;
- the validity of claims to be able to teach processes such as 'observation';
- the fallacy of the notion that 'science processes' can be seen as something separate from the content and context in which the processes are being developed;
- the lack of convincing evidence (in, for example, the APU research) on the transferability of skills and processes;

- an over-simplistic view of progression in the development of the abilities needed to undertake investigative work.

Criticisms of process science have resulted in a shift of emphasis in the way in which pupils are introduced to investigative work. Rather than drawing on a model of progression which builds up to investigations through a hierarchy of discrete 'processes', the emphasis is now on pupils engaging in whole investigations where progression is addressed through increasing levels of sophistication in terms of the associated procedural and conceptual understanding.

The increasing prominence accorded to investigative work has made it the focus of a number of research studies, both small and large in scale. Such a major shift in the nature of practical activity in science lessons has prompted teachers to explore the effects on their pupils. Box 4.3 illustrates an example of such a study which focused on pupils' understanding of the reliability of the measurements they took when carrying out investigations.

Larger-scale studies include that of Foulds *et al.* (1992), reported in Gott and Duggan (1995). This study gathered data on a number of aspects of investigative work, including teaching methods being employed and aspects of progression. This latter aspect drew on the work of the APU to explore the ways in which the number and nature of variables involved in an investigation influenced children's performance. Findings of the study included: performance in investigations varied according to the related science concepts; pupils performed less well in investigations set in 'everyday' contexts than in scientific contexts; and pupils had particular difficulties with investigations involving two independent variables. One particularly positive note about this study was that it was commissioned with a view to informing policy decisions, and subsequent findings influenced the revision of the National Curriculum for Science in England and Wales. The findings are described in detail in Gott and Duggan (1995). The ideas were developed in the Procedural and Conceptual Knowledge in Science (PACKS) project (Millar *et al.*, 1994). The first phase of this two-phase project involved developing a model linking pupils' performance in investigative tasks in science to their understanding of the related science. The second phase explored ideas about the reliability of experimental data in pupils aged 11–16. Box 4.4 summarizes the second phase of the PACKS project, and more

Box 4.3: An example of a small-scale study on practical work (Tompkins, 2000)

Aim
To explore upper primary age pupils' understanding of the reliability of empirical evidence.

Research questions

- What are pupils' expectations of the consequence of repeating an experimental event, and how do they explain variation in repeated measurements?
- How do pupils perceive the need for repeat measurements when performing investigations, and how do they use repeat measurements?
- How do pupils' ideas about reliable measurements in investigations change as they progress from age 7 to age 11?

Research strategy and techniques
The research took the form of a survey of 58 pupils distributed across the 7–11 age range. Data were gathered through the use of pencil-and-paper diagnostic questions supplemented by observation of classes of pupils undertaking investigations. In addition, interviews were conducted with eight pairs of pupils (two in each of the year groups) as they performed 'mini-investigations'.

Main findings
Most pupils believed that repeating an event in exactly the same way would produce an identical result. Variation was attributed to the event not being repeated in exactly the same way. The notion of inaccurate measurement was rarely mentioned. Most pupils believed the purpose of repeat measurements was to confirm previous measurements. The most frequent strategies applied for selecting the final result from a series of measurements were to select the largest value, or the most frequent result, or a value in the middle of the range. Although some changes were detected, the comparatively small sample size study did not suggest any general patterns in the progression of reasoning.

Box 4.4: An example of a larger-scale study on practical work: The PACKS (Procedural and Conceptual Knowledge in Science) project
(Lubben and Millar, 1996)

Aim
To explore ideas about the reliability of experimental data held by pupils aged 11–16. (This study formed the second phase of the project. The first phase involved developing a model linking pupils' performance in investigative tasks in science to their understanding of the related science.)

Research questions
What understanding do pupils have of the validity and reliability of measured data?

Research strategy and techniques
The study took the form of a survey of pupil performance. Two instruments were developed for the survey, each consisting of six written diagnostic questions (probes). These were administered to approximately 400 11-year-olds, 400 13-year-olds and 250 15-year-olds, a total sample of some 1000 pupils. The probes explored ideas about the need to repeat measurements, dealing with anomalous readings and judging reliability of data from a spread of values in a set of repeated measurements.

Main findings
The following are two of the findings from an extensive data set:

- About 35 per cent of 11-year-olds think the purpose of repeated measurements is to obtain two identical results as this identifies the 'true value'. Only 18 per cent of pupils of this age see repeating measurements as a means of estimating the uncertainty in measurements, though this figure rises to 50 per cent by age 14 and 70 per cent at age 16.
- Very few pupils (almost no 11-year-olds and only 13 per cent of 16-year-olds) rejected anomalous values in a set of data before taking an average of readings.

detailed discussion of the study may be found in Lubben and Millar (1996) and Millar and Lubben (1996).

Other studies have focused on aspects of the implementation and management of investigative work in school science. These include the Open-ended Work in Science (OPENS) project (Watson and Fairbrother, 1993), and the ASE–Kings Science Investigations in School (AKSIS) project (Watson, 1997; Watson *et al.*, 1998).

One final – though important – point on investigative work concerns the nature of the work itself. Though current policy and practice emphasizes investigative work, and the 'process skills' approach of the 1980s has largely fallen into disfavour, there is still considerable debate over what might legitimately constitute 'investigations' in science. Successive versions of the National Curriculum for Science in England and Wales have seen a shift from the model of the late 1980s and early 1990s, which placed particular emphasis on control of variables, to a model which stresses the importance of the evaluation of evidence. In part this stemmed from the strong criticisms levelled at the earlier model for the distorted view of investigative work it presented (see, for example, Donnelly *et al.*, 1996). Despite the change, concerns remain that the current model of investigations still presents too narrow a view of the process of scientific enquiry, and is resulting in what might be termed 'institutionalized investigations' – investigations of a very restricted nature and which follow a very prescriptive format – being undertaken in science lessons (see, for example, Watson *et al.*, 1999).

Assessment of practical work

With such diversity of aims, it is hardly surprising that there has been considerable debate over what constitutes a reliable and valid assessment of practical abilities, and the most appropriate means of assessing such abilities. Some of the issues have been considered in earlier sections of the chapter, particularly in the discussion on investigations. The main areas of debate include: the range and nature of skills to be assessed (e.g. Hodson, 1992; Gott and Duggan, 1995); the balance between the assessment of prescriptive and investigative tasks (e.g. Gott and Duggan, 1995); and the extent to which the assessment should be holistic or atomistic in its approach (e.g. Fairbrother, 1991).

In practice, formal assessment of practical abilities has tended to be restricted to a limited number of aims: manipulative skills and techniques, accurate observation and description, and data collection, presentation and interpretation. Two models of assessment have generally been employed to assess practical abilities: the end-of-course examination and course-based teacher assessment. The advantages and disadvantages of each have been well documented (see, for example, Fairbrother, 1991; Jenkins, 1995). The end-of-course practical examination is economical of time and could be described as more objective in the sense that the teacher is not involved in making the assessment. However, it runs the risks of not providing adequate opportunities for pupils to demonstrate the abilities they have developed over the course, and encouraging teachers to focus practical work on those skills and techniques most likely to be tested in the practical examination. Course-based teacher assessment permits a wider range of practical abilities to be tested and gives pupils more opportunities to demonstrate their abilities, but places very high demands on the time and skills of teachers. Procedures also need to be put into place to ensure the reliability of assessments. In countries where there is a strong tradition of the assessment of practical abilities, current practice tends to use a model of teacher assessment of more extended tasks with an investigative emphasis. Evidence to support the use of such a model comes from, for example, the work of the APU, as described earlier. However, even where such a model is used, there is emerging evidence (Keiler and Woolnough, 2002) of the negative impact of assessment, with pupils seeing practical work as game to be played in a certain way to gain marks, rather than as a means of helping develop knowledge and skills.

Two groups of aims are seen as inappropriate or problematic in the assessment of practical abilities, and are therefore either not assessed or form only a very small component of the overall assessment. The first group contains those aims normally associated with routine practical work in course, such as discovering a law or principle, or experiencing a scientific phenomenon. The second group contains the affective aims such as assessment of the extent to which practical work stimulates interest and enjoyment, or the assessment of 'scientific attitudes'. These aims pose particular challenges in terms of carrying out reliable and valid assessment (see, for example, the discussion in Gauld and Hukins, 1980), as they cannot be observed or measured directly and have to be inferred from other observations or behaviours.

Conclusions: where next for practical work?

Although recent policy has been to give prominence to investigations, the general consensus is that a school science curriculum should contain a variety of different types of practical work. Thus, having established that one problem with practical work stems from the diversity of purposes it seeks to fulfil, a logical next step is to attempt to classify different types of practical activity according to their aims. Several authors have attempted to do this. For example, Woolnough and Allsop (1985) suggest that there are three main different types of practical work: *exercises* to develop practical skills and techniques, *investigations* to provide opportunities to act like a problem-solving scientist and *experiences* to obtain a feel for phenomena. Gott and Duggan (1995) propose a similar but slightly longer list: practical work which develops *skills*; practical work which provides pupils with opportunities to relate their *observations* to scientific ideas; acquiring concepts, laws and principles through *enquiry*; verifying particular concepts, laws and principles through *illustration*; and using concepts, cognitive processes and skills to solve problems through *investigation*. It is worthwhile looking back at the aims of practical work given in Tables 4.1 and 4.2 to see how they might fit into each of the categories described.

In an attempt to provide a framework for analysing different types of practical work, a detailed typology, or 'map', has been developed by Millar *et al.* (1999). The map permits practical activities to be classified according to their intended learning outcomes and also to their characteristics in terms of design features, practical context and the records pupils are expected to keep. The potential usefulness of such a map extends beyond the classification of activities as it enables comparisons to be made of activities undertaken by pupils of different ages and of activities undertaken in the different subject areas of science. Additionally, it allows the effectiveness of particular

---

Box 4.5: Implications for practice

- In planning practical work activities for pupils, teachers need to be clear about the specific aims of each activity, and share these with pupils.
- A range of practical activities will be needed to help achieve the aims of practical work. These include activities which develop practical skills and techniques, activities which allow pupils to gain experience of phenomena, and investigations.
- There may be occasions when methods other than practical work will be more appropriate for addressing particular aims.
- Adequate time needs to be allowed for both teacher–pupil discussion and pupil–pupil discussion of the findings of experiments and investigations they undertake.
- Caution needs to be exercised in making any claims about the 'transferability' of skills and abilities developed through practical work, both to other scientific contexts and beyond the confines of science lessons.
- More explicit teaching of particular aspects of investigative work is necessary, particularly in relation to the reliability of data gathered by pupils in investigations.
- Techniques for the reliable and valid assessment of practical abilities need to be formulated with careful reference to the aims associated with particular practical activities.

---

activities to be determined and permits monitoring of the effect of making changes to activities. Box 4.5 summarizes the implications for classroom practice of research into practical work.

Perhaps the clearest messages to come from research into practical work are that no single way of 'doing' practical work can possibly hope to achieve its many and varied aims, and that caution needs to be exercised over the claims made for practical work. The messages emerging from current thinking on practical work are that the emphasis needs to shift from doing to discussing. Such a suggestion certainly poses a challenge to the strong tradition of practical work being at the heart of school science teaching which, in turn, sets an interesting agenda for research. It also ensures that debate over the nature and purpose of practical work will continue for some time yet.

Box 4.6: First stops for further reading

A short and very readable introduction to issues associated with practical work is:
Woolnough, B. and Allsop, T. (1985) *Practical Work in Science.* Cambridge: Cambridge University Press.

A more recent and concise overview of practical work in school science is:
Watson, R. (2000) The role of practical work. In M. Monk and J. Osborne (eds) *Good Practice in Science Teaching: What Research has to Say.* Buckingham: Open University Press.

There are several useful compendia of articles on aspects of practical work. These include:
Hegarty-Hazel, E. (ed.) (1970) *The Student Laboratory and the Science Curriculum.* London: Routledge.
Woolnough, B. (ed.) (1991) *Practical Science.* Buckingham: Open University Press.
Wellington, J. (ed.) (1998) *Practical Work in Science: Which Way Now?* London: Routledge.

A discussion of the criticisms of 'process science' may be found in:
Millar, R. (1989) What is 'scientific method' and can it be taught? In J. Wellington (ed.) *Skills and Processes in Science Education.* London: Routledge.

A good account of issues to do with practical work, particularly investigations, is:
Gott, R. and Duggan, S. (1995) *Investigative Work in the Science Curriculum.* Buckingham: Open University Press.

A frequently cited critique of the aims of practical work is:
Hodson, D. (1990) A critical look at practical work in school science. *School Science Review,* 71 (256), 33–40.

A more theoretical critique is:
Hodson, D. (1993) Re-thinking the old ways: towards a more critical approach to practical work in school science. *Studies in Science Education* 22, 85–142.

An overview of the influential work of the Assessment of Performance Unit (APU) may be found in:
Black, P. (1990) APU science – the past and the future. *School Science Review*, 72 (258), 13–28.

Chapter 5

Context-based Approaches to the Teaching of Science

> 'How did you and your friends get to school this morning? You probably used various forms of transport between you.'
>
> 'Speed is the rate of change of distance moved with time.'
>
> These two extracts come from the opening lines of chapters on forces and motion in two secondary level textbooks, one written in the 1970s and one in the 1990s – and there are no prizes for guessing which is which! They provide just one illustration of a major shift in approaches to teaching over that period – a shift which has seen increasing emphasis on contexts and applications as the starting points for developing scientific knowledge and understanding. What are the effects of using such approaches on pupils and teachers?
>
> This chapter looks at:
>
> - the origins of context-based approaches;
> - links between context-based approaches and other related movements in science education, such as 'STS' (Science–Technology–Society);
> - ways in which context-based approaches have drawn on research evidence;
> - research evidence into the effects on pupils and teachers of using context-based approaches in science teaching.

Introduction

Textbooks and other science curriculum materials have changed significantly over the last twenty years or so, as the above extracts from the 1970s' and 1990s' textbooks demonstrate. On the first page of the 1970s' chapter on forces and motion, the concept of average speed is introduced, defined and a formula given for calculating average speed. Ideas about scalar and vector quantities are then introduced, before going on to describe the three equations of motion. In contrast, the 1990s' text begins by asking pupils to make a list of the different kinds of transport they have used in the last year, and add the advantages and disadvantages of each. Pupils then go on to look at safety features incorporated into different forms of transport, before being introduced to equations of motion in the context of seat belts in cars.

The last twenty years have seen the development of a wide range of materials which use contexts and applications as a starting point for developing understanding of scientific ideas, with approaches variously being described as 'context-based', 'applications-led' or using 'STS' (Science–Technology–Society) links. Examples of curriculum development can be seen on local, national and international scales, and for all age ranges from primary through to tertiary.

Given the widespread interest in context-based approaches to science, one of the most striking features of the area is the comparative *lack* of interaction between research and curriculum development in this area. This is apparent both in the ways in which the development of many of the materials has not been informed by research evidence, and in the comparative scarcity of research into the effects of using such materials. In part, it may be that this lack of interaction is related to the way in which curriculum development tends to be funded, where the priority is the completion of the product – the curriculum materials. Thus time constraints do not permit the luxury of examining research evidence in detail before writing the materials, and there is often little resource left to support research-based evaluation. The widespread interest certainly points to the need for detailed, systematic research into the effects of the materials. Without such research, many of the claims made for context-based approaches, such as their motivating effects on pupils and the resultant enhanced learning of science concepts, run the risk of appearing to draw largely on anecdotal evidence and to owe more to the aspirations of those developing or using the materials than any substantial evidence drawing on research findings.

This chapter begins by considering the origins and meanings of context-based approaches to the teaching of science before going on to review research evidence into the effects of using context-based approaches. These effects are considered under three main headings: the effects on pupils' learning, the effects on pupils' interest in science and teachers' responses. Box 5.1 summarizes the key issues and questions in these areas.

Box 5.1: Key issues and questions

- What are the origins of context-based approaches?
- What are the key features of context-based approaches to the teaching of science?
- How do context-based approaches relate to other linked approaches, such as 'STS' (Science–Technology–Society) or the development of scientific literacy?
- How do context-based approaches draw on research evidence?
- What effects do context-based approaches have on pupils' learning?
- What effects do context-based approaches have on pupils' interest in science lessons and their desire to study science further?
- How do teachers respond to context-based approaches?

What are the origins of 'context-based approaches'?

The term 'context-based approaches' appears to have been applied to some of the activities in science classrooms for around fifteen years, prior to which such activities would probably have been described as attempts to make science 'relevant'. What both approaches share in common is the desire to show young people links between the science they study in school and their everyday life. What distinguishes 'context-based approaches' from 'relevant science' is the point at which these links are normally made. In the former case, the links are made right at the start of the topic, and used as a starting point to introduce and develop scientific ideas. In the latter case, the scientific ideas are introduced first, and then the links are made.

Three factors in particular appear to have provided the impetus for the adoption of context-based approaches to science:

- a concern by teachers and others involved in science education over the seeming irrelevance for their pupils of much of the material being used in science lessons;
- a widely held concern in a number of countries over the comparatively low levels of uptake of science subjects, particularly the physical sciences, in post-compulsory education;
- a concern over science courses provided for non-science specialists.

The origins of context-based approaches in classroom practice stem from the desire of most teachers to make the material they are teaching interesting for their pupils. Indeed, informal evidence suggests very strongly that, for many teachers, the active engagement of their pupils with the material is the single most important factor in evaluating the success or otherwise of a lesson. Many teachers have found through experience that beginning a topic or lesson with some form of story which leads into the science to be covered helps engage interest. A study by Mayoh and Knutton (1997) documented some twelve categories of 'episodes' with which teachers might begin a lesson, including, for example, talking about something which has been in the media or a common out-of-school experience. Context-based approaches could be seen as a logical extension of this strategy. Others involved in science education (e.g. Bybee, 1985; Eijkelhof and Kortland, 1988; Fensham, 1988; Hofstein *et al.*, 1988; Campbell *et al.*, 1994) have also argued strong cases for the motivating effects of context-based approaches.

Context-based approaches have also been developed in response to the concern in many countries over the uptake of physical science subjects. For example, in England and Wales, prior to the introduction of a National Curriculum in 1988, pupils had a choice at age 14 over the subjects they took. Typically, each year 70 per cent of boys and 85 per cent of girls opted out of physics and chemistry at this stage. Though the pattern of educational provision may vary, a broadly similar picture emerges in a number of countries of many pupils opting out of physical science subjects at the earliest opportunity.

It is particularly interesting to note that context-based approaches have their origins in concern over provision for *non*-science specialists rather than those choosing to take science subjects. This concern was for two particular groups. The first of these groups was less academic secondary level pupils, where the approaches and subject matter of traditional academic courses were felt to be inappropriate and alienating for pupils. In the UK, for example, context-based resources – at the time called 'relevant' science – were first developed over twenty years ago for such pupils. Examples of such resources include the projects for *Science for Less Academically Motivated Pupils – the LAMP Project* (ASE, 1978) and *Nuffield Science 13–16* (Nuffield Foundation, 1980). The second group consisted of non-science pupils beyond the compulsory period of schooling, where the *Science In Society* materials (Lewis, 1981) were developed as a course for such pupils. In other countries, the concern over provision for non-science students was at the tertiary level, where a number of localized science courses for non-science majors were developed (e.g. *Science and Culture*, Yager and Casteel, 1968).

Irrespective of their origins, the impact of context-based approaches has been significant, and they are now in widespread use. Counties in which materials and courses with a context-based approach are in use include Australia, Belgium, Brazil, China (Hong Kong), England, the Netherlands, New Zealand, Russia, Scotland, South Africa, Swaziland and the USA, and it may well be the case that the actual use is more widespread.

There are four broad groups into which materials currently fall. In the first group are whole courses which have been specifically developed such that contexts form the framework in which scientific knowledge and understanding are developed in a coherent and systematic way. Examples of such materials tend to be found at the high school level and include in the UK: *Science: The Salters Approach* (UYSEG, 1990–2); *Salters Advanced Chemistry* (Burton *et al.*, 1994); *Salters Horners Advanced Physics* (UYSEG, 2000); *Salters Nuffield*

Advanced Biology (UYSEG/Nuffield Foundation, 2002); the Supported Learning in Physics (SLIP) project (SLIP, 1997); the *PLON* (Dutch Physics Curriculum Development Project, 1988) in the Netherlands; and the STEMS (Science, Technology, Environment in Modern Society) project in Israel (Tal *et al.*, 2001). In some cases, such as in the *Salters'* courses, the content has to comply with an externally imposed specification of curriculum content and, as such, has been perceived as 'a bold attempt to escape from dominant school science' (van Berkel, 2000).

In the second group of materials are whole courses where scientific contexts and applications are the focus of the instruction. Here, the course is driven by the contexts and applications, rather than by the need for comprehensive coverage of science ideas. Such courses have been developed for non-science majors at both the tertiary level, for example *Chemistry in Context* (ACS, 1994), and at the secondary level, for example *ChemCom* (ACS, 1988), *Science in Society* (Lewis, 1981) and AS *Science for Public Understanding* (Hunt and Millar, 2000).

The third group contains units of material developed about particular contexts and applications, and which are generally used to replace some of the more conventional science topics in a course. Smaller-scale interventions (for example, Campbell *et al.*, 2000a; George and Lubben, 2002) would fall into this group. Finally, there are very short (one or two lesson) units used at some point within the teaching of a conventional topic. The *Science and Technology in Society* (SATIS) units (ASE, 1986) are examples of this type of material.

What is meant by 'context-based approaches'?

The term 'context-based approaches' is one which is in common use. It is a term which is applied to a wide range of curriculum materials, and frequently mentioned in debate about 'scientific literacy' and 'public understanding of science'. Additionally, it is clear from looking at resources which claim to have a 'context-based approach' that they all place emphasis on the societal and technological aspects of science. Thus there is considerable overlap with materials developed under the banner of STS.

There are two ways of clarifying the meaning of the term 'context-based approaches'. The first is to examine the literature in the area, and establish the meaning given to the term by those who have either produced, or are writing about, materials which claim to involve 'context-based approaches'. The second is to undertake an analysis of the resources which have been produced. Such an analysis does not appear to have been undertaken before.

Meanings: as taken from the literature

There appears to be comparatively little in the literature exploring specifically the meaning or meanings of context-based approaches. Whitelegg and Parry (1999) suggest that context-based learning can have several meanings:

> At its broadest, it means the social and cultural environment in which the student, teacher and institution are situated. ... A narrower view of context might focus on an application of a physics theory for the purposes of illumination and reinforcement. (p. 68)

The narrower view appears to be that which is taken by those developing context-based curriculum materials, as exemplified by the *Salters* courses and described in Lazonby *et al.* (1992) and Campbell *et al.* (1994). The latter explain how the development team arrived at their fundamental design criteria, one of which concerned the ways in which the scientific ideas is the course were going to be selected:

> The ideas and concepts selected, and the contexts within which they are studied, should enhance young people's appreciation of how chemistry:
>
> - contributes to their lives or the lives of others around the world; or
> - helps them to acquire a better understanding of the natural environment.

Putting this into operational terms, this meant that:

> Units of the course should start with aspects of the students' lives, which they have experienced either personally or via the

media, and should introduce ideas and concepts only as they are needed. (pp. 418–19)

Here, it is clear that applications of science, and pupils' everyday experiences in particular, are to be the starting points for the development of scientific ideas.

The literature on STS materials is more extensive, with several attempts being made to define STS and to characterize materials with 'an STS approach'. In a comprehensive review of a number of STS-related publications (syllabi, curriculum materials, policy statements), Aikenhead (1994) identifies a spectrum of categories of STS materials. This spectrum runs from courses which exhibit 'casual infusion of STS content' by adding short units of STS materials to more conventional content, through courses which develop 'science through STS content', to courses which show 'infusion of science into STS content'. Aikenhead's review also allows him to offer what he describes as 'a succinct definition of STS content':

STS content in a science education curriculum is comprised of an interaction between science and technology, or between science and society, and any one or combination of the following:

- a technological artefact, process or expertise
- the interactions between technology and society
- a societal issue related to science or technology
- social science content that sheds light on a societal issue related to science and technology
- a philosophical, historical, or social issue within the scientific or technological community. (pp. 52–3)

Solomon (1993) lists the following as 'STS features within science education':

- an understanding of the environmental threats, including global ones, to the quality of life
- the economic and industrial aspects of technology
- some understanding of the fallible nature of science
- discussion of personal opinion and values as well as democratic action
- a multi-cultural dimension. (p. 18)

It is worth noting that both Aikenhead and Solomon comment on the difficulties of defining STS precisely. However, as can be seen from the lists above, STS approaches and context-based approaches share a number of common features.

Meanings: as evidenced by the content of 'context-based resources'

This section develops a typology of contexts based on an examination of curriculum materials which are 'context-based' or have an 'STS emphasis'. The common ground for selecting the resources for review is that they draw on applications of science as starting points for developing understanding of scientific concepts and processes.

Two particularly striking features emerge from an analysis of resources. First, there are differences in thy ways the terms 'context-based' and 'applications-led' are interpreted at different levels. Second, a significant majority of the resources produced are intended for use with pupils at the upper high school level.

There are comparatively few formal examples of context-based materials at the primary level. There are likely to be two possible explanations for this. First, science (that is to say science which includes elements of chemistry, physics and biology) is not a compulsory feature of primary school curricula in many countries. Second, comparatively few problems have been reported in engaging the interest of primary age children in science. Indeed, there is a curious contrast in the way in which primary age and secondary age pupils respond to science. At the secondary level, pupils' lack of interest in science is often attributed to its remoteness from everyday life. However, at the primary level, it would appear that what makes science attractive to pupils is its difference from everyday life and use of specialist equipment in specialist locations. It can therefore be argued that one of the principal motivations for producing context-based resources, that of stimulating pupils' interest, does not apply at the primary level, because the interest already exists.

Context-based resources which have been developed at the primary level appear to have two main aims: to show that science is important in everyday life and to show that scientists do a wide variety of jobs.

This latter aspect is something of a 'pre-emptive strike', undertaken in the hope that young children will not develop the stereotypical image associated with scientists and the jobs they do – the white coats, the receding hairlines, the slightly eccentric behaviour and the laboratories of strange apparatus full of mysterious, bubbling and colourful liquids!

Context-based resources at the primary level set about achieving their aims through a 'stories with science in them' interpretation of context-based approaches. Two examples serve to illustrate this approach in action. *Farming Tales* (Chemical Industry Education Centre (CIEC), 1992) looks at the work of environmental technologists, and *Room for Improvement* (CIEC, 1996) introduces ideas about colour, light and electricity whilst designing an ideal bedroom. The pupils' materials for these resources appear as story books, similar to the sorts of reading books pupils will use in English lessons, with a number of central characters telling a 'story' which involves several excursions into science.

The high school level appears to be that where by far the greatest quantity of materials has been developed, particularly at the upper high school level. This is likely to be a reflection of resources being developed where the need is perceived to be greatest. At the lower high school level (around 11–14 years of age), two linked aims are most apparent in the materials. The first is to show young people that science can help them understand and explain things which are going on around them in their everyday lives, and the second is to foster young people's interest in science in the hope that they will want to continue with their study of science beyond the compulsory period. The first of these aims is a logical development from materials developed for the primary age range, taking pupils beyond *knowing* about science being important in everyday life to understanding and explaining some of these situations. The notion of 'story' is still very much a feature of the materials. For example, one course, *Science Focus* (UYSEG, 1992–4), uses the broad context of a community and events in the lives of its inhabitants as a framework for a three-year science programme. Narrower contexts are used to develop understanding in particular areas: ideas about chemical change are introduced in the context of treatments for indigestion, the clothes the people wear allow ideas about the structure and properties of materials to be developed, simple ideas about forces are introduced in the context of the structure of houses and other buildings.

Two further characteristics of context-based materials become apparent in looking at the materials. One is concerned with the approach to teaching and the other with concept learning.

The first of these characteristics, the approach to teaching, is one which is variously described as 'pupil-centred learning', 'participatory learning' or, more commonly, 'active learning'. These terms are applied to activities where pupils have a significant degree of autonomy over the learning activity, making decisions for themselves about aspects of the organization and direction of the activity. Examples of activities commonly classed as involving 'active learning' include small-group discussions, group and individual problem-solving tasks, investigations and role-play exercises. Such activities are not the sole preserve of context-based materials, and examples may certainly be found in other materials. However, it is interesting to consider why such activities have become so closely linked with, and feature so prominently in, context-based materials. Kyriacou (1998) summarizes the educational benefits claimed for such activities. They are:

- intellectually more stimulating and thereby are more effective in eliciting and sustaining pupil motivation and interest;
- effective in fostering a number of important learning skills involved in the process of organizing the activities, such as when organizing their own work during individualized activities, and interaction and communication skills during co-operative activities;
- likely to be enjoyed, offer opportunity for progress, are less threatening than teacher-talk activities and thereby foster more positive pupil attitudes towards themselves as learners and more positive attitudes towards the subject. (p. 42)

Thus there is a clear link in the claims made for both active learning strategies and for context-based approaches: both are felt to increase pupils' interest in the subject. Additionally, active learning strategies are felt to have benefits in terms of promoting pupils' metacognitive skills – skills in developing strategies to help them learn most effectively.

The second of the characteristics is most apparent in context-based courses which ultimately have to meet external curriculum specification, such as a national curriculum or national public examination syllabus. One outcome of introducing scientific ideas on a 'need to know' basis (i.e. they are needed to help explain and enrich understanding of features of the particular context being studied) is that it is unlikely that any one concept area, such as, for example, bonding, will be introduced and developed in full in one particular context, as might be the case in more conventional courses. Rather, the concept will be revisited at different points throughout the course, with different aspects of the concept emerging from different contexts. Such an approach is often referred to as 'drip feed' or a 'spiral curriculum', and clearly has implications for the development of pupils' understanding of scientific ideas.

At the upper high school level (age 15+), the aims of the earlier high school years are pursued further. However, two rather different interpretations of 'context' emerge. At this level, the tension between science courses as a preparation for further study and science courses as 'terminal' courses (i.e. pupils' last formal experience of science in school) becomes increasingly apparent. In some instances, this tension can be resolved by having separate courses for those hoping to study science to a higher level and those planning not to continue with their study of science. Courses which provide a preparation for further study (for some pupils, at least) show a move away from contexts which emphasize the immediate impact of science to the lives of the individual, and draw more on contexts which illustrate 'what scientists do'. For example, *Salters Advanced Chemistry* (Burton *et al.*, 1994), introduces pupils to organic chemistry by looking at the design of medical drugs, whilst the chemistry of the elements in Groups IV and V is covered in looking at how scientists help design fertilizers. 'Terminal' courses, however, place less emphasis on 'what scientists do' and more on 'scientific literacy' through developing understanding of issues which impinge on everyday life. For example, the *AS Science for Public Understanding* (Hunt and Millar, 2000) looks at the science behind issues such as genetic modification of crops, air quality and potential risks associated with ionizing radiations. Elements of both 'what scientists do' and 'scientific literacy' can be identified in the course trying to meet the twin aims of preparation for further study and provision of a 'terminal' course.

Whilst the main focus of this chapter is on context-based approaches at school level, it is worth looking briefly at the current picture at the tertiary (university) level, given that this is one of the places where such approaches had their origins. Two contrasting pictures emerge. 'Enrichment' courses for non-science specialists are aimed at stimulating students' interest and helping them become 'informed citizens', with rigorous, systematic treatment of scientific content not seen as necessary. So, for example, in the *Chemistry in Context* programme developed in the USA (ACS, 1994), extracts from a book on ecology by the then Tennessee Senator, Al Gore, are used as the starting points for exploring the chemistry of global warming. However, in mainstream courses, there are very few examples of context-based materials in use, with the possible exception being materials developed on a comparatively small scale for use in 'problem solving' or 'critical thinking' classes. The view here seems to be that anyone who has got this far can take their science without the 'trimmings'!

In summary, materials which use context-based approaches to science have in common an emphasis on active learning strategies, and employ contexts as a strategy to engage pupils' interest. However, the interpretation of the term 'context' evolves with the level of study from one with a direct relevance to an individual's immediate life and surroundings, to more sophisticated illustrations of the contribution science and scientists make to society, and an increasing emphasis on aspects of scientific literacy.

How do context-based approaches draw on research evidence?

There are several ways in which the development of any curriculum materials *might* draw on research theories and evidence. These would include looking at:

- the findings of specific research studies relevant to the science ideas and teaching approaches in the materials;
- theories about cognitive aspects of learning;
- theories about the development of interest and motivation;

- theories about promoting educational change (given that one aim of the materials is to effect change in practice);
- theories about how to select the content of a curriculum.

Whilst there are certainly some examples of curriculum development where use has been made of the literature in some of the areas above, it is true to say that the majority of curriculum development work has been undertaken with comparatively little reference to research theories and evidence, with decisions on content, approach and dissemination being made largely on the basis of experience. In some ways, this is less of a concern than it might first appear. Experienced classroom practitioners can claim, with some justification, to know what works and what does not work with their pupils, whether or not it is informed by any 'research theory'. This tacit 'craft knowledge' plays an important role in determining approaches and activities employed in science lessons to engage pupils' interest in the subject matter. Practitioners may also claim, again with some justification, that research findings rarely offer clear-cut advice for classroom practice, making it difficult to know which aspects of research might be worth incorporating into curriculum materials.

However, there are examples of context-based materials drawing directly on research evidence. For example, units in the *Science: The Salters Approach* (UYSEG, 1990–2) were developed with reference to the findings of studies on strategies for promoting the interest and involvement of pupils, and girls in particular, in science. Additionally, the structure and approach of selected units (for example, those on electricity, energy and motion) drew directly on the findings of constructivist research (see Campbell *et al.*, 1994, for further details).

What is apparent in the literature on context-based approaches is some attempt at 'retrospective analysis' of curriculum content to link it to aspects of theory, particularly learning theory. For example, Whitelegg and Parry (1999) make links between their context-based *Supported Learning in Physics* materials (SLIP, 1997) and Vygotsky's theories of learning and constructivist research. Central to both these areas is the idea that effective learning takes place when learners are able to merge scientific and everyday versions of events. Campbell *et al.* (1994), in describing the *Salters*' courses, make reference to Vygotsky's work, and also to work on the role of language in developing understanding (Barnes *et al.*, 1969; Lemke, 1990; Sutton, 1992). In a similar vein, a report on the development of context-based materials in Swaziland (Campbell *et al.*, 2000b) makes links with the work of Ogborn *et al.* (1996) on the need for effective scientific explanations to draw on examples from the learner's own surroundings.

The research evidence into the effects of using context-based approaches

This section focuses on the research evidence gathered on the use of context-based approaches. As mentioned earlier, one of the most interesting features of context-based approaches is the comparative scarcity of research-based evaluation. However, as the use of such materials has become widespread, there has been increasing interest in their effects.

The majority of context-based materials have been developed for use at high school level and it is therefore not surprising that the research which has been undertaken has concentrated on effects in this age range. The research can be divided into three main areas:

- the development of pupils' understanding of key scientific ideas (cognitive aspects);
- pupils' responses to science, and their experiences in science lessons (affective aspects);
- teachers' responses to the materials.

To the list above, might be added two further areas: uptake of science subjects by pupils who have followed context-based courses, and effects on 'scientific literacy'. In the latter area, relatively little work has been done, though it would appear to be an area well worth investigating. In the former area, what might appear to be a comparatively easy task is, in practice, not the case. Though it might be possible to gather such data on a local basis or for small-scale interventions, any substantial curriculum development takes place over a number of years, and it is therefore likely that other changes will take place which might also influence uptake of subjects. In a number of instances, curriculum development has taken place alongside or in response to change in curriculum specification, making it impossible to tease out the effects, if any, of the materials developed from externally imposed change.

Box 5.2 summarizes the key research findings.

Box 5.2: Key research findings

- Pupils' interest in and enjoyment of their science lessons are generally increased when they use context-based materials or follow context-based courses.
- Context-based materials help pupils see and appreciate more clearly links between the science they study and their everyday lives.
- Pupils following context-based courses learn science concepts at least as effectively as those following more conventional courses.
- A curriculum development model which involves teachers is more effective than the 'centre–periphery' model in effecting change in practice and alleviating teachers' anxiety when faced with innovation.
- There is a need for further research into the effects of assessing pupils' scientific knowledge and understanding through the use of context-based questions.
- Interest and enjoyment of lessons involving context-based materials does not appear to be translated on a widespread scale into a desire to study the subjects further, though there are some significant localized exceptions to this.

Cognitive aspects: the development of pupils' understanding of key scientific ideas

Studies in this area have tended to be comparative in nature, looking at the understanding of selected chemical ideas demonstrated by pupils who have followed context-based courses and pupils who have followed more conventional courses.

Two studies (Ramsden, 1997; Barker and Millar, 2000) which gathered data in a number of schools on pupils' understanding of key chemical ideas have suggested that there are no significant differences in levels of understanding demonstrated by pupils following either conventional or context-based courses (*Science: the Salters Approach* and *Salters Advanced Chemistry*), though both revealed common areas of difficulty in chemistry. Both studies offer reassurance that the 'drip feed' approach does not impair learning of concepts and, indeed, may have benefits: for example, the gradual introduction and revisiting of ideas (such as chemical bonding and thermodynamics) in different contexts at several points during *Salters Advanced Chemistry* appeared to improve understanding.

Two smaller-scale studies comparing pupils following *Salters Advanced Chemistry* with those following conventional courses provide additional evidence to support the claim that pupils' learning is not adversely affected by context-based approaches. Banks (1997) found that the 'drip feed' approach of the context-based course to teaching ideas about chemical equilibrium appeared more effective than the conventional approach. Barber (2000) used a range of added value performance indicators to compare predicted and actual grades in the A-level chemistry examinations for the two groups of pupils. Her study indicated that there was no particular disadvantage or advantage to pupils in either course in terms of the final examination grade they achieved. Although the pupils took different examination papers, both groups had to meet externally imposed assessment specifications for content, so the study provides some additional evidence to indicate that the learning of pupils on context-based courses is comparable with that of pupils on more conventional courses. Barber's study is summarized in Box 5.3 as an example of a small-scale study.

Eijkelhof and Kortland (1988) report on the evaluation of the context-based physics programme, *PLON*, developed in the Netherlands. Part of the study looked in detail at a particular unit – ionizing radiation – and how pupils made use of scientific knowledge in arguing about controversial issues regarding applications of ionizing radiation. Interestingly, they found that, where the topic was a subject of fierce national debate – dumping nuclear waste into the sea – there was little change in the very limited extent to which pupils drew on their scientific knowledge before and after experiencing the

Box 5.3: An example of a small-scale study on the effects of context-based approaches
(Barber, 2000)

Aim
To compare the responses and achievements of students following a context-based course (Salters Advanced Chemistry) and a more conventional advanced level chemistry course.

Research questions

- What views do students have of their course?
- What are the preferred learning styles of students on each course?
- What understanding do students demonstrate of key concepts?
- How do the final examination grades of each group compare?
- How easy do students find the transition from school to university?

Research strategy and techniques
The research took the form of a case study of 120 17- and 18-year-old pupils in a 'sixth-form' (pre-university) college. The primary data collection techniques were questionnaires and interviews with students, plus a standard test of understanding of key ideas.

Main findings
The study showed that there were some significant differences between the two groups of students in terms of their attitude to their course, with students following the more conventional course feeling they received a good grounding in key chemical concepts, and those following the context-based course particularly enjoying the applied approach and feeling that they were developing a range of useful skills.

There were also noticeable differences in students' preferred learning styles in, for example, preference for being given notes (conventional course) and planning and organizing their own notes (context-based course).

Added value performance indicators showed students' final examination grades were independent of the course followed.

A higher proportion of students following the context-based course went on to study chemistry at university.

context-based module. However, for a topic less publicly debated – food irradiation – much better use of scientific knowledge is made, though in both cases pupils still revealed misconceptions about radiation.

One potentially very interesting area of research on pupils' learning, as yet in an early stage of development, concerns the assessment of scientific understanding through the use of context-based questions. Evidence from one study (Ahmed and Pollitt, 2000) points to the need for particular care in the design of context-based assessment items so that pupils are not over-burdened with reading, and the questions make a valid assessments of the ideas they set out to test.

Affective aspects: pupils' responses to science and their experiences in science lessons

Studies on affective aspects have tended to focus on secondary level pupils, mainly because this is the age group where interest in science declines most noticeably. Two studies (Ramsden, 1992, 1997), gathering comparative data from pupils following a context-based course (*Science: The Salters Approach*) and more conventional science courses, suggested that pupils who had earlier experience of more conventional courses reported increased enjoyment of science lessons, although worryingly some pupils indicated that they did not feel the activities they were doing were 'proper science' as they were enjoyable. Pupils following context-based courses also cited a wider range of reasons for enjoying science than pupils following conventional courses. There was some evidence to support the claim that increased enjoyment of science was reported more frequently by girls than boys. Similar findings emerged from an evaluation of the *PLON* materials in the Netherlands (Eijkelhof and Kortland, 1988).

Despite the increased interest and enjoyment reported by pupils following context-based courses, data on proposed subject choice and career intentions (Ramsden, 1997) indicated that this not translated to any significant extent into a desire to pursue the study of science. Comments made by pupils hinted at a deep-rooted problem concerning the image of science held by young people: doing science is not seen as interesting and enjoyable. There is, however, evidence of localized exceptions where there has been a significant increase in uptake (Pilling, 1999).

Other studies, one with upper secondary age pupils (Key, 1998) and one with upper primary age pupils (Parvin, 1999), have explored pupils' specific responses to the chemical industry, with both demonstrating that pupils using context-based approaches had a more realistic perception of the role of the chemical industry.

Research with pupils has tended to gather data *on* pupils, using their performance on diagnostic questions or their responses to their science lessons to make inferences about particular features of context-based approaches. However, some studies have asked pupils directly for their views on contexts they found particularly interesting and/or helpful for learning. In a study undertaken in Swaziland (Lubben *et al.*, 1996), lower secondary pupils identified three particular contexts as being helpful: personally useful applications, opportunities to contribute their own knowledge and views, and discussion of controversial issues. A study of upper secondary level pupils (Campbell *et al.*, 2000a) following the context-based *Salters Horners Advanced Physics* course (UYSEG, 2000) showed that pupils felt contexts to do with everyday life and hobbies were important for fostering interest. Box 5.4 summarizes this study.

One of the claims sometimes made for context-based approaches is that increased motivation leads to enhanced understanding. This is a complex area in which to gather systematic evidence. Certainly there is evidence to suggest that students appear more willing to engage with scientific ideas when they encounter them in context. For example, in a report of a five-year evaluation of *ChemCom* (ACS, 1988), Sutman and Bruce (1992) found that pupils who would not normally have been expected to respond very positively to chemistry were much more willing to engage with context-based materials than with more conventional materials. Whilst this does not offer direct evidence for improved understanding, it seems reasonable to suggest that, without engagement, understanding is likely to be very limited.

Teachers' responses to context-based materials

Unlike their pupils, most teachers using context-based approaches are likely to have experience of teaching both these and more conventional courses and therefore have views on the relative merits of

---

Box 5.4: An example of a larger-scale study on the effects of context-based approaches
(Campbell *et al.*, 2000b)

Aim
To explore students' perceptions of the effects of particular contexts employed in a context-based advanced level physics course, Salters Horners Advanced Physics (SHAP).

Research question
What are students' perceptions of the effectiveness of particular contexts in stimulating interest and promoting effective learning?

Research strategy and techniques
The study took the form of a survey of ten schools and colleges using SHAP. Data were gathered using interviews, with groups of six students in each school being interviewed at three points during the two-year period of their course. (These data were supplemented by questionnaire and interview data on factors influencing subject choice.)

Main findings
Students view contexts very positively both in terms of stimulating interest and in being helpful to learning.

Contexts of particular interest are those which explain something about which the student wants to find out, relate to everyday experience or centre on contemporary technology.

Most students viewed the contexts as interesting and helpful bridges to the content, though a substantial number did not, either not seeing the context-to-content bridge, or perceiving the context as unnecessary.

Over the period of the course, there was an increase in the number of students perceiving contexts as interesting and helpful bridges to the content.

---

each. A note of caution needs to be sounded about evidence collected from teachers, as many using context-based materials may well have been party to the decision to use them and therefore be particularly positively disposed towards them. In a small-scale study undertaken by Ramsden (1994), teachers using *Science: The Salters Approach* all reported a greater willingness on the part of pupils to engage in tasks in lessons.

One other aspect of teachers' responses is of interest in the context of curriculum innovation, even though it is only indirectly related to the use of context-based materials. An interesting feature of many context-based curriculum development projects is that they embrace a developmental model which is very different to the prevailing 'centre-periphery' model of curriculum innovation, which, in its crudest form, requires decisions taken by a group of centrally based policy-makers to be implemented by teachers. In contrast, a number of context-based projects have involved teachers in some, if not most, of the stages of development, ranging from initial decision-making over content and structure, through writing, to the process of dissemination. Two studies, one in Swaziland (Dlamini *et al.*, 1994) and one in Trinidad and Tobago (George and Lubben, 2002), have gathered evidence indicating that involving teachers in the development process is a key determinant in effecting change in the classroom through alleviating anxieties associated with change. These teachers also reported positive outcomes in terms of their own professional development. One final piece of evidence of potential use to curriculum developers comes from a study by Borgford (1995) on the effects of *Science: the Salters Approach*. This indicated that the development of detailed resources to support teaching through context-based approaches resulted in change in classroom practice irrespective of the commitment of the teacher to the use of such an approach.

Conclusions

Research into the effects of context-based materials indicates that there are a number of benefits of such an approach, particularly in terms of increasing pupils' interest in science by helping them to see links between science and everyday life. There is also evidence that pupils following context-based courses learn science concepts at least as effectively as those following more conventional courses. More generally, research into the use of context-based approaches has yielded important messages about the process of curriculum innovation.

The implications of such findings for practice are summarized in Box 5.5.

Box 5.5: Implications for practice

In those cases where context-based approaches to teaching science have drawn on aspects of research evidence, they form in themselves *implications for practice*. They provide concrete examples of materials which research evidence indicates should increase pupils' interest in science lessons and help them to see links between science and society. In some instances, they should also help develop better understanding of particular science ideas than more traditional approaches.

Additionally:

- Particular care is needed in the design of context-based questions to assess pupils' understanding.
- A more general implication concerns the process of curriculum innovation, which is more likely to produce changes in practice if teachers are involved in the planning and development of associated materials.

The research has also pointed to a number of areas of difficulty, some of which might be more easily remedied than others, and some not specifically linked to the use of context-based approaches. First, it must be a matter of concern that some secondary pupils view the interesting and enjoyable activities in which they engage in context-based courses as not really being what science is about. This has implications for the experiences of science which might be provided for pupils at the primary level. Second, a number of key ideas in science appear to be poorly grasped, irrespective of the approach used in their teaching. Finally, interest and enjoyment in science lessons do not appear to be translated on a widespread scale into a desire to study the subjects further. Here, useful insights will be gained by further research in schools which do report significant increases in uptake. The experiences of those developing and undertaking research on context-based approaches also appears very relevant to current debate about the place of scientific literacy in the core school science curriculum.

Box 5.6: First stops for further reading

A good description of a framework for characterizing science teaching materials which use contexts may be found in:
Aikenhead, G. (1994) What is STS teaching? In J. Solomon and G. Aikenhead (eds) *STS Education: International Perspectives on Reform*. New York: Teachers College Press.

A paper reflecting on the process of developing a large-scale context-based course (Salters Science) is:
Campbell, R., Lazonby, J., Millar, R., Nicolson, P., Ramsden, J. and Waddington, D. (1994) Science: the Salters approach: a case study of the process of large scale curriculum development. *Science Education*, 78 (5), 415–47.

A useful typology of 'episodes' which teachers commonly use as contexts to introduce science ideas has been developed by:
Mayoh, K. and Knutton, S. (1997) Using out-of-school experiences in science lessons: reality or rhetoric? *International Journal of Science Education*, 19 (7), 849–67.

A useful review of context-based approaches may be found in:
Bennett, J. and Holman, J. (2002) Context-based approaches to the teaching of chemistry: what are they and what are their effects? In J. Gilbert (ed.) *Chemical Education Research-based Practice*. Dordrecht: Kluwer Academic Publishers.

Chapter 6

Information and Communications Technology (ICT) and School Science

In the school science laboratory of twenty years ago, it would have been comparatively rare to see a computer. Today, computers, and resources linked to the use of computers, are commonplace in many school laboratories. Moreover, unlike much of the equipment used in science lessons, computers are one resource to which an increasing number of pupils have access at home. There can be little doubt now about the potential for computers to offer access to a range of knowledge and resources. How best might this potential be realized in science lessons?

This chapter looks at:

- the origins of information and communications technology (ICT) in the school curriculum;
- the claims made and possibilities offered by computers and information technology for science teaching;
- research into the ways in which ICT is used in science lessons and its effects on pupils' learning, development of skills and motivation;
- research into some of the problems associated with the use of ICT in school science;
- implications of research for the use of ICT in science teaching.

Introduction: the origins of information and communications technology (ICT) in the school curriculum

Although the 'computer revolution' may seem like a relatively recent phenomenon, computers have been around for a long time. The building of the first programmable computing device, Charles Babbage's Difference Engine, began in 1823. However, it was not until the late 1970s, when several makes of small computers (microcomputers) were coming onto the domestic market, that the enormous potential of computers began to be appreciated. The launch in 1981 of the IBM 5150, the first PC (personal computer) to resemble those used today, was an event with a significance beyond even that which was realized at the time. By the 1990s, two decades of research into linking computers together made the Internet available to computer owners and revolutionized information transfer and communications with the World Wide Web and e-mail. It is hard to imagine now that, in 1992, e-mail was a little-used means of communication and there were just 50 websites on the Internet.

It was during the late 1970s, as microcomputers were becoming more readily available, that people started to think in any significant way about how computers might be used in teaching. Such were the possibilities envisioned that the 1980s saw money being invested by a number of countries on an unprecedented scale in initiatives aimed at getting computers into schools, a trend which continued into the 1990s. One illustration of the growth in the number of computers in schools is provided by data collected by the Department for Education and Employment (DfEE) (1998) in England and Wales: in the mid-1980s there was an average of one computer for sixty pupils, a figure which had risen to one computer for nine pupils just ten years later. On the back of the investment in computers came funding for in-service training to help teachers acquire the skills needed to make use of computers in their teaching. Three factors contributed to this massive investment of money and time. First, there was pressure from within certain sectors of the educational community, particularly from enthusiastic teachers and providers of in-service training, who saw computers as offering a new approach to teaching and learning which would be very motivating for pupils. Outside the educational community, there was pressure from successive governments and from parents for computers to be introduced into schools, with both groups wanting to see young people develop what were seen as essential skills they would need as adults. Related to this, a strong economic pressure was exerted for pupils to be introduced to computers in schools to meet an anticipated rapidly increasing demand in many sectors of the workplace for employees skilled in the use of computers.

The 1980s also saw the introduction of the term *information technology* (IT) into educational settings. Although 'IT' itself is a broad term, covering all aspects of transmitting or manipulating information using some form of technology, its use in the school context tended to be limited to activities involving the use of computers in lessons. In the 1990s, information technology evolved into *information and communications technology* (ICT) to reflect the increasing importance of the Internet and e-mail as communication technologies.

Computers and school science: the possibilities

Looking at the tasks that computers were originally designed to do, it is not surprising that they have become an essential part of much scientific work, and that they offer a range of possibilities for science lessons. The original attraction of computers for scientists in industrial and research laboratories came from their ability to make, record and store large numbers of measurements, to perform complex and sophisticated calculations with these measurements, and to process vast amounts of information for display in a variety of forms. With the arrival of the Internet, and the availability of an ever-increasing number of software packages, computers now have a significant part to play in other tasks, such as modelling ideas, searching for information, and presenting and communication of information. More recent developments, such as alternative input devices (touch screens, concept keyboards, light pens and voice sensitive devices), have further increased the potential of computers as learning tools. Thus ICT provides a whole range of possibilities for the science lesson of today, as summarized below:

- practising problems through 'drill and skill';

- providing tutorial instruction;
- making use of integrated learning systems;
- making use of simulations;
- modelling;
- using databases and spreadsheets;
- data-logging;
- controlling and monitoring experiments;
- graphing;
- working with interactive multimedia (e.g. CD-ROMs);
- accessing information from the Internet;
- presenting and communicating information.

It is worth noting that there is an overlap between some of the activities. For example, modelling often makes use of spreadsheets, and presenting and communicating information is very likely to draw on a number of other activities in the list.

As the list above illustrates, activities making use of ICT can be used for a wide range of purposes. Several attempts have been made to classify different types of ICT-related activities, and a useful summary of these may be found in Scaife and Wellington (1993). These classifications tend to focus on the extent to which the learner has control over the way in which the ICT application is being used. At one end of the spectrum are activities where ICT applications are being used directly to reinforce subject learning, such as in 'drill and skill' practice. In the middle of the spectrum are exploratory activities, such as simulations and modelling, which aim to develop learning and allow pupils to test out ideas. Finally, ICT applications may be used as a tool to save time by simplifying or speeding up the tasks of gathering and processing data, or of accessing information.

A wide range of potential benefits resulting from the use of ICT has been claimed for both pupils and teachers by a number of groups (policy-makers, researchers, some teachers, employers). For example, in the UK, a report by the government body, the National Council for Educational Technology (NCET) (1994), listed well over twenty such benefits, including:

- making pupils' learning more effective;
- increasing pupils' motivation;
- enhancing pupils' sense of achievement;

- providing pupils with access to richer sources of data and information;
- helping pupils become autonomous learners;
- reducing pressure on pupils by letting them work at their own speed;
- enhancing pupils' literacy skills;
- making teachers take a fresh look at the way they teach;
- freeing teachers from administration to focus on pupils' learning.

The wide range of applications and the diversity of the perceived benefits mean that it is impossible to ignore the potential of ICT for science lessons. Harris (1994) suggested that the impact of IT was making itself manifest in science in five particular ways:

- in using communication technologies;
- in using developments in the field of instrumentation and measurement, and the acquisition, handling and processing of data;
- in using modelling and simulations;
- in being able to retrieve, search and manipulate vast quantities of information;
- in making it possible to focus learning on understanding, interpretation and application of information without the need to spend time on lengthy mathematical procedures.

The wide range of applications certainly makes it comparatively easy to answer the question, where *could* ICT be used in science lessons? A more difficult question to answer is where *should* ICT be used in science lessons? The wide range of potential applications also points to a characteristic particularly associated with the introduction of ICT into schools, where a big investment in equipment often precedes thinking on how it might best be used. In science teaching, the key question is *when is ICT an appropriate tool to use to help promote effective learning in science and develop ideas about the way scientists work?* Research findings have an important contribution to make in helping answer this question and in providing evidence to show to what extent the claims made for ICT are justified.

Research into the use of ICT

Although there is a significant literature on ICT in science education, much of it takes the form of articles on applications for use in teaching situations – the emphasis has been on how to use ICT, rather than exploring its effects. The research literature is less extensive, and much of the research evidence which does exist is based on comparatively small-scale studies. It is also the case that the nature and diversity of ICT means that the associated literature is spread across a very wide range of books, journals and other publications, such as reports by government-sponsored bodies or groups with a particular interest in ICT. Moreover, the speed at which developments have taken place and new initiatives have been launched mean that some of the literature is of a transient nature – it dates fairly quickly or is difficult to track down. These factors point to the need for some selectivity in deciding which studies should be included in this chapter. Thus, most of the studies described in the following sections are comparatively recent (1990s onwards), have been reported in books or research journals and have a specific focus on science education.

Box 6.1: Key issues and questions

- What are the possibilities offered by ICT for science teaching?
- When should ICT be used in science lessons?
- What are the effects of using ICT on pupils' learning and development of skills?
- What are the effects of ICT on pupils' motivation?
- What implications does ICT have for the role of the teacher?
- What sorts of problems have been encountered with ICT in schools, and how might these be overcome?

Research into the use of ICT in school science falls into three main areas, as summarized in the list below. Box 6.1 summarizes the key issues and questions which have been asked.

- A number of studies have been carried out on *specific applications of ICT*, such as tutorial programmes, simulations and data-logging. Much of the early research into ICT was of this form, with the majority of studies tending to be small in scale. The focus of this work has been on pupils, with studies exploring effects on pupils' learning and development of skills. However, some additional evidence has also been gathered on aspects such as pupils' motivation and the role of the teacher.

- Work has been undertaken on *more general aspects of the effects of ICT*. These studies have focused both on pupils, for example in exploring possible links between the use of ICT and performance in national tests, and on teachers, for example by looking in detail at the role of the teacher in lessons which make use of ICT.

- Studies have been undertaken into the *problems associated with the use of ICT* in science lessons and in schools more generally. Such studies have tended to focus on managerial and practical issues associated with the use of ICT.

Key research findings are summarized in Box 6.2.

Research into specific applications of ICT in science lessons

The emphasis of this section is on the areas where the most extensive research has been undertaken: tutorial applications, simulations and modelling, data-logging and graphing, and the use of multimedia. Given its enormous potential impact, a short section on the use of the Internet is also included, though research is in its early days. A point worth mentioning is that, as the technology continues to evolve, some of the boundaries are becoming blurred. For example, in communicating information through producing reports, pupils might make use of multi-media authoring to draw on data they have gathered from a range of sources.

Tutorial applications

One of the early uses of ICT was in providing Computer Assisted Learning (CAL): subject-specific software which enabled pupils to

Box 6.2: Key research findings

- There is considerable evidence that the use of ICT in lessons motivates pupils to engage with learning activities in their science lessons. In particular, pupils appear to value the control ICT can give them over their learning.
- The majority of evidence suggests that ICT promotes more effective learning of science concepts and ideas, though there is also evidence to indicate misunderstandings can sometimes be introduced or reinforced.
- There is evidence to suggest that ICT helps pupils with the development of skills in science lessons. For example, pupils' abilities to interpret graphical information are enhanced by the use of ICT.
- There is conflicting evidence over the extent to which ICT skills developed in one particular subject are 'transferable' to other subjects and situations.
- Pupils in schools with good ICT provision and teaching do better in national tests and examinations than pupils in less well-resourced schools.
- Teachers, through their questioning of pupils and directing of pupil activity, have a vital role to play in maximizing the effectiveness of ICT in science lessons.
- There are many barriers to the successful implementation and effective use of ICT in science lessons. A number of these arise from practical and managerial issues (e.g. lack of time, training and technical support), whilst others concern pedagogy (e.g. the need to plan around whole science lessons being based in dedicated computer rooms can result in the technology driving the learning, rather than serving as a means to enhance it).

reinforce basic learning or, at a slightly more sophisticated level, provided pupils with instruction in the form of a tutorial-style programme on the material being covered. Development of these applications has resulted in Integrated Learning Systems (ILS), programmes which provide pupils with individualized instruction in the form of an intelligent tutorial system which provides almost immediate feedback on performance. The systems also keeps a record of performance for access by the teachers. A detailed review of research into ILS may be found in Underwood and Brown (1997). The emphasis of such research has been to explore how and what pupils learn, and has generally shown that the use of ILS does result in gains in learning, though with less success in developing abilities to reason and to apply what has been learned. Research has also provided evidence that ILS has a number of other benefits in terms of pupils being well-motivated, remaining on task and reporting increased confidence as a result of immediate feedback.

In a recent study using ILS, Rogers and Newton (2001) explored its potential for supporting investigative work in practical science with 13- and 14-year-old pupils. This involved enhancing standard ILS software to incorporate data-logging software. A further dimension of the study involved exploring the role of the teacher in lessons where ILS was being used. A combination of observation and interview data, together with the records kept as part of the ILS, suggested that the software had been successful in promoting pupils' abilities to collect and manipulate data, and also that pupils had enjoyed the approach. Pupils were, however, less good at making links between the data they had collected and the associated science, and that teacher intervention was needed at this point. This study therefore provides additional evidence of the benefits and limitations of tutorial applications of ICT.

Simulations and modelling

Simulations and modelling are related, though slightly different, applications of ICT. In *simulations*, users explored a model built into a computer programme. In science lessons, this allows pupils to gain experience in some form of phenomena which are, for example, potentially hazardous or where the timescale does not permit easy replication in a school science laboratory. *Modelling* software, as its name implies, allows users to develop their own models. Primarily this is achieved by taking away the drudgery of time-consuming and repetitive calculations. At the simplest level, modelling software can be used to manipulate particular kinds of data. In science lessons, this allows pupils, for example, to explore relationships between variables. At a more sophisticated level, content-free modelling software allows pupils and teachers to use simple programming languages to devise and explore their own models. (More details of the evolution of modelling software packages and their potential applications may be found in Ogborn, 1990; Scaife and Wellington, 1993; and Cox, 2000.) Many of the features of computer simulations and models have led to them being seen as useful complements to practical work in school science, or, in some instances, even as replacements.

Although simulations and modelling have a number of advantages, there are also limitations. For example, Scaife and Wellington (1993) point out that the use of simulations and models may over-simplify processes, leading pupils to conclude that the ease with which variables can be controlled and manipulated in a computer programme is an accurate reflection of how this might happen in reality.

Several studies have explored effects of the use of simulations and modelling. Two studies with a focus on pupil learning were the Conceptual Change in Science Project undertaken in the UK (O'Shea *et al.*, 1993; Hennesey *et al.*, 1995), and the Model-based Analysis and Reasoning in Science (MARS) project, undertaken in the USA (Raghaven and Glaser, 1995). The former focused on the teaching of aspects of mechanics to 12- and 13-year-olds, and took the form of an experimental study, whilst the latter looked at the teaching of ideas about forces to 11- and 12-year-olds. The Conceptual Change in Science Project provided evidence that pupils who used the simulation and modelling packages performed better than those who did not in post-test (and delayed post-test) questions exploring their knowledge of mechanics. There was, however, mixed evidence on the extent to which prior misconceptions were altered. In some cases, these decreased, whilst in others there appeared to be no change. The study also indicated that the teacher was important in focusing and developing discussion during and after the use of the software. The MARS project, which did not involve the use of control groups, also indicated that, by providing pupils with situations in which they could test out their own ideas, they became better able to cope with more complex situations involving forces. Other findings included improved pupil motivation, and the central role played by the teacher in guiding pupils, challenging their ideas and in helping them reflect on and apply the ideas they had encountered when using the computer models.

Studies which have focused on the development of skills have yielded conflicting evidence. One of the most widely used modelling programmes of the 1980s was LOGO, a simple programming language used in science lessons and elsewhere. Some studies have suggested that pupils using LOGO were better able to solve problems and think logically, and that these abilities were transferred to a range of subjects (Papert, 1980; Cathcart; 1990). However, other studies, such as that of Pea *et al.* (1986) did not support these findings. There are parallels here with the work done on transferability – or otherwise – of skills developed through practical work. More recent work, such as the study by Rogers and Newton (2001) described earlier, has made more modest claims about the extent to which the use of models helps pupils manipulate and interpret data. There would appear to be a need for more work in this area, particularly given the current prominence in school science of investigative work and its associated skills.

Two other ICT applications linked to modelling are databases and spreadsheets, as they enable pupils to input data and then manipulate it to explore patterns and test hypotheses. They also enable data to be presented in a variety of different pictorial and graphical forms. Though there are numerous examples of applications of databases and spreadsheets in the literature, and many claims made for their benefits (see, for example, Carson, 1997), there is little in the way of detailed research on their use.

Data-logging and graphing

Data-logging (referred to as microcomputer-based labs, or MBL, in the USA) involves using electronic sensors during practical work to take measurements and then send them to a computer for processing. Examples of measurements which can be taken by sensors include temperature, light level, sound level, pH and concentration of oxygen. Using computers in this way provides an opportunity to free pupils from time-consuming data collection so that they can spend more time analysing and interpreting data. A further potential benefit is that measurements can be displayed graphically in 'real time' (i.e. as a process is taking place).

Possibly because data-logging and graphing were two of the earlier applications of ICT to be incorporated into science lessons, their effects have been researched in some detail. Three earlier studies (Brasell, 1985; Mokros and Tinker, 1987; Nakhleh and Krajcik, 1993) were undertaken with high school pupils in the USA. In keeping with the research tradition in the USA, all involved experiments and all reported that pupils who had used data-logging (MBL) demonstrated superior performance in interpretation of graphs over those who had not. This improvement was attributed to the fact that pupils could see their results in 'real time' and that the time saved in not having to plot the graphs allowed pupils to focus on interpreting the data. Of particular interest in the Brasell study was the finding that pupils who had used the sensors, but not been shown the graphical display until twenty minutes later, showed no gains in ability to interpret graphs, providing evidence that the benefit is derived from the immediacy of the display. More recently, Barton (1997a, 1997b) undertook a study in the UK which explored the abilities of 12–13- and 14–15-year-old pupils to interpret graphs based on the properties of components of electrical circuits. The study involved a comparison of three approaches: data-logging, traditional practical work and non-practical work. For the majority of pupils, there was no obvious link between the approach and the ability to interpret the graphs, though pupils who used data-logging were able to give more detailed interpretations, and this appeared to be linked to the fact that they had been able to generate more data than those using traditional practical activities.

A note of caution is sounded by Rogers and Wild (1996), who make a useful distinction between properties and potential benefits of data-logging. For example, their work and the work of others (e.g. Newton, 1997) show that the property of data-logging to display data in 'real time' may not be a benefit, as pupils report being bored if all there is to do is sit passively and watch a screen as data are being displayed. The benefit comes, they argue, from the steps the *teacher* takes to engage the pupils with the data, a finding supported by evidence from Barton's work described in the previous paragraph.

Interactive multimedia and the Internet

Interactive multimedia involves working with a variety of different inputs from a CD-ROM or the Internet. These inputs may take the form of text, sound, drawings, photographs, animated drawings and video clips. Interactive multimedia and access to the Internet are resources to which pupils are most likely to have access at home as well as in school. The potential impact of interactive multimedia is significant, particularly on textbooks as the traditional pupil learning resource. There are already some examples of textbooks being developed in tandem with interactive multimedia resources, such as in the *Salters Nuffield Advanced Biology* (*SNAB*) project materials (UYSEG/Nuffield Foundation, 2002), though their use and effects have yet to be evaluated.

A review of the use of multimedia in science education was undertaken by Hartley (1994). At this relatively early stage of using multimedia in science teaching, evidence was emerging to indicate that pupils were motivated by the use of multimedia, and that its use stimulated conversation between pupils, but much of the conversation focused on aspects of procedure rather than development of scientific knowledge and understanding.

Advances in multimedia technology have resulted in CD-ROMs being developed for use in science lessons which allow pupils to perform 'virtual experiments'. Although some of these concentrate on practical activities which are difficult to do in the school laboratory, others have provided an alternative to normal practical work in science lessons. Collins *et al.* (1997) report on work done in exploring the effects of such software in a range of school subjects, including science. Here, both pupils and teachers reported benefits. For pupils, these included being able to see and try things several times, being able to generate results quickly and easily, and knowing they would get the 'right' answer as experiments always worked. Teachers valued safety aspects and ease of gathering data. However, teachers were concerned about abilities and experiences pupils might not gain if too much practical work became 'virtual'. These included drawbacks such as not being able to assemble and use simple apparatus, or smell a gas. There was also evidence that some of the visual images provided by the software were potentially misleading. For example, one package prompted a pupil to ask if electric current changed from red to blue when it went through light bulb.

Additional detailed evidence on the effects of the use of multimedia in science lessons comes from a study by Wellington (1999). This involved the evaluation of a two-year project, the Chemistry

School project, undertaken in the late 1990s and which involved the development, trial and use of multimedia technology for use in chemistry teaching. The study gathered data from just over fifty schools, in the form of a questionnaire sent to all the schools, and in-depth case studies involving observation and interview with both pupils and teachers in six schools. The study identified some of the barriers to facilitating use of the software (discussed later in the chapter). From the teachers' point of view, the material was seen as providing 'added value' for pupils in the form of, for example, motivation, flexibility in study routes and rates, variety of activity, freeing the teacher to spend more time with individual pupils and a perception of improved pupil learning. However, drawbacks were also identified, such as pupils playing with software rather than learning, and the temptation to use software at the expense of practical work. Pupils were generally very positive, though many did comment that there was a danger of potential over-use of multimedia leading to boredom and a lack of variety in activity.

Use of the Internet

The arrival of the Internet in schools has added an additional dimension to interactive multi-media, as well as opening up a new means of communication and access to huge resources of information. Some of the possibilities and potential problems for science teaching are discussed by Jackson and Bazley (1997), though research into the use of the Internet in science lessons is in its infancy. Some work, though not specifically with a focus on science lessons, has indicated that the Internet offers interesting possibilities for enhancing learning through computer-mediated communication. For example, Noss and Pachler (1999) have shown that pupils are motivated to engage in writing when they are able to access information quickly and easily and send it to someone (such as an electronic pen-pal) for almost instant feedback. Given the enormous potential of the Internet as a learning medium, it seems likely that it will receive considerable research attention in the next few years.

Box 6.3 illustrates a small-scale teacher study into the use of the Internet as a teaching resource in science.

Box 6.3: An example of a small-scale study on the use of ICT (Leaver, 1999)

Aim
To compare students' and teachers' perceptions of Internet-based resources developed to support the teaching of industrial chemistry.

Research questions

- In what ways do teachers make use of Internet-based resources in their teaching of industrial aspects of chemistry?
- What views do teachers have on these resources?
- What views do students have on these resources?

(An additional aspect of the study involved exploring the use of on-line questionnaires to gather research data.)

Research strategy and techniques
The research took the form of a survey. Data were gathered from both teachers and pupils through the use of on-line questionnaires linked to the website developed for the study. Data were therefore collected from an opportunistic sample – those who visited the website and completed the on-line questionnaires. Though some 50-plus responses were received from teachers, the response from students was disappointingly low (8 replies), and the data therefore not analysed.

Main findings
The study showed that the three main uses of Internet resources were: giving out a website address for students to follow up in their own time (half the respondents); adapting web-based material for handouts (one third of respondents); adapting web-based material (one-third of the respondents). Teachers targeted those resources which had strong visual impact, were perceived as up-to-date, and which provided data with which their students could work.

Research into more general effects of the use of ICT

A considerable amount of data on the more general effects of the use of ICT has emerged from work on its applications, as described in the previous section. There is evidence to suggest that the use of ICT can be motivating for pupils, though it is worth noting that this motivation is linked to the way in which the ICT is used, and is more apparent in some groups than others. For example, Somekh and Davies (1997) argue that computers are seen by females as a male province, and the evidence suggests that boys are more likely than girls to have a computer at home, are more interested in the use of computers and tend to take a more active role than girls when ICT is used in science lessons.

The role of the teacher has also been identified as crucial in helping pupils derive maximum benefit from the use of ICT. This latter finding has resulted in a shift of emphasis in research from a focus on the *nature* of ICT applications being used to *how* they are being used. Rogers and Newton (2001) describe the role of the teacher in lessons involving the use of ICT as one which includes:

- pointing out what pupils have learned already and building upon this, e.g. looking for further instances and recognising them;
- prompting pupils to make *links* between observations or some other knowledge;
- helping to interpret the implications for science and keeping the science questions to the fore;
- helping reduce the possibility of 'early closure' of pupils' discussion. (p. 421)

A comparatively recent development in research has explored possible links between the use of ICT in schools and the standards achieved by pupils in national tests and examinations. Recent studies by the British Educational Communications and Technology agency (BECTa) (2001a; 2001b) have sought to compare the performance of pupils in schools well-resourced for ICT with those less well-resourced. (BECTa was formerly the NCET – the National Council for Educational Technology.) Data were gathered from 2500 primary schools and 418 secondary schools in the academic years 1998–9 and 1999–2000. In order to classify levels of ICT provision, school inspectors graded schools as very good, good, adequate or unsatisfactory in terms of provision, though it should be noted that there were subjective elements in this judgement, as no specific criteria were applied. The judgement was made on the basis of quality and quantity of hardware and software, but did not take into account staff skills or training. Schools were also banded according to their socio-economic context so that comparisons could be made between schools with similar pupil intakes.

The studies showed that pupils at schools with 'good' ICT resources achieved significantly better results in national tests in English, mathematics and science at age 11 and 14 and in national examinations at 16+ than pupils at schools with 'poor' ICT resources. This finding was independent of the socio-economic banding of the school. Achievement was higher in schools where ICT was used routinely in maths and science lessons, and the best results were seen in schools where ICT was used across the whole curriculum. The studies did, however, reveal a key difference in resources level between primary and secondary schools: good ICT facilities were found across the range of socio-economic bands in primary schools, whereas good ICT facilities in secondary schools were linked to higher socio-economic bands. BECTa concludes that there is evidence of a 'digital divide' opening up in secondary schools, with adverse consequences for the achievement of pupils in less privileged schools. Box 6.4 summarizes the study on secondary school pupils.

Research into problems associated with the use of ICT

The scale of investment in ICT has been massive, and it is therefore scarcely surprising that a point was reached where people started to look at the 'returns'. Towards the end of the 1980s, questions were being asked from within and beyond the education sector about the ways in which ICT was being used in lessons, the expertise which had been acquired by teachers and the knowledge and skills being acquired by pupils. Underpinning these questions was the concern that the impact of ICT has been less than had been anticipated, and the reality in the classroom was falling short of the aspirations of those promoting the use of ICT in schools. For example, a report on use of ICT in schools in the mid-1990s (McKinsey and Co., 1997),

Box 6.4: An example of a larger-scale study on the use of ICT
(British Educational Communications and Technology Agency
(BECTa), 2001b)

Aim
To explore links between the standard of ICT provision in secondary schools and performance on national tests.

Research question
To what extent is the performance on national tests of pupils in
schools of similar socio-economic banding linked to the provision and use of ICT resources?

Research strategy and techniques
The study took the form of a survey of 418 secondary schools
which were inspected in the academic year 1998–9. Data on
pupils' performance in national tests were obtained from the
Qualifications and Curriculum Authority (QCA). These were
supplemented by data from the Department for Education and
Employment (DfEE).

Main findings
Pupils in schools with good ICT resources achieved better
results in national tests at age 14+ in English, maths and science
than those in schools with poor ICT resources. This applied to
both the 1999 and 2000 cohorts.

Pupils in schools with good ICT resources obtained better
results in national examinations at age 16+ than those in
schools with poor ICT resources. This applied to both the 1999
and 2000 cohorts.

Pupils in schools of similar socio-economic banding did better
in schools with good ICT resources than those with poor ICT
resources.

Pupils in schools where ICT was routinely used in science and
maths lessons did better than pupils in schools where ICT was
used infrequently.

The more widely ICT was used across the curriculum, the
better the performance in national tests in English, maths and
science at 14+, and the better the performance in national
examinations at 16+.

showed that fewer than 5 per cent of science teachers were making use of ICT in their lessons.

Evidence from surveys such as those undertaken by McKinsey and Co. (1977), Goldstein (1997) and Poole (2000) suggested that the problems in science lessons arose from a mix of educational and practical reasons. Though many of these were not unique to science, they were, arguably, brought more sharply into focus in science (and maths) lessons because these subject areas initially appeared the more natural 'home' for many ICT applications, and expectations were therefore higher. Reasons for problems being encountered included:

- doubts held by teachers over the value of ICT in promoting learning in science lessons;
- the lack in many ICT resources of a clear rationale for their inclusion in teaching;
- lack of adequate training for teachers;
- a lack of time for teachers to plan for effective use of ICT in their lessons;
- the planning difficulties associated with banks of networked computers being located centrally in rooms which had to be booked in advance;
- teachers feeling threatened by the presence in the classroom of a new, powerful source of information;
- lack of confidence on the part of many teachers with hardware and software;
- shortage of computers;
- lack of technical support;
- unrealistic expectations about the nature and speed of change on the part of those implementing initiatives.

An additional, though less obvious problem, arises from the fact that many schools have centrally located networks of computers. Rather than teachers being able to make decisions about how they can best use ICT to enhance the learning they wish to bring about, they often have to work out what sort of learning experiences they can provide when they have booked a computer room for a whole lesson. Thus, the technology is driving, rather than supporting, learning.

Other studies, such as those of Wellington (1999) and Newton (2000), though focusing on specific applications of ICT, have provided evidence of the persistence of many of the problems listed above. The studies have also identified factors which are more likely to lead to the successful implementation of ICT into science lessons, the most important of which appear to be a positive overall ethos towards the use of ICT within the school, and time for staff not just to undergo training but also plan for the ways in which ICT might be incorporated into their teaching and develop confidence in using ICT. However, some evidence of improving teacher confidence has been provided by a survey in England and Wales undertaken to establish the impact of an investment of over £2.3 million in ICT training for teachers through the New Opportunities Fund (NOF) scheme. Data gathered showed that 73 per cent of teachers reported themselves to be confident in the use of ICT in their teaching, compared with a figure of 63 per cent two years previously (Department for Education and Skills (DfES), 2001), though these figures do not reveal anything of what happens in practice in lessons.

Conclusions

There can be little doubt about the potential of ICT as a resource for learning in science lessons. Though the reality in many classrooms may fall short of the aspirations, there is, nonetheless, a growing body of research evidence to support the value of including ICT in science lessons.

Research has shown that the use of ICT improves pupils' motivation in science lessons and their learning of science ideas. Certain ICT applications, such as data-logging and simulations, can free pupils from tedious and time-consuming data collection and processing so that more time can be spent on thinking about and interpreting their data – key aspects of scientific activity. Research evidence also indicates that these skills are enhanced through the use of ICT.

One of the most important messages to emerge from the research relates to the role of the teacher. As much, though not all, of this evidence has been gathered incidentally in studies focusing on other aspects of the use of ICT, this is an area which would certainly benefit from more detailed work. Making use of ICT certainly requires teachers to think differently about the ways in which they plan for pupils' learning in their lessons. However, the expertise they have developed in, for example, questioning pupils, directing activities and helping pupils to make links between the various tasks in which they are engaged appear just as relevant and essential in lessons which make use of ICT as they are in other lessons.

Box 6.5: Implications for practice

- The provision of resources and training for teachers are insufficient to bring about an increase in the use of ICT in science lessons. There is also a need for time to be spent in school planning for the use of ICT.
- ICT-based activities are a means, not an end. Simply using ICT in lessons is insufficient to bring about learning and develop skills. A clear rationale is needed for incorporating ICT into lessons such that its use is in keeping with the planned lesson outcomes.
- Some ICT applications available for use in science lessons are incompatible with the provision of banks of computers in centrally located rooms. If ICT is to be used to best effect in science lessons, sufficient hardware and software need to be readily accessible in the normal teaching areas.

Implications for practice are summarized in Box 6.5. It is clear that in-service training for teachers will not, in itself, lead to a significant increase in the purposeful use of ICT in science lessons: creating time for planning is essential if ICT is to be used appropriately and effectively as part of good teaching. Linked to this, practical issues to do with the location of equipment also need to be addressed.

The emphasis of this chapter has been on reviewing the evidence on the ways in which ICT can be used to enhance pupils' experiences in science lessons, and the role the teacher can play in this. Whilst it is reassuring to find that many traditional teaching skills are as relevant to the use of ICT as they are to other teaching situations, it is also clear that ICT has the potential to continue to change significantly many of the experiences traditionally offered to pupils. With some well-resourced schools already investing in sets of laptop computers, the prospect of every pupil having access to an individual computer during lessons gets closer. This has enormous implications for the ways in which pupils can access information and the ways in which such information might be supplied. Teachers will still be needed, but increasingly easy access to ICT means that there are already moves to develop alternatives to the traditional teaching resource – the pupil text-book. This will certainly be an area of future research into the use and effects of ICT.

Box 6.6: First stops for further reading

Though advances in ICT have been rapid, many of the general issues to do with its use have been debated for a number of years. Thus a useful starting point for an overview of the area is:
Scaife, J. and Wellington, J. (1993) *Information Technology in Science and Technology Education*. Buckingham: Open University Press.

Three reviews of research related to the use of ICT in science teaching are:
Cox, M. (2000) Information and communications technologies: their role and value for science education. In M. Monk and J. Osborne (eds) *Good Practice in Science Teaching: What Research has to Say*. Buckingham: Open University Press.
Harlen, W. (1999) *Effective Teaching of Science: A Review of Research* Chapter 3. Edinburgh: Scottish Council for Research in Education.
Newton, L. and Rogers, L. (2001) ICT for teaching science – some prospects from research. In L. Newton and L. Rogers, *Teaching Science with ICT*. London: Continuum.

A compendium of articles on ICT in science lessons may be found in a special edition of School Science Review. *Though a number of these focus on ways in which ICT can be used, some draw on research evidence, and one takes the form of a review:*
Rodrigues, S. (1997) The role of IT in secondary school science: an illustrative review. *School Science Review*, 79 (287), 35–40.

For specific links between ICT and practical work, a useful article is:
Barton, R. (1998) IT in practical work: assessing and increasing

the value-added. In J. Wellington (ed.) *Practical Work in Science: Which Way Now?* London: Routledge.

There are many books on the wider use of ICT. Although primarily written for students on initial teacher education courses, a useful compendium of articles covering a range of issues is: Leask, M. and Pachler, N. (1999) *Learning to Teach Using ICT in the Secondary School*. London: Routledge.

Chapter 7

The Role of Language in School Science

> 'Language is a system of resources for making meanings ... any particular concept or idea makes sense only in terms of the relationship it has to other concepts and ideas. ... In order to talk science, we have to express relationships between the meanings of different concepts ... Ultimately, doing science is always guided and informed by talking science, to ourselves and with others.'

The extract above comes from the introduction of a book called *Talking Science* (Lemke, 1990) and it illustrates the central role language plays in science teaching – a role which extends well beyond the specialist vocabulary associated with science subjects. Language is one of the most important ways by which ideas are communicated, and the fact that so many pupils find science ideas hard to understand suggests that this process of communication does not always work very well. It is therefore hardly surprising that a significant area of research in science education has focused on the use of language in science lessons. What has this work revealed about, in Lemke's words, how 'doing science' relates to 'talking science' (and reading and writing science)?

This chapter looks at:

- how teachers use language, particularly when they are asking questions and explaining in science lessons;
- how pupils use language when talking, writing and reading;

- difficulties pupils may encounter with language in science lessons;
- ways in which language may be used in science lessons to help develop understanding.

Introduction

At one level, the importance of language in science lessons has always been recognized: in order to understand science subjects, pupils need to become familiar with a wide range of specialist vocabulary. Though obviously important, this aspect of language is only part of the story. Understanding science is more than just *knowing the meaning* of particular words and terms, it is about *making meaning* through exploring how these words and terms relate to each other. For this to happen, teachers and pupils need to be able to communicate effectively with each other, and this places language at the heart of science teaching.

The last two decades or so have seen increasing recognition being given to the crucial role played by language in learning, whether in science or in other subjects. A number of factors have contributed to the interest. One is the impact of the work of the Russian psychologist, Lev Vygotsky, on education. One of the most important elements of Vygotsky's theory of development concerns the role of language in learning. (More information about Vygotsky's work may be found in Appendix 2.) Vygotsky's often-quoted remark that 'Children solve practical tasks with the help of their speech as well as their eyes and hands' is of particular relevance to science lessons (Vygotsky, 1978: 26). The very influential work of Douglas Barnes and his co-workers (Barnes *et al.*, 1969; Barnes, 1976) on classroom talk and James Britton on classroom writing (Britton, 1970; Britton *et al.*, 1975), which will be described later in the chapter, was also significant in focusing attention on language. In England and Wales, the publication of the Bullock report, *A Language for Life* (Department of Education and Science (DES), 1975), further highlighted the importance of language by recommending that all teachers, irrespective of their subject, should see themselves as language teachers. Similar moves were apparent elsewhere, such as in the writing across the curriculum movement in the USA. The 1990s saw a formal requirement for pupils to be taught reading, writing, speaking and listening skills in all subjects in the National Curriculum for England and Wales (Department for Education and Employment/Welsh Office (DfEE/WO), 1995).

For science teaching specifically, many of the areas of research described in other chapters of this book have pointed to the importance of language as a means of developing understanding. For example, a constructivist approach to learning (see Chapter 2) emphasizes the need for careful questioning to elicit pupils' ideas and the importance of providing opportunities for pupils to clarify their thinking through discussion, and effective investigative work (see Chapter 4) requires pupils to articulate hypotheses and describe patterns in the data they gather. An expectation of scientific literacy (see Chapter 5) is that pupils draw effectively on the ideas and language of science to contribute to informed discussion. (In this context it is worth noting that 'scientific literacy' differs from what is sometimes referred to as 'science literacy'. The former concerns the ability to understand and discuss scientific matters, whereas the latter is about the development of talking, writing and reading abilities in science lessons.) Finally, the selection of appropriate language is clearly a vital aspect of assessment (see Chapter 10).

Within a broad framework of talking, writing and reading there are many ways in which language is used in teaching, including describing, questioning, explaining discussing and formulating arguments. Language is not, however, the only means of communicating information and developing understanding. Visual representation through the use of images and symbols is also important. This is particularly true of science, which makes extensive use of graphs, diagrams, charts, mathematical symbols, and the scientific 'shorthand' of chemical symbols, formulae and equations. This wide variety of methods of communication means that science can be described as a *multi-semiotic system*. (Semiotics is the study of language, signs and symbols and how they are used to communicate meaning.) Whilst visual representation is clearly very important in science, the focus of this chapter will be on the role of language in science lessons.

An overview of the literature on the use of language in science lessons

Several important questions have been asked – and continue to be asked – about language in science lessons. These are summarized in Box 7.1. Much of the initial work, undertaken in the 1970s and early 1980s, concerned pupils' understanding of scientific terminology and other vocabulary associated with the teaching of science. From the late 1970s onwards, the ideas of Barnes and Britton on the role of language in developing understanding were gaining ground, and exerted a strong influence on publications in the 1980s and into the early 1990s. Publications during this period tended to take the form of documents drawing on research to make recommendations for practice in science lessons (e.g. Davies and Greene, 1984; Bulman, 1985; Bentley and Watts, 1992), or 'position papers' putting forward commentary and ideas on the current status on the role of language in science education (e.g. Sutton, 1992).

Box 7.1: Key issues and questions

- What factors have contributed to language in science lessons becoming the focus of so much attention?
- What difficulties do pupils encounter with the specialist vocabulary of science and other terms associated with such vocabulary? How might these difficulties be overcome?
- What are the key features of teachers' and pupils' talking (classroom discourse) in science lessons? To what extent do these help or hinder the development of understanding?
- What role does writing play in science lessons? To what extent should pupils be encouraged to use a range of writing styles (genres) in their writing?
- What role does reading play in science lessons? How might reading be used most effectively?
- How do the many recommendations for strategies to employ in the classroom draw on research into the use of language and theories of language development?

There are three prominent strands to work from 1990s onwards. One is an increased interest in relating theories of language development to the teaching of science, in part as a means of providing theoretical underpinning or justification for some of the recommendations for practice. The second is a focus on the analysis of talking (often called *discourse analysis*) in science lessons and the ways in which this might hinder or help develop understanding. The third, and most recent, is an exploration of the nature and purpose of writing styles (*genres*) in science. The current prominence being given to developing literacy has seen a re-emergence of publications making recommendations for practice (e.g. Henderson and Wellington, 1998; Staples and Heselden, 2001), drawing in particular on discussion of the role of writing genres in science lessons.

Characterizing research on language and science education

There are several different ways in which research on language in science education can be characterized. One way is to look at whether the emphasis is on teachers or pupils, and on the spoken or written word. Thus one can look at matters relating to teacher talk, pupil talk, pupil writing and pupil reading, though there is inevitably some overlap between these areas. A second way is to look at the extent to which the research is seeking to identify potential *problems* with language, or seeking to identify the potential *benefits* of language. For example, studies such as those concerned with the readability of texts appear to be taking an initially negative stance and aim to identify barriers presented by language to learning and understanding. Other studies, such as those concerned with pupil–pupil talk, appear to seek to explore the positive contribution of the use of language in the development of understanding and learning. Finally, the research can also be characterized according to the research approach adopted. Work on 'problem' areas has tended to use a reductive and quantitative approach to the analysis of the use of language. In contrast, work on the potential benefits of language in developing understanding has drawn on a more qualitative and interpretative approach to analysis. The emphasis of the research work has tended to be on 'problem' areas and, whilst there is no shortage of literature describing activities aimed at developing language skills and abilities in science lessons, far less has been done by way of evaluating the effects of such activities.

For the purposes of this chapter, the research has been summarized in the following sections:

- vocabulary in science lessons;
- talking in science lessons;
- writing in science lessons;
- reading in science lessons.

Much of the work described in the first section consists of the earlier, quantitative work on factors which affect pupils' ability to understand what they hear and read about in science lessons. Although this work is clearly of relevance to talking, writing and reading, it is worth considering separately as it forms a comparatively cohesive area of research with clear implications for practice. It has also largely taken place without reference to theories on language development and the literature on language as a means of developing understanding.

One final, but very important, dimension to language research concerns the teaching of science in a language other than the first language of the learner. Those for whom English is a first language are privileged in that much scientific writing is done in English. Many learners in science have to cope with the additional difficulty of the medium of instruction being a second or even third language. This can only serve to exacerbate many of the problems encountered by first language learners. A detailed review of this aspect of language and science education may be found in Rollnick (2000).

Box 7.2 summarizes the main research findings on language and science teaching, with each of the main areas being discussed in detail in the following sections.

Vocabulary in science lessons

The most immediately apparent language problem in science is the vast technical vocabulary with which pupils need to become familiar in order to be able to make sense of what they hear, read and have to use when writing in their lessons. It is therefore not surprising that earlier work on language focused on *words* and the difficulties they might pose for pupils. In the late 1970s and early 1980s, several

---

Box 7.2: Key research findings

- Although pupils do encounter some problems with the technical vocabulary of science, they experience more difficulty with other commonly used terms which may not always be explained ('the language of secondary education') and the use of logical connectives.
- Language is often used in science as a means of describing and recording events, but it also has a key role to play in exploring and developing understanding.
- Science lessons are dominated by teacher talk.
- Teachers' use of questions and styles of explanation can often discourage pupils from putting forward their own ideas and thinking in any depth about ideas.
- Few opportunities are provided for pupils to engage in small-group discussions.
- There is considerable debate over writing in science lessons: using more personal language can be less alienating for pupils and help them develop their ideas, yet pupils can only develop 'science literacy' if they are able to use scientific writing genres.
- Extended reading rarely occurs in science lessons, thus reducing pupils' exposure to scientific writing genres and their opportunities to develop the critical reading skills associated with scientific literacy.
- Although the literature contains many suggestions aimed at improving practice, relatively little evaluation of such strategies has taken place.

---

studies were undertaken on the readability of school textbooks (e.g. Johnson, 1979; Knutton, 1983). The studies used a variety of standardized measures of readability, many of which involve counting features of text such as the length of sentences and the use of polysyllabic words. (A detailed description of common measures of readability may be found in Wellington and Osborne, 2001.) The average reading ages of a number of texts emerged as higher than the chronological age of pupils, with reading ages of between 15 and 21 being found in physics and chemistry textbooks written for 13–16-year-olds! Because it tends to focus on surface features of text, work on readability has its limitations (see, for example, Slater and Thompson, 1984; Merzyn, 1987; Reid and Hodson, 1987). Calculations based on sentence and word length ignore matters such as the layout of text and the role of illustrations, both of which have been shown to influence a reader's motivation to engage with the text and the ability to understand what is being read.

A further limitation of many measures of readability is that they reveal nothing of the *nature* of the words in the text and hence the overall 'understandabilty' of what is being read. In order to address this, Wellington (1983 and elsewhere) has proposed a four-level taxonomy of words in science. At the lowest level are *naming* words (e.g. tibia, fulcrum), followed by *process* words (e.g. distillation, photosynthesis), then *concept* words (e.g. work, salt) and, finally, *mathematical* 'words' and symbols. As Wellington notes, concept words pose the most problems: first, because they are abstract; second, because language development in science results in some words changing from naming words to concept words (e.g. gas, salt); and, third, because some may have both everyday and scientific meanings (e.g. work, salt). Chapter 2, on constructivist research, has shown how such words cause problems for pupils.

Whilst the work described above has confirmed that the language of science can pose difficulties for pupils, other research has suggested that the problem is less to do with the technical vocabulary of science than might be expected. Some indication of this came from studies by Douglas Barnes and his co-workers, begun in the 1960s. Drawing on detailed observations of lessons in a range of subjects at secondary school, Barnes *et al.* (1969) described three types of language used in lessons:

- specialist language presented;
- specialist language not presented;
- 'the language of secondary education'.

The observations revealed that, when compared with other subjects, not only did science lessons contain the highest proportion of specialist words, but that science teachers also drew extensively on a specialist vocabulary that was not explained to pupils – 'specialist vocabulary not presented'. Barnes (1969: 51) cites an example of a teacher describing the extraction of chlorophyll from grass as being done in 'an enclosed system' and 'under reflux conditions', with the teacher assuming that both terms would be understood by the pupils. Barnes also uses the term 'the language of secondary education' to describe words one would expect to find in textbooks and other official documents which set out to discuss topics in an impersonal manner, but which would not normally be encountered except in schools. Language in this category included words and phrases such as: in terms of, subject to, factors, determines, assumption, complex, theoretically, becomes apparent. 'Specialist language not presented' and 'the language of secondary education', Barnes argues, all add to the difficulties faced by pupils in lessons.

In seeking to explore further possible difficulties encountered by pupils in science lessons, a widely cited study by Cassels and Johnstone (1985) involved exploring pupils' understanding of 95 words which were judged to be most troublesome in science lessons. In producing their list of words, Cassels and Johnstone drew on an earlier study undertaken in Australia by Gardner (1972; 1974). Words in the list were not scientific words, but words commonly used in science lessons, such as classify, characteristic, constituent, initial and relative. These words were then incorporated into a research instrument which consisted of a series of multiple-choice items which required pupils to select the appropriate use of a word, as illustrated below:

Which sentence uses the word <u>classify</u> correctly?

A   Classify the dishes with soap and water.
B   Classify the argument by expanding the main points.
C   Classify the rocks according to their age.
D   Classify the crystals together. (Cassels and Johnstone, 1985: 33)

Respondents were asked to select the sentence in which the word was used correctly. The instrument was used with pupils in 200 secondary schools. The study revealed that many words were poorly understood by pupils (such as agent, incident, component, negligible, random, uniform). This was particularly the case for words which are used in everyday contexts but which have special meanings in science. The study also showed that that these difficulties in understanding tended to persist during schooling. An implication of this is that teachers are aware of the demands of the technical vocabulary of science, and therefore take steps to explain it, but are less aware of problems posed by frequently employed non-specialist vocabulary. Subsequent studies (e.g. Pickersgill and Lock, 1991; Meyerson *et al.*, 1991) have provided further evidence of the difficulties pupils have with non-specialist vocabulary and words with multiple meanings.

One final area of work on words in science concerns *logical connectives* – words, phrases and clauses used as links in sentences to improve the cohesion of the text. Logical connectives are employed frequently in science, and examples include: because, this shows, hence, therefore, for example, respectively, furthermore, consequently, although, conversely, moreover, similarly. (Technically, logical connectives are normally adverbs, adverbial clauses or subordinate conjunctions.) In a study of some 16 000 secondary-age pupils (Gardner, 1977) found over 70 logical connectives which hindered pupils' understanding of sentences, including words such as consequently, hence, conversely, respectively, moreover. A later study by Byrne *et al.* (1994) has provided additional evidence to support Gardner's findings, and the sample from the small-scale teacher study (Valentine, 1996) summarized in Box 7.3 also identifies similar problems for pupils. One outcome of the work on logical connectives has been the simplification of language used in science textbooks through the removal of logical connectives to make shorter sentences. It is worth noting, however, that concern has been expressed about the over-simplification of language in pupil resources resulting in pupils finding it more difficult to engage with formal scientific writing (e.g. Sutton, 1992; Wellington, 2001).

Beyond words and their meanings

Studies such as those described above have served to draw attention to a communication gap between teachers and pupils, and resulted in significantly more attention being paid to language in resources produced for pupils (see, for example, strategies suggested by Long, 1991). Words are important, but it is through talking, writing and reading that understanding is developed. The remainder of this chapter therefore focuses on these aspects of language use in science

Box 7.3: An example of a small-scale study on language
(Valentine, 1996)

Aim
To identify problems with logical connectives in chemistry teaching at upper high school level, with a focus on possible differences between students with English as a first language and students for whom English was not the first language.

Research questions

- What problems do students have understanding logical connectives in scientific writing?
- To what extent are there links between these problems and whether or not students have English as their first language?

Research strategy and techniques
The research took the form of a case study of just over 60 17- and 18-year-old students taking A-level chemistry. The primary data collection technique was a questionnaire containing 40 items testing understanding of connectives in everyday and scientific contexts. These items were developed from those used in earlier studies (e.g. Gardner, 1977). These data were supplemented by interviews with students which gathered further data on their use of connectives and asked them to comment on those they found difficult.

Main findings
The study showed that some connectives (such as hence, as to) posed difficulties for all students, though, not unexpectedly, students with English as a first language had fewer problems overall. There was an indication from the interviews, more noticeable in students for whom English was not their first language, that students focused on what they saw as the 'key words' in text, and that these key words tended not to include any logical connectives in the text.

lessons. However, it is helpful to set the research in each of these individual areas in the context of theories about the role language plays in learning.

The research undertaken by Barnes and his co-workers (Barnes *et al.*, 1969; Barnes, 1976), though not recent, has much to say which is still relevant today. It was ground-breaking in terms of the way in which it conceptualized language as a tool for learning and certainly provided much of the impetus for research into the way in which language is used in science lessons. In addition to the work described earlier in the chapter, Barnes also used his extensive lesson observations to identify a dimension of teaching which he called 'Transmission–Interpretation'. Some teachers saw their role as one involving the *transmission* of knowledge and understanding to pupils. Others taught in a way which suggested they saw knowledge as something to be shared, and that their role was to help pupils with the *interpretation* of this knowledge. Barnes went on to characterize the ways in which teachers used writing in their lessons. *Transmission mode* teachers essentially saw writing as a means of acquiring or recording information, and placed an emphasis on the product. *Interpretation mode* teachers saw writing as a means of promoting cognitive and personal development, with the emphasis being on the processes involved in generating the written product. The most significant outcome of Barnes's work for science teaching has been the trend to develop activities for use in lessons which move science teaching towards the interpretation end of the Transmission–Interpretation dimension. The view of language associated with this move has been summarized by Sutton (1996):

> The popular image of science presents language as a medium for describing – for getting an account of the world as it is, an 'objective' record of what happens, independent of human beings. Yet ... it is more of a tool for trying out ideas, for figuring out what is going on, for interpreting the situation. (p. 5)

Like Barnes, Sutton makes the distinction between language used as a *labelling* system for describing and informing, and language used as an *interpretative* system for clarifying and making sense of new experiences. Sutton also argues that too little interpretative use of language is made in science lessons.

A further issue to which Barnes's work points is one which forms a dimension of sociolinguistic theory – the notion of power and status being conferred on those with particular forms of knowledge and the ability to use their associated language. Socio-linguists would argue that those who are able to talk the specialist language of science are members of an exclusive group, who may exercise power and control through the ways in which they use this language in their interactions with others. Teachers in Barnes's transmission mode of teaching would – though probably without being aware of it – be exercising this power and control. Although such ideas may seem rather removed from everyday classroom interactions, they are certainly linked to debates over the nature of writing which is appropriate for science lessons, as will be seen later. A useful overview and more detailed discussion of these ideas may be found in O'Toole (1996).

Talking in science lessons

Observation of numerous science lessons has shown that the dominant activity is talking, with teacher-talk generally predominating! A study by Newton *et al.* (1999), who observed 34 science lessons given to 11–16-year-old pupils in seven schools, revealed teachers' questions, instructions and explanations occupied somewhere between one-third and a half of lesson time, with pupils spending around three-quarters of their time listening to the teacher or doing practical work. Similar findings have been reported by Wilson (1999), who also noted that over half of teachers' talking involved giving explanations.

Research on talking in science lessons has focused on four main areas:

- teachers' questions;
- teachers' explanations;
- pupils' questions;
- pupils' discussions.

Teachers' questions

Asking questions, together with explaining and giving instructions, constitute the major part of the subject-related talking done by teachers in their lessons. Much of the questioning that occurs in lessons takes the form of what Shapiro (1998) aptly describes as teachers trying to 'pull' the ideas they want from pupils. Although such dialogue may include open questions, the answers ultimately being sought are clear in the teacher's mind. Far less use is made in lessons of questions which challenge pupils to think, or which seek to explore pupils' ideas and explanations, as was demonstrated by constructivist researchers (see Chapter 2). The 'pulling the ideas out' style of questioning exemplifies a typical classroom dialogue of three parts (a triadic dialogue) variously called Initiation–Response–Evaluation (IRE) (Sinclair and Coulthard, 1975) or Initiation–Response–Follow-up (IRF) (Mehan, 1979). In such a dialogue, the teacher asks a question, a pupil answers and the teacher comments on the answer. Lemke (1990) suggest that much of the dialogue which takes place in science lessons takes this form and he goes on to argue that such dialogue, by simply requiring pupils to engage in recall or description, discourages pupils from engaging in any real thinking about ideas.

A study which provides some evidence of teachers expanding their repertoire of questioning strategies is that of Koufetta-Menicou and Scaife (2000), who examined teachers' style of questioning in detail through a comparison of lessons using CASE (Cognitive Acceleration through Science Education) materials (see Chapter 3) and normal science lessons. One aim of the study was to see if CASE lessons, where the focus is on challenging pupils' thinking, resulted in teachers varying their style of questioning. Data were gathered through observation of 38 lessons in two secondary schools. Analysis of the data allowed questions to be classified into one of nine types, and revealed that much of the questioning which did take place still took the form of seeking recall or descriptive answers from pupils. However, there was evidence of a wider range of questions being used in CASE lessons, particularly questions asking pupils to justify ideas and support them with evidence, suggesting that the use of such materials was having some effect on the nature of questions asked by teachers.

Teachers' explanations

Most science teachers would see explaining as a fundamental part of their job – and the nature of the subject means that there is much explaining to be done in science lessons. This crucial aspect of teacher talking has been explored in detail in a major study by Ogborn *et al.* (1996). Prior to this, comparatively little work had been done to explore and characterize the nature of teachers' explanations in science lessons. Through extensive observation of secondary science lessons, Ogborn *et al.* (1996) identified four characteristics of explanations and four main styles of explaining. Their four characteristics of explanations were:

- creating differences (establishing that there is a difference between what the teacher and pupil know);
- constructing entities (giving meaning to various elements which will form part of the explanation, e.g. talking about lungs, blood, oxygen, carbon dioxide and haemoglobin in advance of an explanation of respiration);
- transforming knowledge (using stories or analogies to help pupils grasp ideas);
- putting meaning into matter (using demonstrations to give meaning to ideas).

Ogborn *et al.* (1996) point out that explanations generally incorporate all the above characteristics at the same time. The four styles of explanation were:

- 'Let's think it through together' (the teacher collects and reshapes ideas from the class);
- 'The teller of tales' (the teacher telling a story);
- 'Say it my way' (the teacher lays out explanatory forms of words and these are practised by the class);
- 'See it my way' (a given scientific theory is used to rationalize facts and phenomena).

These characteristics and styles of explanation are proposed as a language for describing explanations. The research did not set out to make an judgements about the effectiveness or otherwise of particular explanations, though Ogborn *et al.* (1996) conclude that the obvious next question arising from their work is 'what explanations work well, when and for whom?' Box 7.4 provides a summary of the study by Ogborn *et al.* (1996).

One aspect of explanations which emerged from the Ogborn *et al.* (1996) study as being frequently employed by teachers was their use of analogies. Some research has been undertaken specifically on analogies and yielded mixed evidence of their usefulness. For example, Black and Solomon (1987) looked at the use of analogies in the teaching of current electricity, and concluded that teaching pupils' analogies did not appear to confer any advantage when answering test questions. In contrast, other studies (e.g. Thiele and Treagust, 1991; Glynn *et al.*, 1995) found evidence that analogies could help in the process of developing understanding, particularly where pupils were taught explicitly.

Work on classroom discourse has revealed just how complex teacher–pupil interactions can be, which, in turn, creates considerable methodological challenges for analysis and interpretation of data. Some attempts have been made to apply quantitative methods to discourse analysis. For example, in order to look at the cohesion and clarity of classroom discourse, Rodrigues and Thompson (2001) used a Cohesive Harmony Index (CHI) to analyse video data of a lesson on materials with 14-year-olds. (The CHI involves making a detailed breakdown of the discourse followed by the application of a formula to provide a measure of the cohesiveness of the discourse.) The study demonstrated that, even when discourse was coherent, pupils did not always appear to grasp the point being made by the teacher as there were few opportunities for discussion and clarification of ideas. Whilst such an approach provides some insights into the nature of classroom interaction, it also points to the limitations of quantitative methods for such analysis.

Analysis of classroom discourse has largely drawn on qualitative methods, which can lead to problems over interpretation. For example, in a detailed analysis of an extract from a lesson on forces, Klaassen and Lijnse (1996) illustrate how the same dialogue may be open to a number of different interpretations depending on judgements made about the nature and value of pupils' contributions by those doing the analysis. The work of Ogborn *et al.* (1996) has provided one example of a framework for describing and analysing

Box 7.4: An example of a larger-scale study on language
Ogborn *et al.* (1996)

Aim
To explore the nature of explanations used by teachers in science lessons and develop a language for describing explanations which might be helpful in the analysis of classroom discourse. (Note: the study did not set out to explore the effectiveness – or otherwise – of particular explanations.)

Research questions
What are the characteristics of explanations used in science lessons? What styles of explanations are used by teachers?

Research strategy and techniques
The study took the form of a survey of a range of science lessons taught by twelve teachers in four secondary schools. Data were gathered by means of lesson observations and audio tape-recordings of the lessons.

Main findings
Four characteristics of explanations and four main styles of explaining were identified from analysis of the data. (These are explained in more detail in the text.)
The characteristics of explanations were:

- creating differences;
- constructing entities;
- transforming knowledge;
- putting meaning into matter.

The styles of explanation were:

- 'Let's think it through together'
- 'The teller of tales'
- 'Say it my way'
- 'See it my way'.

classroom discourse which has been derived from empirical data. An alternative framework has been proposed by Mortimer and Scott, who draw on Vygotsky's ideas to propose a 'flow of discourse' model of analysis. Their ideas are discussed in detail in Scott (1998) and Mortimer and Scott (2000). Identifying appropriate strategies for the analysis of classroom discourse appears to be a developing area of research in science education.

Pupils' questions

Although a number of studies have been undertaken on teachers' use of questions, comparatively little has been done on pupils' questions. One reason for this may be that analysis of classroom discourse reveals that pupils ask very few subject-related questions in lessons. Wray and Lewis (1997), reporting on the findings of a three-year study of pupils' writing in non-fiction, suggest that teachers are often reluctant to encourage pupils to ask questions is case they expose ignorance on the part of the teacher. Lemke (1990) suggests that pupils probably ask far more subject-related questions in their minds than out loud, and argues that it is when pupils ask questions that glimpses are provided of 'much of the miscommunication and confusion that occurs in everyday classrooms'.

One study which has focused specifically on pupils' questions is that of Watts *et al.* (1997), who sought to explore the extent to which pupils' questions might be indicative of their 'frame of mind' and reveal something of their understanding. Watts *et al.* draw on an analysis of extracts from classroom discourse from a number of secondary science lessons to propose a useful classification of questions from pupils which are indicative of particular periods of conceptual change. The three types of questions are:

- consolidation, where pupils are trying to sort out their understanding and seeking reassurance that they have grasped the right idea (e.g. 'Is it because ... ?');
- exploration, where pupils are seeking to expand knowledge and test ideas they have formed (e.g. 'If ... would ... ?');
- elaboration, where pupils attempt to reconcile different

understandings and resolve conflicts (e.g. 'But what happens if . . . ?').

Watts *et al.* (1997) argue that teachers need to pay more attention to what is revealed by their pupils' questions, and provide explicit opportunities in lessons for pupils to practise asking questions.

Pupils' discussions

Interest in the possibilities offered by pupil–pupil discussions first arose when Barnes (1969) demonstrated that subject-related dialogue which took place between pupils differed considerably from that between pupils and their teachers. In the absence of an authoritative adult, pupils engaged in *exploratory* talk – talk in which ideas were discussed and negotiated, a process which Barnes likened to Piaget's concept of accommodation. In contrast, much of the teacher–pupil discourse in lessons took the form of *presentational* talk – teachers presenting pupils with information or pupils answering teachers' questions by presenting them with information. Since that time, much has been written about the desirability of using small group (pupil–pupil) discussion in science lessons, and a number of strategies have been suggested for promoting such discussion, such as the use of 'concept cartoons' (Naylor and Keogh, 2000), generating concept maps and focusing on the science in topic issues. As yet, little research has been done to evaluate the effects of small-group discussions on pupils' learning. There is evidence, however, that such discussion continues to be used only very infrequently in lessons. A study by Newton *et al.* (1999) indicated around just 2 per cent of lesson time was occupied by pupil–pupil discussions, with teachers reporting the main reasons for its infrequent use being a lack of confidence and time on their part, and a feeling that pupils did not value such an activity. Other problems are likely to include a lack of clarity of purpose, and well-structured materials to support discussions.

Some insights into effects of the use of pupil–pupil discussions are provided in a study by Solomon (1992). This involved the analysis of recordings of discussions which formed part of an STS (Science–Technology–Society) course for pupils aged 16+. Pupils were shown video extracts of science applications (e.g. kidney donation, risks and costs of nuclear power), then asked to discuss what they had seen. The analysis revealed three phases to the discussions:

- 'framing' (deciding what was going to be discussed);
- 'negotiating and persuading' (clarifying ideas, checking out others' ideas, views and understanding);
- 'reaching judgements'.

Though the study revealed little evidence of logical thinking and reasoned argument, there was some evidence that understanding of the science associated with the issues increased through discussion, and that the nature and quality of discussion improved with experience.

A comparatively recent move in school science has been to promote the use of *argument* and the development of argumentation abilities in lessons. This work has links with both pupils' discussion and pupils' writing. The work draws on a model of argument developed by Toulmin (1958), and which is described in detail in Newton *et al.* (1999). In essence, the model identifies four main types of statement which contribute to an argument:

- claims (what is going to be established);
- grounds (data to support the claims);
- warrants (justifications for linking data to particular claims);
- backings (basic assumptions to justify particular warrants).

To help develop argumentation abilities, Osborne *et al.* (2001) have developed a set of materials to support the process of argument in science lessons, many of which relate to common misunderstandings. The activities involve pupils interpreting evidence and justifying their interpretation. The materials are supported by *arguing prompts* for teachers (questions such as 'why do you think that?', 'how do you know?') and *writing frames* to help pupils structure their ideas. (Writing frames are discussed in more detail in the next section.) Osborne *et al.* (2001) suggest that the use of such strategies will allow science teachers to claim genuinely that they are helping pupils to develop their abilities to reason and think critically. These materials appear to offer a very useful means for promoting effective pupil–pupil discussion, and it will be interesting to see what effects they have.

Writing in science lessons

Together with listening to their teacher and doing practical work, writing is the activity on which pupils spend most time in their science lessons. Writing is also most frequently cited by pupils as the activity they like *least* in science lessons (e.g. Ramsden, 1997; Osborne and Collins, 2001). The reasons for this are two-fold. First, writing can be boring, particularly when it simply involves copying – from textbooks, worksheets or the board. Second, writing can be hard – it places additional linguistic demands on pupils by requiring them to express themselves more coherently than is likely to be the case when talking. In science this problem is exacerbated by the conventional use of impersonal language in reporting (e.g. 'a test tube was taken ... ').

One strand of the literature on writing in science focuses on 'writing science'. The use of an impersonal reporting style was first challenged by Britton *et al.* (1975), who argued that children needed to use language in different and more informal ways in order to learn effectively in science. (There are overlaps here with what has been said about the role of spoken language in developing pupils' understanding.) The notion of using a more personal, exploratory style of writing was very much in keeping with the 'student-centred' views of education of the time, and led to a number of recommendations for practice being made to diversify the nature of, and audience for, the writing which pupils undertook in their science lessons. These included writing stories and plays, writing newspaper articles, writing instructions to a younger child on how to do something, producing posters and writing poems. Little research has been undertaken on the effects of using such activities, though some discussion of issues raised by their use may be found in Sheeran and Barnes (1991).

There are two opposing views on appropriate ways of writing in science. Advocates of the use of more expressive, personal writing (e.g. Sutton, 1989; Prain and Hand, 1995) see it as a natural development from ordinary speech and an important means of developing understanding, with the added advantage of not having the alienating effect on pupils associated with more traditional writing. For others (e.g. Halliday and Martin, 1993; Keys, 1999), a failure to introduce pupils to scientific writing genres is seen as a failure to develop 'science literacy' in pupils and therefore denying them access to scientific writing with its associated status. O'Toole (1996) sums up this view by arguing that:

> If science teachers, textbook writers and examiners expect students to act on information presented in a particular style, and expect them to use that same style to demonstrate the degree to which their activity has been successful, then those teachers, writers and examiners would seem to have a responsibility to both let students know precisely what they expect and help them meet those expectations. (pp. 134–5)

The debate on writing style, together with the increasing prominence being given to developing literacy, has resulted in the current interest in teaching about genres of writing in science lessons.

One classification of writing genres is that of Wray and Lewis (1997), whose focus was on non-fiction writing across the curriculum. They identified six non-fiction genres:

- recount (retelling of events to inform or entertain);
- report (presentation of information);
- explanation (explaining processes involved in natural or social phenomena, or how something works);
- procedure (giving a sequenced step of instructions);
- persuasion (promoting a particular point of view or argument);
- discussion (presenting arguments and information from differing viewpoints before reaching a conclusion based on the evidence).

(This framework, supplemented by the genres of analysis and evaluation, formed the basis of the National Literacy Strategy implemented in 2001 for 11–14-year-olds in England and Wales.) Within Wray and Lewis's framework, they suggest that the three genres of report, explanation and procedure are those which are most likely to be used in science lessons.

Martin (1993) has identified five major scientific writing genres, of which the first three in his list appear to predominate:

- experiment (documentation of research);
- explanation (small reports focusing on scientific processes);
- report (organizing information – most commonly used in scientific textbooks);
- biography (life and contributions of one or a group of scientists);
- exposition (presenting arguments for a position on a controversial topic).

Current thinking on writing in science lessons advocates the view that pupils should be encouraged to write in a range of genres, and provided with instruction in their science lessons to help them achieve this. (This must also imply the need for support for teachers.) For example, Rowell (1997) argues writing in science should relate to three dimensions:

- hermeneutic (interpretative) activity (writing in which pupils use their own language to interpret information to help with their understanding);
- knowledge transforming activity (writing in which pupils begin to make use of scientific genres to formulate problems and evaluate evidence);
- discursive practice (writing in which pupils use scientific genres to convey their understanding).

Practical suggestions for broadening the range of writing activities in science lessons, drawing on work on genres, are beginning to appear in the literature (e.g. Staples and Heselden, 2001). Linked to the work on genres is the notion of using *writing frames* to provide help and support for pupils in their writing. Writing frames provide sentence stems for pupils to complete. Thus, for example, a writing frame for a discussion in which pupils were required to present arguments and reach a conclusion might contain the sentence stems such as: 'There is discussion about ... '; 'Supporters of this idea say ... and ... '; 'However other people say ... '; 'My view is ... '

As yet, little research has been undertaken into the use of writing genres in science lessons. One study in the USA (Hand *et al.*, 1999) reports on the use of a teaching module for use with 16–17-year-old pupils with a specific focus on writing in different genres. The study identified teacher knowledge and confidence as being a key factor in using the materials, and the need for pupils to be made explicitly aware of the nature and purpose of different writing styles in science. It seems likely that the next few years will see work being done on teachers' use of different types of writing with pupils, and the effects of such writing on pupils' knowledge, understanding and views of science.

Reading in science lessons

Reading – or reading which occupies any extended period of time – rarely happens in science lessons. In part this is because of the prominence given to practical activity in lessons, but it is also likely to be related to the drive for readability: many modern school science textbooks now have a 'magazine-like' appearance, with short paragraphs of text interspersed with a variety of illustrations and snippets of information. This has led to such books being criticized (e.g. Sutton, 1992) as failing to develop the critical reading abilities associated with scientific literacy. (A good review of the development of textbooks in science lessons may be found in Wellington, 2001.) More recently, the role of reading in science has received attention in the context of writing genres. For example, Kearsey and Turner (1999) undertook a detailed analysis of one modern school science textbook and demonstrated that the text switched between everyday and scientific styles of writing – on occasions even within the same paragraph of text – causing difficulties for pupils in making sense of what they had read and in identifying appropriate language for their responses. Unsworth (2001) has also developed and applied a framework for analysing explanations in textbooks which looks potentially very helpful in identifying features of effective explanations.

The most prominent area of work on reading in science began in the 1980s and focused on the promotion of 'active reading' in science. One of the most important and influential publications of this period was *Reading for Learning in the Sciences* (Davies and Greene, 1984). Drawing on a detailed analysis of textbooks of the time, they identified seven different *frames of text* which they list in an order of what they conclude is increasing complexity:

- instruction (providing instructions for a task, e.g. an experiment);
- classification (identifying similarities and differences in order to group objects or phenomena, e.g. solids, liquids and gases);
- structure (describing the names, properties, location and function of parts, e.g. of a tooth);
- mechanism (similar to structure, but making reference to associated phenomena, e.g. the role of air in the aneroid barometer);
- process (describing and explaining stages of particular phenomena, transformations and actions which cause these, e.g. the processes involved in the rock cycle);
- concept–principle (defining features of a concept or examples and applications of a principle, e.g. characterizing electric current);
- hypothesis–theory (testing ideas and reaching conclusions, e.g. in describing Pasteur's work on vaccination).

Davies and Greene (1984) describe a number of strategies for encouraging pupils to interact with different frames of text, and introduced the concept of Directed Activities Related to Text (DARTS) which require pupils to work on texts in a way which may help them develop skills associated with reading for learning. (Full details of this work, together with many examples, may be found in Davies and Greene, 1984.) More recently, Wray and Lewis (1997) have proposed a number of strategies for extending pupils' interaction with non-fiction texts. As with writing in science, little evaluation has been undertaken of the effects of utilizing such strategies in science lessons.

Conclusions

A number of messages appear to emerge from the extensive literature on language in science teaching, and implications for practice are summarized in Box 7.5. Some of the messages are clear, and it is

---

Box 7.5: Implications for practice

- Pupils will need help to become familiar with a variety of terms they encounter in their lessons which extend beyond the more obvious technical vocabulary of science.
- Teachers should reflect carefully on their use of questions to ensure they are not discouraging pupils from putting forward their own ideas and questions.
- There appears to be a good case for providing more opportunities in lessons for pupils to talk and write about science in ways which help them develop their own thinking and ideas rather than simply recording and describing information.
- There also appears to be a good case for incorporating strategies into lessons which make more use of reading and which encourage pupils to think about what they are reading.
- The current focus on literacy suggests that support will be needed for both teachers and pupils if instruction is to be provided for pupils on the use of different writing genres.
- There is a need for detailed evaluation, including teacher evaluation, of the many suggestions for practice to explore their effectiveness in use.

---

comparatively easy to see what their implications are for classroom practice. The early work on words in science points to the need for vigilance when talking to pupils and in producing text for pupils to ensure that new terminology – which might not be obviously 'scientific' – is explained appropriately.

Much of the rest of the research has pointed to the complexity of classroom interactions and the challenges of analysing and interpreting data on such interactions. One outcome of attempts to provide a clearer picture of this complexity of interaction is that research is shifting from a focus on language to explore language as one component in a repertoire of communication modes employed in science lessons (Kress *et al.*, 2001). Research has, however, helped identify several aspects of language use in teaching where change would seem desirable. For example, research has shown that the dominant activity in science lessons is teacher talk. Whilst this in itself might not be a problem, there are questions over the usefulness of some of the talk. Teachers' use of questions in science lessons often discourages pupils from putting forward their own ideas or from thinking in depth about the ideas they are encountering; much teacher talk is presentational and little encouragement is provided for pupils to ask questions; few opportunities are provided for pupils to engage in small-group discussion in order to explore and develop their ideas. Problems have also been highlighted about writing and reading in science lessons. Scientific writing genres often fail to engage pupils and can be difficult to understand, yet an over-reliance on more personal writing styles can reinforce the notion that scientific writing is unattractive and deny pupils access to the information in such writing. Little reading takes place in science lessons, thus pupils are not provided with opportunities to develop either scientific literacy or science literacy. The reading which does take place often does not promote active engagement with ideas or encourage pupils to think. Whilst much of this might appear rather negative, a range of strategies has been proposed or recommended for practice, and resources generated for use in lessons, with more recent examples drawing on research into writing genres.

The literature demonstrates very clearly the widespread interest in language in science education, and an important next step for research is to gather data on the effects of strategies which have been proposed for enhancing the role of language in promoting learning in science lessons.

Box 7.6: First stops for further reading

A good introduction to work in the area, including recommendations for practice is:
Wellington, J. and Osborne, J. (2001) *Language and Literacy in Science Education.* Buckingham: Open University Press.

A concise review of research on language and science education, together with discussion of related issues is:
Jones, C. (2000) The role of language in the teaching and learning of science. In M. Monk and J. Osborne (eds) *Good Practice in Science Teaching: What Research has to Say.* Buckingham: Open University Press.

Two widely cited books, the first presenting a fairly theoretical discussion of the use of language in science lessons and the second a very positive view of the role of language in science, are:

Lemke, J. (1990) *Talking Science*. New York: Ablex Publishing Corporation.

Sutton, C. (1992) *Words, Science and Learning*. Buckingham: Open University Press.

Two books about the classic and influential work of Barnes and his co-workers are:

Barnes, D., Britton, J. and Rosen, H. (1969) *Language, the Learner and the School*. Harmondsworth: Penguin. (Now in its fourth edition, 1990.)

Sheeran, Y. and Barnes, D. (1991) *School Writing: Discovering the Ground Rules*. Buckingham: Open University Press.

Though not recent, an informative and helpful book on the nature of text and the role of reading in science is:

Davies, F. and Greene, T. (1984) *Reading for Learning in the Sciences*. Edinburgh: Oliver Boyd.

A comparatively accessible discussion of theories of language development and how they relate to science teaching may be found in:

O'Toole, M. (1996) Science, schools, children and books: exploring the classroom interface between science and language. *Studies in Science Education*, 28, 113–43.

Chapter 8

Pupils' Attitudes to Science and School Science

Everyone involved in science education wants pupils to enjoy the science they study in school and to see how it relates to their lives. Yet, there cannot be many science teachers who have escaped hearing in their lessons 'This is *boring*, Miss/Sir!' or who have not worried about how few of their pupils seem to want to continue with their study of science beyond the compulsory period. Why is it that so many young people appear to be alienated by science?

This chapter looks at:

- attitudes pupils have towards science and school science, and why many of these are both negative and persistent;
- ways of gathering data on attitudes, and problems associated with gathering reliable and valid data;
- research evidence on strategies which have been employed in science lessons to try and promote a more positive response to science from pupils.

Introduction

One aim of science education is to help young people understand something of the key ideas in science and gain an appreciation of the importance and impact of science on society. However, pupils' feelings about the science they encounter in their lessons are just as important as the science ideas they learn, for these feelings exert a significant influence on their dispositions towards science. The importance attached to these *affective* aspects of learning is illustrated by the regular revision and alteration teachers make to their teaching of topics, and even of whole courses, in order to try and increase their pupils' engagement with science. This importance extends beyond the desire to make pupils respond more positively in lessons. There can be few people in science education today who are not concerned about the low numbers of pupils taking science subjects, particularly chemistry and physics, in post-compulsory education. Much of the evidence points to affective factors as being particularly influential in determining subject choices. It is therefore not surprising that a considerable amount of research effort has been devoted to exploring this area.

In looking for insights into the situation, considerable attention has been paid to pupils' *attitudes* to science, and Box 8.1 summarizes the key issues and questions which researchers have addressed in this area. This chapter will attempt to draw together what has emerged from a very diverse area of research, and identify those aspects which seem to be most fruitful in terms of providing answers to some of the questions in Box 8.1 – or demonstrating why answers might be quite difficult to find.

Box 8.1: Key issues and questions

- Why have attitudes received so much attention?
- What is meant by 'attitudes'?
- How might attitudes be measured?
- What problems are associated with the measurement of attitudes?
- What attitudes do young people appear to hold towards science and school science, and why?
- What action, if any, could or should be taken to alter the situation?

The importance of attitudes

Three characteristics are apparent in the research literature on attitudes to science. First, there is a lot of it! Second, there appears to have been a peak of interest and activity in the 1970s and the early 1980s, with much less being written in the last decade or so. Third, a substantial proportion of the literature focuses on the problems and difficulties associated with research into attitudes to science.

The existence of a large volume of literature on attitudes to science reflects the importance attached to affective factors in influencing pupils' responses in lessons. Interest in attitudes to science is not new, as demonstrated in the extract below, from the Report of the Committee to Enquire into the Position of Natural Sciences in the Educational System of Great Britain (Thomson, 1918):

> The traditional science course is much too narrow, is out of touch with the applications of science, and does not satisfy the natural curiosity of pupils. More attention should be paid to those aspects of the sciences which bear directly on the objects and experiences of everyday life. (p. 21).

Indeed, concern about pupils' involvement and engagement has been a virtually permanent feature of science education for several decades (Bennett, 2001). Research into attitudes to science originates from the 1960s and 1970s. At this time, it was becoming clear that the plans of the post-war government to increase numbers studying science and technology at the tertiary level were failing to come to fruition – the places were there, but not the students to fill them. The Department of Education and Science therefore set up a committee to look at the flow of candidates into science and technology courses in higher education. This committee – the Dainton Committee – reported its findings in 1968 (DES, 1968), documenting what became known as the 'swing from science'. The report also introduced an additional dimension into the problem: not only were comparatively small numbers of *pupils* electing to continue with their study of science once they reached a point of choice, but one group – *girls* – was scarcely represented at all in the physical sciences. The effects of this situation being recognized were two-fold. First, the 1970s and early 1980s saw considerable research effort being devoted to exploring the reasons why young people, and particularly girls, appeared to be alienated from science, with a significant part of this effort exploring aspects of pupils' attitudes to science. One of the most wide-reported research studies was the Girls into Science and Technology (GIST) project (Whyte, 1986). (Chapter 9 explores gender issues in science education in more detail.) Second, the 1980s saw a number of initiatives being taken to increase the levels of participation of young people, especially girls, in the physical sciences. Such initiatives took the form of legislation and curriculum development. In England and Wales, for example, a National Curriculum was introduced in 1989, specifying that science had to be studied by all pupils throughout the period of compulsory schooling. A significant trend in curriculum development was the production of materials which emphasized the social applications and relevance of science. Examples of such materials include the *Science and Technology in Society (SATIS)* units (ASE, 1986), and *Science: the Salters Approach* (UYSEG 1990–2).

Interest in attitudes

The decrease in frequency of articles on attitudes to science in recent years may be explained by a mix of practical and educational factors. The relentless pace of reform in the last decade has meant effort has had to be focused elsewhere. There is also a sense of the seeming intractability of some of the questions involved. What is meant by attitudes? How might they be measured? What could, or should, be done with the information obtained? Moreover, this intractability appears to be coupled with a seeming inevitability in the answers, with newer studies simply confirming the same general conclusions of earlier work, and any recommendations arising from such work appearing to do little to remedy the situation. Despite this, it is clear that pupils' attitudes to science contribute significantly to the low levels of participation in science at the post-compulsory level and, as such, cannot be ignored. More encouragingly, as will be seen later in this chapter, there are examples of initiatives which do appear to have resulted in pupils responding more positively to science, and these do suggest possible ways ahead for research in the area.

Problems with research into attitudes

Anyone first encountering the literature on attitudes to science could be forgiven for thinking they have entered something of a minefield when they start reading about problems with research into attitudes. A number of concerns have been raised and criticisms levelled at the work, including:

- the lack of precision over definitions of key terms;
- a failure to draw on ideas from psychological theory;
- little consensus over what data should be gathered and which techniques should be used to gather the data;
- a lack of standardization of instruments, with a proliferation of small-scale, 'one-shot' studies;
- poor design of instruments and of individual response items within instruments;
- failure to address matters of reliability and validity appropriately;
- inappropriate analysis and interpretation of data;
- a lack of appreciation of ethical considerations.

The key features of the main areas of difficulty are summarized below, and more detailed discussion may be found in major review publications and discussion papers (e.g. Gardner, 1975; Ormerod and Duckworth, 1975; Schibeci, 1984; Munby, 1990; Ramsden, 1998; Osborne *et al.*, 1998; Simon, 2000).

It is clear from reading accounts of different studies about 'attitudes to science' that different interpretations have been placed on the terms 'attitude' and 'science'. The term 'science' is, perhaps, the less problematic of the two to consider. One issue concerns the use of 'science' as an umbrella term to encompass biology, chemistry and physics (and possibly other areas). Earlier work (for example, Kelly, 1986) has demonstrated that pupils respond differently to the different disciplines within science, suggesting that any instrument designed to gather data on attitudes needs to explore responses to each of the sciences separately.

The matter of where pupils experience 'science' and how this influences their attitudes also needs to be considered. For most pupils, much of their formal experience of science is likely to come about through their science lessons at school, where they will engage in a variety of activities structured in such a way as to give them some appreciation of scientific concepts and methods of scientific enquiry. Outside school, pupils may also participate in a number of different activities or hobbies which could be classed as scientific. In addition, they will certainly receive a variety of other messages about science, not only from their experiences in science lessons, but also from sources such the media, books, friends and relatives. These messages will relate to who scientists are, what sorts of jobs they do, how they behave and what effects scientific activity has on everyday life. Thus pupils' disposition towards science will be influenced by a variety of experiences, each of which need to be considered separately when gathering information on attitudes. This important point is considered further later in the chapter.

Where the term 'attitude' has been employed, it has generally — though not exclusively — been used to encompass some dimension of pupils' feelings about the science they encounter and, possibly, how these feelings relate to their knowledge of science and influence behaviour. However, as Gardner (1975) has pointed out, the term *attitude* is used in two different ways with reference to science. He makes the distinction between *attitudes to science* and *scientific attitudes*. The former refers to the views and images young people develop about science as a result of influences and experiences in a variety of different situations. The latter is more closely associated with 'scientific method' or, in Gardner's words, 'styles of thinking' which encompass skills related to the undertaking of practical work, and other more general dispositions towards the beliefs and procedures of science. A more detailed consideration of scientific attitudes may be found in Gauld and Hukins (1980). The distinction between attitudes to science and scientific attitudes is not, perhaps, as clear-cut in reality as it might appear, as both are associated with behaviours, dispositions and beliefs. However, using Gardner's distinction, the work on attitude, as it concerns responses to science and possible links with career choice, is based essentially in the area of attitudes *to* science.

It is also the case that different terminology has been employed in studies covering much of the same ground. Thus, for example, information on 'attitudes' to science can be found in studies of pupils' 'interest' in science, their 'views' of science, the 'images' they hold of science and their 'motivation' to study science. A fuller account of this aspect of attitude research may be found in Ramsden (1998).

In order to clarify the meaning of the term 'attitude' it is necessary to turn to psychological theory. Oppenheim (1992) discusses the problem of definition in detail and concludes:

> ... attitudes are normally a state of readiness or predisposition to respond in a certain manner when confronted with certain stimuli ... attitudes are reinforced by beliefs (the cognitive component), often attract strong feelings (the emotional component) which may lead to particular behavioural intents (the action-tendency component). (p. 175)

In other words, attitudes are a function of what you know, how you feel about what you know and how this influences your likely behaviour. The implication of this definition is that data need to be gathered in all three of these areas. The literature on psychological theory also points out that attitudes cannot be observed, but need to be inferred. Thus it is very important to gather data in a number of strands (sometimes called 'attitudinal constructs') in order to make valid inferences about attitudes. This clearly has implications for research into attitudes to science which, as mentioned earlier, may arise from experiences in several different areas.

Several of the other problems associated with research into attitudes to science stem from the lack of precision in the definition of key terms. For example, failure to separate 'science' into 'biology', 'chemistry' or 'physics' raises questions about the validity of the data interpretation – which component of science do pupils have in mind when they are making their responses? There are also issues to do with reliability of data. Many studies assume that attitudes are sufficiently stable for measurements only to be needed at one point in time. Yet such an approach is ignoring the message from psychological theory that there is a cognitive component to attitudes.

It is interesting to compare research into attitudes to science with another area which has received considerable attention, that of children's misunderstandings of key ideas in science (see Chapter 2). In this latter area, there are well-established procedures for gathering data involving the use of diagnostic questions followed up by interviews. No such parallel exists with research into attitudes to science as the area is characterized by lack of consensus over what data should be gathered and which techniques should be employed. Moreover, many of the studies reported are small-scale and undertaken by single researchers who are often teachers. Given the complexity of the literature and the criticisms which have been levelled at much of the work, it is scarcely surprising that such studies usually involve the design of a new instrument, tailored to the situation of the researcher. It is highly likely that such studies generate insights for the individual researcher. However, one outcome of this characteristic of research into attitudes is a lack of standardization of instruments, with a proliferation of what are often termed 'one-shot' studies – studies involving the development of a new instrument which is only used on the one occasion. This lack of standardization in instruments makes comparisons between studies problematic.

The issue of ethics and attitude research is one which has received rather less attention than might be expected. Generally, people worry about attitudes because they want to change them! Many of the studies on attitudes to science have been undertaken by concerned individuals or small groups of people who aim to provide their pupils with what they perceive to be an improved experience of science. Though such work is worthwhile, it does not always take account of the fact that views on what might constitute a 'positive' attitude to science, in some areas at least, will involve value-judgements and could be open to debate. For example, few people are likely to take issue with the aim of fostering a more positive attitude to science in girls through the use of images of female scientists, or using science lessons to promote an attitude of respect for living things. However, there would be considerably less consensus about the aim of promoting more positive attitudes to the impact of industry on society, as this could be perceived as the indoctrination of a particular set of values.

Gathering information on attitudes to science

The importance of gathering data in a number of different strands, sometimes called 'attitudinal constructs', has already been mentioned. For attitudes to science, such strands are likely include:

- dispositions towards school science;
- dispositions towards science outside school;
- dispositions towards the relevance and importance of science to everyday life;
- dispositions towards scientists;
- dispositions towards scientific careers.

A number of different methods may be employed to gather data on attitudes. A fairly consistent feature of attitude research has been the use of instruments (sometimes called 'attitude inventories') designed to gather written, fixed response data which lends itself to quantitative analysis. There are several publications which give details of methods of construction of such inventories, strategies for checking reliability and validity, analysis techniques and indications of potential strengths and drawbacks (e.g. Henerson *et al.*, 1987; Oppenheim, 1992; Coolican, 1995).

Very often, fixed response attitude instruments make use of Likert-type scales. These present the respondent with a series of statements (sometimes called 'items') and invite responses on a scale which frequently has five points. For example, respondents may be presented with a statement such as 'Science causes more problems than it solves', and asked to say whether they strongly agree, agree, are neutral, disagree or strongly disagree. Numerous examples of such studies may be found in the literature, for example in the work of Hadden and Johnstone (1983) looking at secondary school pupils' attitudes to science, Koballa (1984) on high school pupils' attitudes towards energy conservation, Qualter (1993) on the interest shown by girls and boys in scientific topics, and Hendley *et al.* (1995) on secondary pupils' attitudes to a range of subjects including science.

Thurstone-type rating scales may also be employed to gather fixed-response data. Here, respondents are presented with a series of statements and select those which most closely resemble their own points of view. Items on a Thurstone-type inventory could include statements such as 'Science causes more problems than it solves' and 'Science occasionally causes problems'. The statements have previously been presented to a panel of 'judges' who have placed them at a point on a scale which they feel is indicative of a positive attitude to science. Frequently, an 11-point scale is employed. Of the two statements above, the latter is likely to indicate a more positive attitude than the former, and would therefore have a higher ranking in the scale. Examples of attitude studies employing Thurstone-type scales include those of Smail and Kelly (1984) on attitudes of 11-year-old pupils to science and technology, Johnson (1987) on gender differences in science, and Craig and Ayers (1988) on the effect of science experience in primary schools on pupils' interest in secondary science.

The last category of fixed-response items are semantic differential scales. These scales involve presenting respondents with a statement and asking them to rate their response at a point on a bi-polar scale. An example of an item in an inventory employing semantic differential scale would be:

Studying science at school is...

Boring ----------|-----------|----------|-----------|----------|----------|----------Interesting
       extremely   quite   slightly undecided slightly   quite   extremely

Examples of inventories using semantic differential scales can be found in the studies of attitudes to science undertaken by Krynowski (1988).

The majority of the studies on attitudes have relied on gathering evidence from pupils in written form, sometimes supplemented by the examination of formal records of data such as subject choices, examination grades and career destinations. There are also some limited examples of qualitative data on attitudes being collected through the use of interviews. For example, Piburn and Baker (1993) investigated attitudes to science through interviews conducted with pupils who were asked to imagine what they would do about attitudes to science if they were teachers.

Considerably less use has been made of attitude inventories seeking open responses through employing, for example, sentence stems for respondents to complete or presenting respondents with stimulus situations (e.g. photographs or descriptions of situations) and inviting responses. Such approaches are examples of indirect or *projective* techniques, which have a long history in psychological research as a means of probing deeper aspects of attitudes (the Rorschach 'inkblots' are probably the most familiar in this group).

Projective techniques involve the interpretation of unstructured responses in order to reveal information on attitudes, and the validity of this interpretative element has given rise to some criticism. One example of an attitude-related study which has drawn on open responses is the Views on Science–Technology–Society (VOSTS) study undertaken in Canada (Aikenhead and Ryan, 1992). This study involved presenting 16- and 17-year-old students with statements such as 'Science and technology help you solve practical problems in your everyday life', and then asking them for their views on the statement. These open responses were then categorized, and the categories used as the basis of a fixed-response instrument, where students were presented with the same statements and had to select one from around six or seven options. The key feature of this instrument was that the items it contained were expressed in the students' own words. Whilst detailed interpretation of the findings was not undertaken, the methodology and the data collected offer a different and potentially very informative approach to the collection of data on attitudes to science.

What has emerged from research on attitudes

Despite the problems associated with attitude research discussed earlier in the chapter, the findings which have emerged from studies are remarkably consistent over a period of almost three decades. Box 8.2 summarizes the main findings. The persistence of largely negative perceptions of science is very worrying, particularly when set in the context of the number of changes which have been made to the structure and content of school science since people first became concerned about young people's attitudes to science. The seeming lack of success of such initiatives points to the difficulty of implementing any strategies which appear to make a significant difference to young people's perceptions of science. Thus, when science is increasingly becoming an area of knowledge which shapes the age in which we live, it is particularly disturbing to see that so many pupils want so little to do with it.

If the findings of studies on attitudes to science are examined in more detail, it becomes clear that there are two sorts of science to which young people are responding: the first is the science they

---

Box 8.2: Key research findings

- Pupils see school science as a hard subject.
- Pupils see science and school science as not relevant to everyday life and not relevant to most people.
- Pupils see science as causing environmental and social problems.
- School science is more attractive to males than females.
- Interest in science declines over the years of secondary schooling.
- Negative dispositions towards science are more strongly associated with the physical sciences rather than the biological sciences.
- Pupils feel more negatively disposed to school science than to science more generally – or, at least, the technological products of science.
- Considerable care is needed in the design of research instruments to measure attitudes.
- There is some evidence that science curriculum materials which contextualize science and emphasize its applications are successful in fostering a more positive response to science in pupils.

---

encounter in their science lessons and the second is the science they encounter in the world outside school, or science in society. It therefore becomes important to try and separate out where possible which of these 'sciences' are contributing to the perceptions above.

The evidence on attitudes to school science is fairly clear-cut. A number of studies have shown that young people entering secondary school generally feel very positive about science and are looking forward to science lessons (e.g. Ormerod, 1973; Hadden and Johnstone, 1983; Smail and Kelly, 1984; Johnson, 1987). However, other studies show that attitudes to school science become less positive over the years of secondary schooling (e.g. Whitfield, 1979; Kelly, 1986; Institute of Electrical Engineers (IEE), 1994; Hendley *et al.*, 1995). By the age of 16, a significant majority of pupils report that the science curriculum is over-full and lacks relevance to their lives (e.g. Ramsden, 1997; Osborne and Collins, 2001). Whilst it is the case that attitudes to school and most school subjects decline over this period, the decline is most marked for *physical* science subjects and more marked for girls than for boys. Studies have also demonstrated that physical science subjects are seen by pupils as more difficult than other subjects (e.g. Havard, 1996; Hendley *et al.*, 1995), and that this perceived difficulty is a significant factor in influencing choice of A-level subjects (Cheng *et al.*, 1995). Moreover, in a study undertaken in England and Wales, Fitz-Gibbon and Vincent (1994) demonstrated that pupils opting for A-level physical science subjects were more likely to get lower grades than if they chose other subjects. (Chapter 10 gives more details of this study.) Whilst the findings of this study really demonstrate that it is more difficult to get good grades in physical science subjects, rather than the subjects being intrinsically more difficult, such an outcome could only serve to reinforce the view of physical sciences as difficult subjects.

The picture is less straightforward for attitudes towards science in society. On the one hand, studies have consistently demonstrated that negative attitudes are held as a result of science being seen as responsible for environmental problems (e.g. Ormerod, 1973; Smail and Kelly, 1984; Woolnough, 1990). Such attitudes often seemed to be formed as a result of reports of science presented in the media. On the other hand, there is also evidence to suggest that positive attitudes also exist. For example, the large-scale IEE survey of pupils in the UK revealed that 87 per cent thought science and technology was important in everyday life. The study also indicated that pupils tended to see 'science' in terms of technological products used directly by themselves as members of society, such as computers and televisions. Thus the pupils' views of the 'science' they saw as important were rather different to the more theoretical science they were likely to be encountering in school. A study by Sjøberg (2000) has also provided interesting evidence of variation in attitudes from country to country, with pupils in developed countries generally demonstrating much less interest in science and having a much more negative image of science and scientists than pupils in developing countries.

In a nutshell, the evidence that is available would seem to indicate attitudes to science are not particularly positive overall, but attitudes to school science are *more* negative than attitudes to science in society, or, more precisely, the technological products of science used by society. At first sight, this finding is very disappointing, but it can also be seen more positively, as teachers are in a strong position to influence what happens in science lessons.

Two examples of studies of attitudes to science are shown in Boxes 8.3 and 8.4. The first study is a small-scale study undertaken by a teacher-researcher in her own school, who wanted to evaluate the effectiveness of particular strategies and teaching materials adopted in her school to foster more positive responses to science in pupils. The second study is a larger-scale study, and one which collected data from adults rather than pupils. However, it is included as it employed a range of techniques to gather data, many of which could be adapted for use with a younger sample.

Some implications and ways ahead

What could and should be done about attitudes to science? Is there a need for further research, or do we know what there is to know, and what is important now is to try and identify effective action to remedy the situation? If there were easy answers to these questions, research into attitudes to science would not have been going on for well over twenty years!

Taking the second of these questions first, it is unlikely that interest in attitudes will decline as long as there is concern over pupils' less-than-positive responses in lessons and over the comparatively low numbers of young people studying science subjects beyond the compulsory period. Thus the general case for attitude research is probably the same as it always has been: a desire to create the climate which best helps young people make sense of, and feel positive about, their experiences in science lessons.

There also appears to be a case for saying that further research would be informative, given the changes in school science provisions which have taken place in the last decade or so. A number of countries have implemented intervention strategies aimed at broadening the appeal of science, many of which seek to emphasize the links between science and society. Some of the thinking which has informed these moves is the suggestion that, if pupils know more about science and how it is used, their attitude will 'improve'. This is an argument which is certainly open to debate – attitudes may or

Box 8.3: An example of a small-scale study of pupils' attitudes to science
(Smith, 1994)

Aim
To explore the effectiveness of strategies and teaching materials introduced to foster more positive responses to science in pupils.

Research question
Are students' attitudes to science indicative of their general attitude to school and is there a gender bias in such attitudes?

Research strategy and techniques
The research took the form of a case study of 128 15-year-old pupils in a secondary school. Data were gathered using an attitude inventory inviting Likert-type responses to 40 items grouped into four constructs (strands):

- Pupils' attitude to school.
- Pupils' attitude to school science.
- Pupils' academic self-image.
- Pupils' interest in things scientific (e.g. science TV programmes, 'hands-on' science exhibitions).

A limited number of follow-up interviews was also conducted.

Main findings
The study showed that lower ability pupils, especially boys, had a very negative academic self-image and attitude to school. However, there were no discernible trends in responses to school science, with similar attitudes being demonstrated by both female and male pupils across the ability range. Overall, these attitudes were more positive than those reported in other studies, a finding which was attributed to specific strategies adopted by the Science Department in the school to stimulate pupils' interest in science.

Box 8.4: An example of a larger-scale study of pupils' attitudes to science
(Office of Science and Technology and the Wellcome Trust, 2000)

Aim
To inform those concerned with the development of policy and practice in science communication.

Research question
What is the situation concerning science communication and public attitudes to science in Britain?

Research strategy and techniques
There were two components of the research: a survey of the various ways in which the facts, issues and policies involved in science and medicine are brought to the attention of the public, followed by a questionnaire survey of attitudes of the general public towards science. The questionnaire gathered quantitative data from a sample of 1839 adults. Prior to this, qualitative data had been gathered through 'scoping' group discussions to determine the issues to be explored in the questionnaire.

Main findings
The application of statistical techniques (factor and cluster analysis) allowed the identification of six attitudinal clusters, given the following labels:

- *Confident believers* who are interested in science because of the benefits it brings.
- *Technophiles* who are in favour of science but concerned about the way in which it is regulated.
- *Supporters* who are 'amazed' by science and feel they can cope with rapid change.
- *Concerned* who are interested in a range of topical issues and know that science is an important part of life.
- *Not sure* who are neither anti- nor pro-science as they do not know much about how it affects their lives.
- *Not for me* who are not interested in science, but appreciate its importance.

may not change, and the change might not be such that science is viewed more positively. However, it is still likely that what pupils *know* about science has changed. It is highly desirable that any further work goes beyond simply arriving at the same general conclusions of earlier studies. Case studies to illuminate practice would seem to offer a useful way ahead, focusing on particular locations where pupils do seem to be positively disposed towards science.

Turning now to what might be done about attitudes to science, it is clear that there are legitimate areas of concern. For many young people, their attitudes appear have an adverse effect on their engagement with science in school and their views on careers involving science. Indeed there is evidence (e.g. Ramsden, 1997) that career plans are a strong determining factor in influencing choice of subjects, with many able young people citing the chief reason for not choosing science subjects being the lack of appeal of jobs involving science. Of particular concern is the evidence emerging which indicates that experiences in science lessons appear to do little to foster more positive attitudes to science over the period of secondary schooling.

It is less clear what might constitute appropriate and effective action to try and alter the situation, particularly as there is little evidence to suggest that many of the intervention strategies adopted have influenced young people's responses to science in any significant way and on a large scale. In terms of curriculum content, there are clearly decisions to be made about what it is appropriate for young people to *know* about science. Beyond that, it is up to the individual to decide how they feel and how this will influence behaviour. For example, if a pupil has a negative attitude to science because they have gained a picture of science as something which 'causes pollution', it could be argued that this attitude is based on limited knowledge. It therefore seems reasonable that a science course should draw attention to some of the ways in which society has benefited from science. However, if in the light of this knowledge, the pupil concludes that the benefits of science do not outweigh the drawbacks, this is a legitimate view to hold, even though it might not be shared by those involved in science education. There are also decisions about the *sort of science* young people should know about. The facts and theories of science – or some of them, at least – are important, but it is equally important that pupils find out about how such knowledge is acquired and applied, and how decisions are reached about what could and should be done with the knowledge. Current debate and discussion on the nature of the school science curriculum is exploring views on where the balance should lie between these two areas, with a number of people arguing for a shift of emphasis from fact and theories to applications and decisions about using knowledge, or, in the words of Osborne and Collins (2001), moving to a curriculum which emphasizes an education *for* science rather than an education *about* science.

Box 8.5: Implications for practice

- Pupils see their experiences in science lessons as being important factors in determining their responses to science, and pupils who elect to study science subjects beyond the compulsory period are very likely to cite their teachers and the teaching they received as stimulating their interest in science. Both these factors suggest it would be desirable to undertake case studies of practice in selected schools which do appear to be particularly successful at encouraging pupils to continue with their study of science.
- Curriculum materials which introduce science concepts through applications of science and the ways in which science affects everyday life do increase pupils' interest in the science they are studying. Such materials also appear to increase pupils' desire to study science further. These findings suggest it would be desirable to undertake more detailed evaluation of the effects of specific components of such materials.
- It is desirable for science teachers to teach their main subject specialism as science teachers report greater levels of confidence and feel they are best able to motivate pupils when this is the case.

In the midst of what often appears a very gloomy picture of attitudes to science, there are some indications as to where action *might* be effective. Box 8.5 summarizes the main implications for practice which have emerged from the research. There is considerable evidence to suggest that teachers feel that what goes on in science lessons exerts a significant influence on pupils' attitudes. More significantly, the evidence demonstrates that *pupils* see their teachers and the teaching in their science lessons as being important factors in determining how they feel about science (e.g. Piburn and Baker, 1993; Woolnough, 1994). Pupils who do go on to study science subjects are very likely to cite their teachers and their experiences in science lessons as being the most significant factors in stimulating their interest in science. As yet, however, comparatively little research has been done to explore this aspect in more detail and establish teachers' and pupils' views on exactly what does appear to make a difference.

From the limited work undertaken, two features in particular emerge, both of which have implications for the staffing of science lessons and the teaching approaches adopted in lessons. First, and unsurprisingly, science teachers are happiest and feel that they are doing a good job when they are teaching within their main specialist area (Woolnough, 1994). Second, pupils following courses which place a particular emphasis on approaching science concepts through contexts and applications, such as *Science: the Salters Approach* (UYSEG, 1990–2), report higher levels of interest and enjoyment in their science lessons than pupils following more traditional science courses (Ramsden, 1997). Other data gathered from schools indicate that this interest is translated into increased numbers opting for science subjects beyond the compulsory period. For example, schools moving from a more traditional A-level chemistry course to a context-led course, *Salters Advanced Chemistry*, report a significant increase in numbers choosing chemistry (Pilling, 1999).

Conclusions

As long as there is concern about numbers choosing to study science, there will be concern about attitudes to science. However, the concern about attitudes extends beyond the desire for more people to study science when they have a choice and also encompasses the need to ensure that all young people are adequately informed about science. The evidence which has emerged from work on attitudes to science is that, despite the initiatives and reforms of the past two decades, attitudes have largely remained consistent and negative.

However, within this, there are indications that a curriculum which uses applications as starting points and which helps pupils see how science relates to their lives is likely to make more pupils respond more positively to science.

From the research perspective, there is clearly a need to explore in much more detail the effects on pupils of following particular types of science course. Attitude research has certainly demonstrated that pupils respond differently to the different *areas* of science, namely biology, chemistry and physics. What it has yet to do is to explore any links between attitudes and the *nature of the approach adopted* to the teaching of science. Attitudes are influenced by knowledge, and it may well be that what pupils following courses which emphasize the applications *know* about science differs from what pupils following other courses know. Such information will help provide a sound basis on which to make informed decisions about aspects of curriculum provision and classroom practice which are likely to be effective in promoting more positive attitudes to school science.

Box 8.6: First stops for further reading

An overview of issues in attitude research may be found in:
Ramsden, J. (1998) Mission impossible: can anything be done about attitudes to science? *International Journal of Science Education*, 20 (2), 125–37.

A review of evidence gathered on pupils' attitudes is in:
Simon, S. (2000) Students' attitudes towards science. In M. Monk and J. Osborne (eds) *Good Practice in Science Teaching: What Research has to Say*. Buckingham: Open University Press.

Two studies which draw on contrasting research techniques to gather data on attitudes are:
Osborne, J. and Collins, S. (2001) Pupils' views of the role and value of the science curriculum. *International Journal of Science Education*, 23 (5), 441–67.
Kelly, A. (1986) The development of children's attitudes to science. *European Journal of Science Education*, 8 (4), 399–412.

A paper tracing the origins of concern about attitudes is:
Bennett, J. (2001) Science with attitude: the perennial problem

of pupils' responses to science. *School Science Review*, 82 (300), 59–70.

Two 'classic' reviews of work on attitudes to science are:
Gardner, P. (1975) Attitudes to science: a review. *Studies in Science Education*, 2, 1–41.
Schibeci, R. (1984) Attitudes to science: an update. *Studies in Science Education*, 11, 26–59.

Chapter 9

Gender Issues in School Science

> ## GIRLS TAKE MORE TOP GRADES FOR FIRST TIME
>
> ### The Missing Half

Above is a headline from *The Times Educational Supplement*, published in the UK in August 2000. The article reported that girls had just stormed one of the 'last remaining bastions of male exam supremacy' by winning more top grades than boys in A-level examinations at 18+. Below it is the title of a book which contains a collection of articles exploring issues to do with girls' involvement and achievement in science education, edited by Alison Kelly and published in 1981.

The headline points to an area which has received a particularly high profile in the last few years, an area often portrayed as that of boys' underachievement. Yet for those working in science education, as the book title indicates, gender issues – the 'girls and science problem' – are nothing new, for they have been the focus of research for almost three decades as a result of concerns about girls' levels of participation in science. What is the 'girls and science problem', and how might it be addressed?

This chapter looks at:

- the differential involvement of girls and boys in science;
- the differential achievement of girls and boys in science;
- research evidence into possible explanations for differential

involvement and achievement;
- strategies which have been proposed to increase girls' interest and levels of participation in science, and research into their effects;
- boys' underachievement and how this relates to school science.

Introduction

The first upsurge of interest in gender issues in science education occurred in the late 1960s. In the UK, the publication of a report by the Dainton Committee (DES, 1968) documented a 'swing from science' in the school-age population as a whole (see Chapter 8), and also established that the numbers of boys studying physical science subjects beyond the compulsory period far outweighed the number of girls. Specifically, the report made reference to an 'untapped pool of ability' in the female school-age population. The report was published at a time when the promotion of equality of opportunity for women was high on the political agenda. In the UK, for example, the Sex Discrimination Act was implemented in 1975, making it illegal to discriminate on the grounds of sex in employment, education and the provision of goods, facilities and services. One outcome of this legislation was a very close scrutiny of the school curriculum, a scrutiny which revealed very different provision being made for boys and girls in a number of subjects, including science. This picture was certainly not unique to the UK, and thus, for a mix of both educational and political reasons, the under-representation of girls in the physical sciences became the focus of considerable attention. One indicator of the widespread interest and concern was the setting up in 1981 of the first of what has become a series of international conferences on gender issues in science education, the GASAT (Gender and Science and Technology) conferences.

By the mid-1980s, the area was broadening out from a focus on gender to address more widespread issues of equity associated with race, ethnicity, class and socio-economic status. The significant increase in educational reform and legislation at that time also shifted the focus of interest away from gender and science. For example, the Education Reform Act in England and Wales, which made a broad, balanced science course part of the curriculum for all pupils throughout their period of compulsory schooling, was seen by some as a solution to girls' under-involvement in school science.

The focus of interest shifted again in the 1990s, where one outcome of the more elaborate systems of reporting and accountability introduced during that period has been the emergence of a growing body of evidence to suggest that girls were regularly outperforming boys in a range of subjects at secondary level. For example, in England in 1984, 27.2 per cent of girls and 26.3 per cent of boys gained five or more passes with A–C grades in 16+ examinations. By 1996, the figures were 49.3 per cent for girls and 39.8 per cent for boys. Moreover, as the newspaper headline at the beginning of this chapter illustrates, girls appear to have continued to gain ground on boys. For these reasons, boys' underachievement has been the focus of widespread research interest since the mid-1990s.

Key issues and questions in gender and science education are summarized in Box 9.1.

Box 9.1: Key issues and questions

- What is the 'girls and science problem'?
- What are the possible explanations for girls' under-involvement in science, particularly the physical sciences?
- What are the effects on involvement of factors such as ability, societal and cultural context, schools, teachers, mixed and single-sex teaching, the image of science, personality, attitudes and assessment strategies?
- How does the achievement of girls in science compare with that of boys?
- What strategies have been proposed to encourage girls to pursue their study of science, and what have been their effects?
- What are the implications for science teaching of the current more general and widespread concern about boys' underachievement?

Research on gender and science education

There are three areas of literature relating to gender issues in science education. The first two are very clearly focused on science provision, one looking at the *differential involvement* and the other at the *differential achievement* of girls and boys in science. The literature in these areas is largely found in science education books and journals. There are also strong links between work on differential involvement in science and that on attitudes to science, partly because gender appears to be an influential factor in determining attitude. The third area concerns the 'underachievement' of boys, with a rapidly expanding literature which extends well beyond science education publications. These three broad areas, differential involvement, differential achievement and boys' 'underachievement', form a useful framework for discussing the research evidence on gender issues in science education. Box 9.2 provides a summary of key research findings on gender and science education.

The differential involvement of girls and boys in science

The literature from the 1970s and 1980s on the differential involvement of girls and boys in science is extensive and wide-ranging. From an initial focus on documenting the nature and extent of the problem of the under-representation of girls in science, the area developed very rapidly to explore a variety of possible reasons for the differential involvement of girls and boys in science, and physical science subjects in particular. Arising out of this work, a variety of strategies was proposed to encourage more girls to continue with their study of science.

The nature and extent of 'the problem'

Though the 'girls and science problem' has received much attention, it is important to be clear about the nature of the problem. The early work in the 1970s indicated there were four dimensions to the problem. First, data from a range of sources served to provide a

Box 9.2: Key research findings

- The 'girls and science problem' originally identified in the 1970s and 1980s was one in which girls were under-represented in the physical science, and boys' achievements in these subjects were superior to those of girls.
- Currently, fewer girls than boys choose physical science subjects, particularly physics, but girls now outperform boys in most science subjects except physics.
- There is no evidence to suggest that girls and boys have any significant inherent differences in ability.
- Boys generally have a more positive attitude to science than girls, and the masculine image of science has a strongly alienating effect on girls.
- Girls' confidence and levels of achievement are likely to increase when single-sex teaching groups are used in science. There do not appear to be similar benefits to boys.
- Measures of performance are dependent on the assessment strategies employed, with girls doing particularly well when assessment involves course work and project work.
- Strategies aimed at increasing girls' participation in science are effective in increasing girls' (and boys') interest in science lessons, though have not had significant impact overall on levels of participation. Impact has been greatest where strategies have been implemented in situations where there is a more general commitment to ensuring equality of opportunity.
- Researchers with a particular interest in gender issues argue that a radical reconstruction of science is necessary so that it reflects females' contributions and attributes, leading to a gender-inclusive curriculum which appeals to both girls and boys.
- The views, actions and classroom practices of teachers have a critical influence on girls' (and boys') involvement and achievement in science.

picture of considerable differences in levels of participation in science between girls and boys at school and beyond. For example, a survey carried out in England and Wales in 1973 (DES, 1975) revealed that, in national examinations at 16+, the ratio of boys to girls gaining passes in physics was over 3:1, with the corresponding figure for chemistry being 2:1. However, these figures need to be set in the context of overall entry figures, where, for example, just 16 per cent of boys and only 5 per cent of girls gained passes in physics. Thus, whilst there was clear evidence of the differential involvement of girls and boys in science, the 'girls and science problem' was really one facet of a much larger problem concerning numbers taking science. Two decades later, legislation such as the National Curriculum in England and Wales has ensured that the majority of girls and boys leave school with qualifications in biology, chemistry and physics. However, such legislation has had little impact on numbers choosing to continue their study of physical sciences, and girls continue to be under-represented in the physical sciences beyond the compulsory period of study.

A second dimension to 'the problem' emerged from work on possible explanations for the differential involvement of girls and boys in science. In the 1970s, evidence from international surveys such as that of the International Association for the Evaluation of Educational Achievement (IEA) from 1970–3 indicated that boys were outperforming girls in physical science subjects, with differences being most apparent in physics (Coomber and Keeves, 1973; Kelly, 1978). More recent studies (see later in this chapter) suggest that girls' overall performance in science is now superior to that of boys.

The third aspect of 'the problem' was, in part, a response to the need to provide equality of opportunity. Encouraging more girls to pursue their study of science was seen as a means of improving their status and employment prospects. Within this, studying science at school was seen as important in order to equip all young people with knowledge and skills to prepare them for life in an advanced technological society. Such an argument for the inclusion of science in some form in the curriculum is at least as relevant today as it was in the 1970s.

Finally, there was a shortage of people in the 1970s with appropriate qualifications to fill scientific and technical jobs, and girls were seen as a significant but largely untapped resource to alleviate this shortage. This political dimension to the problem resulted in initiatives such as 1984 being designated Women into Science and Engineering (WISE) year in the UK. Today, though technological developments have reduced the number of jobs in some areas, there is still a shortage of well-qualified scientists.

More recently, Kreinberg and Lewis (1996) have proposed a model which describes six stages in the work on girls' under-involvement in science. The stages are:

1. not noticing the absence of women in science;
2. searching for the missing women;
3. looking for explanations of why there are so few women in science;
4. studying women's experience in science;
5. challenging the current paradigm of science;
6. transforming and reconstructing a gender-free curriculum.

Stages 1, 2, 3 and 4 equate with the work of the 1970s and early 1980s, with work since that time largely addressing stage 5, plus some limited attempts to move to stage 6.

Looking for explanations for differential involvement

The research in this field divides into a number of areas, some of which are overlapping. These areas are inherent differences (both physiological and cognitive), societal and cultural influences, school and teacher effects, the image and nature of science, personality, attitudes to science, learning styles and assessment strategies. This section considers the evidence that has been gathered in each of these areas.

Inherent differences

In the opening section of her book *The Missing Half: Girls and Science Education*, Kelly (1981) quotes an extract from an article on the education of women written by Felter in a 1906 edition of *Education*

Review. Felter argues that 'girls should not be taught physical sciences except at the most elementary level because the expenditure of nervous energy involved in the mastery of analytic concepts would be injurious to their health'. In a similar vein, Walton (1986), in a review of attitudes to women in science, quotes Swinburne from the *Westminster Review* in 1902: 'When we come to science we find women are simply nowhere. The feminine mind is quite unscientific ... .' A century later, anyone reading these extracts is likely to do so with wry amusement. Nonetheless, considerable research effort has been devoted to exploring possible differences between boys and girls, particularly differences in intellectual ability, which might explain differential involvement and achievement in science.

One dimension of intelligence which has received considerable attention in the context of science is 'spatial ability' (more correctly termed 'visuo-spatial ability'). As its name implies, it is concerned with the visualization and manipulation of relationships such as, for example, being able to extract smaller and simpler shapes from within more complex diagrams. A number of studies in the 1960s had shown that pupils who did well in maths and physical science subjects also scored highly on tests of spatial ability, and also that boys tended to obtain higher scores than girls on such tests. These findings led researchers to hypothesize that such differences were genetic in origin. Maccoby and Jacklin (1975) undertook an extensive review of studies on spatial ability, concluding that, after the age of 12, boys obtained higher mean scores than girls in tests of spatial ability. However, a reworking of the data by Hyde (1981) showed that sex differences accounted for only a very small percentage of the variance in the scores, and Whyte (1986), in reporting on the GIST project (see later in this chapter), demonstrated that girls who had followed a six-month programme of activities aimed at improving spatial ability performed as well as boys in spatial ability tests.

Further evidence to support the notion that there are no significant inherent differences in ability between boys and girls comes from the analyses of Harding (1983) and Linn and Hyde (1989), who concluded that, though boys performed better than girls on certain types of test, the differences were small, they were unlikely to be biologically determined and were in no way sufficient to explain the discrepancy in numbers of males and females taking the physical sciences. Such conclusions have resulted in research shifting to focus on links between performance and styles of assessment.

Societal and cultural influences

Numerous studies have been undertaken to explore the possible effects of societal influences on girls' and boys' subject choices, particularly in relation to science. Work by Archer and Lloyd (1982) with very young children showed that, by the age of three, children already had a very clear idea of gender-appropriate behaviour, and that parents treated little boys and girls very differently, encouraging the former to be more adventurous than the latter. Children's out-of-school hobbies and interests and their career aspirations have been explored (e.g. Johnson and Murphy, 1986; Johnson, 1987; Ditchfield and Scott, 1987; Dawson, 2000). Boys have emerged as much more likely than girls to have hobbies which involve making models or playing with electrical and mechanical devices, and such interests, it has been argued, are more likely to predispose boys to be interested in physical science subjects and to provide them with opportunities for acquiring skills and knowledge which can later be consolidated in science lessons. Other data (e.g. Whyte, 1986) showed that boys' career aspirations meant they were more likely to need to study physical science subjects.

Although the pattern of under-representation of girls in science in prevalent in many countries, there are exceptions. For example, in Thailand, where science has a high status, roughly equal numbers of girls and boys in the 15–18-year-old age group elect to study science beyond the compulsory period. This suggests that cultural expectations play a role in determining subject choices.

Whilst work exploring societal and cultural effects is informative, it points to areas for action which extend well beyond those which can be addressed in science curriculum policy and practice.

School and teacher effects

Work on school effects has looked at curriculum structure, the dynamics of classroom interactions, the impact of the sex of the teacher and provision of role models, and the effects of mixed and single-sex teaching groups.

Surveys in the 1970s, such as that undertaken in England and Wales by the DES (1975), showed that far fewer girls than boys were offered the opportunity to take physics beyond the compulsory period (then age 14) due to factors such as the timetabling of physics against, for example, home economics. Action resulting from equal opportunities legislation has removed this barrier to access for girls.

Studies of classroom interactions have gathered evidence of the differential treatment of girls and boys by some science teachers which resulted in the reaffirmation of stereotypes and discouraged girls from participating in science. For example, observation of interactions in science lessons showed teachers spent more time interacting with boys than girls (Crossman, 1987). A marking exercise (Spear, 1987) yielded the disturbing result that teachers were more likely to award higher grades and more likely to predict success in science if they thought the work had been done by a boy.

The preponderance of male teachers in physical sciences, resulting in an absence of female role models, has also been investigated. Here, however, Eggleston *et al.* (1976) established that the sex of a teacher was less influential than the teaching style adopted and than the level of awareness and response to potential gender-related problems in science lessons.

An area which has received considerable attention is that of teaching in mixed or single-sex groups. An early and classic large-scale study was undertaken by Dale (1974), who concluded that pupils gained greater social benefits from mixed schools, though boys' achievement was better in mixed schools than in all-boys' schools, a finding which also emerged in a more recent study by McEwen *et al.*, (1997). The picture for girls in Dale's study was less clear-cut, but there was some evidence to suggest that girls obtained better results in all-girls' schools. Certainly girls in such schools were more likely to take science subjects, and more likely to get better results. A later study by Harding (1981) provided additional evidence of the superior performance in science of girls at all-girls' schools. One outcome of such findings has been for schools to experiment with single-sex teaching in science in order to encourage more girls to take science subjects, and Box 9.3 describes a small-scale experimental study exploring the effects of teaching science to

Box 9.3: An example of a small-scale study on gender
(Dawes, 1996)

Aim
To compare the effects of mixed and single-sex group teaching on 14-year-old pupils' performance and behaviour in science lessons.

Research questions

• What effects do the use of mixed and single-sex groups have on pupils' performance in science?
• What effects do the use of mixed and single-sex groups have on pupils' behaviour in science lessons?
• What are pupils' and teachers' views of the use of mixed and single sex groups in science teaching?

Research strategy and techniques
The research was both a case study in that it was undertaken in one school, and an experiment in that it involved gathering data from eight classes of around twenty-five pupils, half taught science in single-sex groups and half taught in mixed groups. The previous experience of all pupils was of mixed-sex groupings. Data were gathered through questionnaires and interviews with both staff and pupils. These were supplemented by baseline data of pupils' performance on national tests gathered at the start of the year and end-of-unit test results gathered within the science department.

Main findings
The study showed that there were no significant differences in the academic performance of either boys or girls, whether taught in mixed or single-sex groups. Girls, boys and teachers all viewed single-sex groups more positively than mixed-sex groups, with all citing factors to do with a more purposeful atmosphere in lessons in the single-sex groups. Girls from the single-sex groups also reported increased interest in science, increased confidence in their abilities in science and an increasing willingness to contribute in science lessons.

mixed and single-sex groups. Interest in the outcome of using single-sex groupings for teaching has intensified in the light of more recent work on boys' underachievement. For example, Jackson (2002a) has shown that girls' confidence and performance improved when taught in single-sex groups, though there were no similar benefits for boys.

The image and nature of science

There is substantial evidence in the literature that science is perceived as 'masculine'. Debate has centred on the extent to which this perception arises from the way science is presented to pupils, or from science itself being inherently masculine. Kelly (1985) identified four senses in which science could be considered to be masculine. First, the majority of those who choose to study it are male, so that it is seen as a predominantly male area of activity. Second, it is packaged for learning in ways which suit the interests and motivations of boys. Third, behaviours in science classes are such that boys and girls act out appropriate gender roles. Finally, Kelly suggested that, because it has been socially constructed in a patriarchal, male-dominated society, science is itself inherently masculine.

In the 1970s and 1980s, the prevailing view was that only a very limited picture of science was projected in school science, and that this picture needed to be broadened so that science was more 'girl-friendly'. Many of the suggestions for practice and intervention strategies proposed at this time were based on this view. However, this view has been criticized as one which sees 'girls' as the problem, rather than 'science', and the last twenty years has seen a developing body of literature (e.g. Manthorpe, 1982; Kelly, 1985; Bentley and Watts, 1986; Weinreich-Haste, 1986; Harding, 1991; Roychoudhury *et al.*, 1995; Keller and Longino, 1996; Kenway and Gough, 1998; Gilbert, 2001; Heywood and Miller, 2001) which draws on radical feminist perspectives to argue that science itself is the problem, and that there will be no significant increase in the involvement of girls in science until science is reconstructed so that it reflects women's contribution to science and the attributes women bring to science, such as empathy and a toleration of ambiguity. This standpoint has gained in support as the evidence mounts up to suggest that many of the initiatives of the 1980s have had little significant impact. This is also the area which has formed the focus for the majority of the most recent writing on gender issues in science education.

Personality

The association of science with characteristics such as objectivity, lack of emotion and a concern with things rather than people ('masculine' characteristics) has resulted in a number of studies being undertaken to explore possible links between personality and the study of science. Smithers and Collings (1981) undertook a survey of 17- and 18-year-olds, and found that the girls who had chosen to study science subjects formed a distinct group, who were more intelligent, less person-oriented, tougher minded and had a more negative self-image than girls who had not chosen science subjects. Head and Ramsden (1990) showed that girls choosing science were likely to be realistic decision-makers who preferred to focus on facts, were organized and dependable, and disliked ambiguity.

Other studies exploring aspects of personality have drawn on theories of moral development. For example, Head and Shayer (1980) used Loevinger's ego development scale (Loevinger, 1976) to explore maturation and subject choice, establishing that physical science subjects tended to be chosen by less mature boys and more mature girls. Head (1980, 1985) developed these ideas into a model linking personality characteristics and preference for science, arguing that a school science which was presented as impersonalized, unemotional and offering clear, precise answers to problems would be an attractive and conventional choice for boys who were wary of expressing emotions and happy with a secure, controllable world. Conversely, such a science would be unattractive to the majority of girls who would need to have reached a particular level of maturity to make unconventional subject choices. There are links between this work and that of Harding and Sutoris (1987), who looked at 'object relations' theory of development and how the ways in which boys and girls are nurtured might affect subject choice. Object relations theory suggests that a child who is deprived of emotional support at too early a stage of development is more likely to develop a need to be in control and a desire for certainty, making science as presented in schools an attractive choice.

Harding (1996) summarizes the problems for science and school science caused by its appeal to a limited range of personality characteristics:

> Much of the physical science curriculum in schools is presented in a depersonalised, abstract form which attracts to it a certain type of emotionally reticent person, usually male, who has developed the need to control, to abstract, and to suppress ambiguity. Not only does this exclude many girls and women, but it constrains the development of science, permitting only certain ways of knowing – the ones in which the chief practitioners are comfortable. There are other dangers, too. Because nurturance, relational responsibility and person-orientation are poorly represented in the chief practitioners, those values will not be influential in the development of new science and technologies. Thus, there are created for the planet and its peoples hazards which could be avoided if school science were modified, and the straight-jacket around science itself loosened. (p.13)

Attitudes to science

Attitudes to science have been discussed in detail in Chapter 8 and are therefore summarized only briefly here. Many young people have a negative view of science, believe it to be a difficult subject, see it as not particularly relevant to everyday life, and think that most scientists are male and that science is for males. A meta-analysis (i.e. analysis of analyses) of studies on gender differences in attitudes (Weinburg, 1995) showed that negative attitudes to science are more prevalent amongst girls than boys, though less so in the case of more able girls.

Linked to work on attitudes, several studies of pupils' interest in particular science topics have been undertaken (Johnson, 1987; Woodward and Woodward, 1998; Sjøberg, 2000; Breakwell and Robertson, 2001). The studies have consistently demonstrated that boys show a preference for physical science topics and girls for biological/medical topics. Sjøberg (2000) also provided some interesting data on the effect of context on interest, as he explored the effect of putting the same science ideas into different contexts by, for example, presenting the topic of sound in physics variously as 'acoustics and sound', 'how the ear can hear', 'music, instruments and sound', and 'sound and music from birds and other animals'. Boys were more interested in the first option, and girls in the last, with the middle two options being more gender-neutral. Such a finding suggests that context in which science ideas are taught, rather than the ideas themselves, is an important influence on interest.

Learning styles and assessment strategies

Several differences between girls and boys have been established in terms of the ways they tackle problems and answer questions. Studies such as that of Harding (1979) and Murphy (1982) showed that boys performed better in multiple-choice tests than girls, with boys being more willing to guess when they did not know an answer and girls omitting to answer such questions. Coursework and project work improves pupils' marks overall, but most noticeably for girls (Murphy, 1993; Hildebrand, 1996), a finding which resulted in the reduction in the coursework requirements in 16+ examinations in England and Wales.

Drawing on the findings of the work of the Assessment of Performance Unit (APU), Murphy (1991) found that the setting of tasks in science was treated differently by boys and girls. Girls tended to see contextual features as integral to the task, whereas boys considered issues in isolation. Head (1996) suggests that this cognitive style of extraction is more common to males than females. These findings suggest that answering problems set in context may be more problematic for girls than boys. Other evidence of different ways of working may be found in a study by Murphy (1999), who looked at styles of talk in lessons whilst pupils were undertaking tasks, and showed that girls were more likely than boys to talk to each other about tasks and offer support as tasks were being done. Elwood and Comber (1996), in a review of gender differences in performance in examinations at 18+, examined writing styles and noted that boys' preferred writing style, which tends to be short and factual, is more in keeping with the sort of answers required in science examinations than that of girls, who prefer extended, reflective writing. Elwood and Comber went on to suggest that the ability to extract information is equated with overall cognitive ability by teachers, with the result that, in science lessons, girls' styles of learning are devalued and their abilities called into question.

Work in two particular areas provides the most compelling evidence of the influence of styles of assessment. The first area relates to data from national and international surveys (see, for example, Gipps and Murphy, 1994 and Murphy, 1996). Where these involve a range of different types of assessment strategy, such as in the APU surveys, there is variation in performance between girls and boys, with girls achieving better performance in some areas and boys in others (see next section). However, where the assessment is made largely or exclusively through the use of multiple-choice items, as is the case in a number of the international studies, boys normally outperform girls. The second area concerns the use of extended investigations, such as in *Salters Advanced Chemistry* (Burton *et al.*, 1994) and *Salters Horners Advanced Physics* (UYSEG, 2000), where girls are performing significantly better than boys when assessed in such investigations (Pilling, 2002).

Findings such as those described above clearly have to be borne in mind when interpreting the research evidence on the differential achievement of girls and boys in science.

The differential achievement of girls and boys in science

Literature on the differential achievement of girls and boys in science dates from the 1970s, with particular focus on patterns and trends in the performance of girls and boys in national and international surveys of achievement. This literature is of relevance to the current and widespread interest in boys' 'underachievement', though the fact that differences in girls' and boys' performance are smallest in the sciences (and mathematics) means these subjects have received less attention than others.

Much of the data on differential achievement has come from national and international surveys of performance, and more information on these may be found in Chapter 10. Both the first and second studies of the International Association for Educational Achievement (IEA), undertaken in 1970–3 and from 1983–6, established a gender gap in favour of boys in all branches of science. This gap was greatest for the physical sciences, and increased with age, though it was narrower in the second study than the first. The gap in performance was attributed to boys' better performance on questions testing understanding rather than recall (Keeves, 1992). A similar pattern of performance was found in the National Assessment of Educational Progress (NAEP) surveys undertaken in the USA in 1978. However, the Third International Mathematics and Science Study (TIMSS) reported no statistically significant differences overall in performance for either 12–13-year-olds or 14–15-year-olds, except in chemistry for the former group (Keys *et al.*, 1996). The first survey of the Organization for Economic Co-operation and Development/ Programme for International Student Assessment (OECD/PISA, 2001), or 'PISA' survey, undertaken in 2000, again indicates that boys no longer have the edge over girls. It is worth noting here that the earlier studies used multiple-choice questions to gather their data, whilst the PISA study made more use of open-ended questions.

In contrast to the picture which emerged from international studies in the 1970s and 1980s, the national surveys of performance of 11-, 13- and 15-year-old pupils carried out in England, Wales and Northern Ireland by the APU in the 1980s (APU, 1988a; 1988b; 1989b) showed that performance depended on the nature of the assessment and the construct being assessed. Girls' performance was superior to that of boys on practical tests which involved making and interpreting observations, whilst boys were better at applying physical science ideas.

Data from national tests are also informative, though they require care with interpretation. An analysis of gender differences in performance in science of pupils in England and Wales (Gorard *et al.*, 2001) shows there are now no significant differences in attainment in science between boys and girls at both 14+ and 16+ for lower attaining pupils, though a small and decreasing gap in favour of boys is apparent in upper-ability pupils. However, this study looked at only the 'aggregate' marks for biology, chemistry and physics. A detailed analysis of the General Certificate of Secondary Education (GCSE) examination results at 16+ (Bell, 1997), which involved breaking aggregate marks for 'science' into separate marks for biology, chemistry and physics, revealed that boys do significantly better in physics than girls, with 60 per cent of boys attaining the equivalent of a grade C compared with 49 per cent for girls.

Overall, the evidence suggests that girls now outperform boys in all subjects apart from physics at most levels during schooling, and that the gap in performance appears to be widening. Changes in assessment strategies have played a significant part in contributing to this picture.

Strategies for encouraging more girls to continue with their study of science

Several strategies have been proposed for increasing girls' levels of participation in science. Some of these have been implemented on a small scale, and others on a much larger scale. Two of the most significant programmes are the Girls into Science and Technology (GIST) programme, which ran in England from 1979–83 (see, for example, Whyte, 1986), and the continuing programme originally implemented in Victoria in Australia in the mid-1980s by the McClintock Collective (Rennie *et al.*, 1996). This group was formed in 1983 and takes its name from the scientist, Barbara McClintock, whose Nobel Prize-winning work in 1983 brought a different perspective to the conduct of scientific research.

The GIST project, though undertaken in the early 1980s, remains important in that it raised awareness and informed research and action on an international scale. Box 9.4 summarizes the key aspects of the project. Reflecting back on the GIST project after fifteen years or so, Smail (2000: 150) concludes that the most important outcome was 'the way in which it raised the issue of the low number of women in science ... so that it became a legitimate topic for conversation rather than a taken-for-granted feature of the education system and workforce'. She also notes that, in undertaking the work, the research team came to realize the difficulties of implementing change in classroom practice.

Arising out of the GIST project, and other studies (e.g. Smail, 1984; Whyte, 1986; Ditchfield and Scott, 1987), was a number of recommendations for enhancing the appeal of science for girls, often referred to as a 'girl-friendly science'. The list overleaf provides a summary of these suggestions:

Box 9.4: An example of a larger-scale study on gender: the GIST (Girls into Science and Technology) project
(Whyte, 1986; Smail, 2000)

Aims
To explore the processes by which children's attitudes to science, engineering and technology changed during the early years of secondary school; to investigate, by working with teachers, how the gendered nature of subject choice could be affected by teachers' attitudes and behaviour.

Research strategy and techniques
The study took the form of both an experiment and action research. An attitude inventory was used with pupils in ten schools. Teachers in eight of these schools (deemed 'action schools') then worked with the research team to develop and implement an intervention package which included modification of curriculum materials to make them more girl-friendly, lunch-time science clubs for girls, observation of lessons and feedback to teachers, visits by women scientists, parents' evenings and class discussions on careers and subject choices. Most school used some, but not all, of these strategies. During and after the intervention, data were gathered from teachers on their views, data on pupils' subject choices were collected and the attitude inventory used again with pupils.

Main findings
The initial pupil attitude data revealed many of the patterns discussed in this chapter. Following the intervention, there was some increase in the numbers of girls in the 'action schools' opting to study physical science subjects (e.g. 4 per cent for physics).

Girls' attitudes to physical sciences following the intervention were much more positive.

Improvements were most apparent in the schools where there was a commitment to change and a willingness to innovate, where women were in positions of authority, science teachers were female and positive about encouraging more girls into science and girls were made aware of the low numbers of girls taking physical sciences.

Data from the teachers showed that, even where the intervention had been embraced positively by senior management, many teachers were unwilling to make changes in their classroom practices.

- surveying resources for gender bias and taking action to remove this;
- taking positive action in science lessons to addressing sex-stereotyping issues;
- including material about the life and work of both female and male scientists;
- emphasizing the human applications of science;
- relating physical science principles to the human body;
- using personal experience as a starting point for the development of scientific ideas;
- broadening the range of activities used in science lessons;
- providing opportunities for pupils to explore opinions on science-related social issues.

Some of these strategies have had an impact, such as in the case of the unsubtle sex-stereotyping of textbooks of the 1970s (Walford, 1980; Smail, 1984). Women are no longer portrayed in traditionally feminine roles or as passive observers of scientific activity. Recent studies (e.g. Matthews, 1996; Sjøberg, 2000) with the popular 'draw-a-scientist' test (Chambers, 1983) suggest changes to resources have contributed to a shift in pupils' perceptions, with more pupils, particularly female pupils, now likely to draw pictures of female scientists.

The evidence on the effects of other strategies is more mixed. Certainly interest in science lessons has increased. For example, two large-scale curriculum development projects, *Science: The Salters Approach* in the UK (UYSEG, 1990–2) and *PLON* (Dutch Physics Curriculum Development Project, 1988), though not aimed specifically at increasing girls' levels of participation in science, did incorporate many of the 'girl-friendly' strategies. Evaluation studies (e.g. Jörg and Wubbels, 1987; Ramsden, 1990 and 1992) have shown these projects increased girls' (and boys') interest in science lessons though have not resulted in any significant increase overall in numbers choosing to continue with their study of science.

However, there are examples of interventions which indicate that localized action by individuals or small groups can have an impact on levels of participation. For example, Head and Ramsden (1990) used a personality inventory as one component of an evaluation of secondary physics materials which emphasized social applications of science, and included a broader range of teaching activities. Not only did significantly more girls elect to continue with their study of physics after experiencing the materials, but they also displayed a wider spectrum of personality types than those formerly choosing to study physics.

The work of the McClintock Collective in Australia seeks to move beyond 'girl-friendly science' to promote a different kind of science in the classroom, a 'gender-inclusive science' which involves 'communication, creative science, developing practical skills, personal growth and science as a human activity' (Kreinberg and Lewis, 1996). In terms of what happens in the classroom, however, there is an overlap with 'girl-friendly science' strategies, as there is a strong emphasis on using personal experience as a starting point for developing scientific ideas, providing opportunities for pupils to explore opinions on science-related social issues and using interactive, collaborative activities which draw on pupils' linguistic and imaginative abilities. Such strategies have been demonstrated to be effective, not only in stimulating girls' interest in science, but also in increasing numbers choosing to study physical science subjects. The work of the McClintock Collective has enabled the group to propose a model to explain gender differences in science-related attitudes, perceptions, classroom behaviour and learning outcomes (Rennie *et al.*, 1996). This model illustrates the crucial nature of the teacher in influencing pupils' views, beliefs and performance in science and subsequent subject choices, a feature which is apparent in much of the work done on evaluating the effects of intervention strategies.

Boys' underachievement

In many ways, things have come full circle in debate on gender issues. Much of the current literature focuses on boys' underachievement, with calls being made for action to be taken to offer boys equal opportunities for success. Interestingly, the concern over boys is described by Weiner *et al.* (1997) as something approaching a 'moral panic' – a panic which, they argue, was not apparent in the 1970s and 1980s when girls were seen as the underachievers. One factor which is certainly contributing to the interest is the drive to raise standards, with intervention strategies aimed at raising boys' achievement seen as a very obvious way in which schools could improve their overall performance.

The literature in the area draws extensively on analyses of published test and examination data. Research has focused on possible underlying explanations for the differences and, to a lesser extent, on evaluating the effectiveness of strategies aimed at improving boys' performance. It is beyond the scope of this chapter to review the research findings in detail, and a number of comprehensive reviews exist (e.g. Powney, 1996; Arnot *et al.*, 1998; Ofsted, 1998; Howe, 1999). In essence, the work has pointed to girls' improved performance arising from new approaches to teaching and assessment, and the positive impact of targeted equal opportunities policies. Boys' lower attainment has been explained in terms of changing notions of masculinity and new attitudes to school and work. In this context, the concept of 'laddish' behaviour is one which is receiving considerable attention in the literature. Jackson (2002b) links such behaviour with 'self-worth' theory. Boys want to convey the image that they could succeed academically, but they are choosing not to, and therefore use 'laddish' behaviour as a protective mechanism to avoid implications of lack of ability.

There is some concern within science education that the focus on boys' achievement is diverting attention from the continuing problem of levels of involvement, as the Department of Trade and Industry (DTI, 1997) in the UK noted in its review of strategies aimed at encouraging girls into science:

> In recent years, girls have made considerable advances in their academic achievements . . . to the point where the debates have focused on 'underachieving' boys rather than the difficulties faced by girls. Whilst this is a proper concern, it needs to be recognised that the world of science, engineering and technology is still, in the main, a masculine domain. (para. 25)

A further problem for science education concerns the nature of what, if any, action needs to be taken to address issues relating to boys' levels of achievement. Differences in achievement are smallest in science subjects and, as Head (1999) points out:

> The dilemma for those involved in science education is whether the physical sciences should be left alone, as they are one of the

few areas in which boys do relatively well, or should reforms be pursued even if boys then become disenchanted. (p. 77)

Conclusions

What are the main conclusions from research on gender issues in science education, and what are the implications for science teaching? The six-stage model proposed by Kreinberg and Lewis (1996), described earlier in this chapter, is helpful in pulling together the main strands of the work on levels of participation. Much has certainly been done to document the position of females in science and to explore the possible reasons for their under-involvement. The findings of work on explanations of differential involvement and the documenting of females' experiences in science have given rise to a wide range of strategies being proposed to increase girls' levels of participation. Though there are some examples of successful intervention, the overall picture of under-representation has not changed significantly, resulting in current work being targeted at the last two stages in Kreinberg and Lewis's model: challenging the current paradigm of science, and transforming and reconstructing a gender-free curriculum. Whilst there continues to be debate over how radical any reform needs to be, it is encouraging to see that there is an overlap between the recommendations arising out of research on gender and science, and recent work aimed at restructuring the science curriculum to emphasize learning *about* science, rather than learning *for* science (see Chapter 1).

The work which has been done on levels of achievement in science has demonstrated conclusively that differences in ability are negligible and in no way account for the differential involvement. Though the picture in the early years of gender research was one of boys outperforming girls, this has now changed, with girls having the edge at all levels in all science subjects other than physics. Improvements in girls' performance are linked to changes in assessment techniques. Box 9.5 summarizes the implications of research in gender and science for classroom practice.

Research on gender issues has certainly helped identify features of successful intervention strategies. Such strategies have been based on research findings and undertaken in situations where there is a

---

Box 9.5: Implications for practice

- Teaching resources should be surveyed for gender bias, and such bias should be removed, or openly challenged where removal is not possible.
- Teaching resources should ensure that the contributions of both male and female scientists to the development of scientific knowledge are acknowledged.
- Appropriate personal experience, contexts and science-related social issues should be used as the starting point for developing scientific ideas as these are likely to increase both girls' and boys' interest in science.
- A range of activities should be used in science lessons to ensure appeal to both girls and boys. Girls tend to do better at interactive, collaborative activities which draw on linguistic and imaginative abilities.
- A range of assessment strategies should be employed to ensure that no one strategy which favours either boys or girls predominates.
- Teaching pupils in single-sex groups should be approached with caution, and seen as one possible strategy in a more wide-ranging review of a school's curriculum and classroom practice.

---

commitment to fostering girls' interest in science and, more generally, ensuring equality of opportunity. Within this, the views, actions and classroom practices of individual teachers have been shown to be critical in increasing girls' participation, confidence and achievement in science.

Box 9.6: First stops for further reading

Several books which are compendia of articles provide a good overview of the issues current at the time of writing. These include:
Kelly, A. (1981) *The Missing Half: Girls and Science Education.* Manchester: Manchester University Press.
Kelly, A. (1987) *Science for Girls?* Buckingham: Open University Press.
Harding, J. (1986) *Perspectives on Gender and Science.* London:

Falmer Press.
Parker, L., Rennie, L. and Fraser, B. (eds) (1996) *Gender, Science and Mathematics: Shortening the Shadow*. Dordrecht: Kluwer Press.

A good recent article summarizing key features of earlier work is:
Murphy, P. (2000) Are gender differences in achievement avoidable? In J. Sears and P. Sorensen (eds) *Issues in Science Teaching*. London: RoutledgeFalmer.

A largely theoretical review paper discussing issues emerging from feminist writing on science education is:
Kenway, J. and Gough, A. (1998) Gender and science education: a review 'with attitude'. *Studies in Science Education*, 31, 1–29.

More general articles on gender issues, some of which have a science focus, may be found in:
Murphy, P. and Gipps, C. (1996) (eds) *Equity in the Classroom: Towards Effective Pedagogy for Girls and Boys*. Buckingham: Open University Press.

A good review and discussion of issues to do with gender and achievement may be found in:
Arnot, M., Gray, J., James, M., Rudduck, J. and Duveen, G. (1998) *Recent Research on Gender and Educational Performance*. London: The Stationery Office.

Chapter 10

The Nature and Purpose of Assessment in School Science

'*You don't fatten cattle by weighing 'em.*' (An expression used by Texan cowhands)

Like all analogies, the one above has its limitations! Yet it probably sums up the feeling many teachers have about the way in which assessment – or a particular approach to assessment – has come to dominate the curriculum and therefore drive much teaching. The last decade of the twentieth century certainly saw assessment come very much to the forefront of debate as it became increasingly associated with accountability and the production of 'league tables' of the performance of pupils in tests, both nationally and internationally. Thus an activity which has an important part to play in teaching and learning has come to have negative connotations associated with it. Why has this happened? What role should assessment play in science teaching?

This chapter looks at:

- the purposes of assessment in science;
- different types of assessment;
- difficulties associated with assessment;
- testing and standards;
- the role of teachers in assessment;
- national and international comparisons;
- what research has suggested about the role of assessment in science teaching.

Introduction

Assessment of pupils' performance in science plays an important and necessary role. It provides information about pupils' progress and achievements – information which should be of interest to the pupils themselves, to their teachers and to their parents. In the words of Black (1990), quoting from an earlier report he co-authored (DES/ WO, 1988):

> Assessment is at the heart of the process of promoting children's learning. It can provide a framework in which educational objectives may be set and pupils' progress charted and expressed. It can provide a basis for planning the next educational steps in response to children's needs. By facilitating dialogue between teachers, it can enhance professional skills and help the school as a whole to strengthen learning across the curriculum and throughout its age range (p. 27).

However, it is undeniable that assessment has been the subject of continuing debate and argument over matters such as the form it might take, what should be assessed, the extent to which teachers should be involved, how often assessment should take place and what should be done with data on pupils' performance. The current drive to raise standards has only served to intensify this debate.

Many of the issues and questions to do with assessment are not unique to science, so this chapter will therefore consider the more general aspects of assessment, relating them to science where appropriate. There are two areas which have received particular attention in science. One is the assessment of practical abilities, which has been discussed in Chapter 4. The second concerns methods of conducting and interpreting data from international surveys of pupils' scientific abilities, an area which has been the focus of increasing interest in recent years, again linked to the drive to raise standards.

Traditionally, a distinction has been made between *summative assessment* and *formative assessment*, the former being used for reporting and the latter for diagnosis. (These terms are discussed in more detail in the next section.) Summative and formative assessment form two broad areas under which research on assessment in science may usefully be discussed. Box 10.1 summarizes key issues and questions about assessment in the context of science education.

Box 10.1: Key issues and questions

- What are the purposes of assessment?
- How are issues of reliability and validity addressed in assessment?
- What are the benefits and drawbacks of norm and criterion referencing?
- What role do (or could) teachers play in summative assessment of pupils' knowledge and skills in science?
- What messages emerge from the results of national tests and examinations in science?
- What messages emerge from international surveys of pupils' performance in science?
- What is the relationship between assessment and raising standards?
- What role does formative assessment play in science teaching?

The purposes of assessment

A number of different ways of characterizing the purposes of assessment may be found in the literature. The most common is to distinguish between formative and summative assessment, and Table 10.1 summarizes the characteristics normally associated with each of these styles of assessment. It is worth noting that the two terms,

Table 10.1 Characteristics of summative and formative assessment

Summative assessment	Formative assessment
• takes place at the end of a teaching block; • aims to measure and report on learning outcomes in order to make a variety of comparisons; • uses formal methods; • is a well-established and traditional form of assessment; • is associated with accountability.	• takes place during teaching; • aims to establish progress and diagnose learning needs in order to support individuals; • uses both formal and informal strategies; • is a comparatively recent development in assessment; • is associated with pupils' educational development.

summative and formative, are relatively recent in origin, being first used by Bloom *et al.* (1971).

Gipps and Stobart (1993) provide a more detailed description of the purposes of assessment in terms of six possible purposes for which it might be used. These are:

- screening (testing groups of pupils to identify those who may need special help);
- diagnosis (using tests to identify individual pupils' strengths or, more usually, weaknesses);
- record-keeping (recording scores on tests);
- feedback on performance (using assessment results to provide information to a variety of groups);
- certification (to provide qualifications which signify particular levels of competence or knowledge);
- selection (to identify selected pupils who are capable of the particular levels of competence and performance required for a possible next step, such as university entrance).

Gipps and Stobart go on to suggest that one way of classifying these six purposes is the extent to which they are *professional* or *managerial*. A professional assessment is one which helps teachers in the process of educating their pupils, whereas a managerial assessment is one which is associated with accountability and managing in the education system. Thus screening and diagnosis are assessments undertaken mainly for professional purposes, certification and selection are undertaken mainly for managerial purposes, whilst record-keeping and feedback can be done for either purpose. Subsequently, Stobart and Gipps (1997) have described the professional and managerial purposes of assessment as assessment *for* learning and assessment *of* learning.

Some of the potential limitations and difficulties associated with assessment arise from the diversity of reasons for which assessment might be undertaken. An effective assessment system needs to give careful consideration to the aspects of a curriculum which are going to be assessed, the ways in which the assessment should be carried out, how the results will be interpreted and the uses which will be made of the results. Where the assessment is summative, care is also needed in the design and selection of assessment items. As this chapter will show, each of these aspects has its associated difficulties.

General issues in assessment

This section considers briefly some of the general issues which need to be addressed in developing assessment models, such as the importance of reliability and validity, and norm and criterion referencing.

Reliability and validity as key aspects of assessment

Assessment can take many forms, ranging from formative techniques used by teachers in their teaching, through end-of-topic tests administered by individual teachers or departments, to national and international tests, examinations and surveys of performance. As Black (1998) points out, the central feature of any assessment is that is should be dependable, and that those who need to use the results of the assessment can have confidence in them. Thus, issues of *reliability* and *validity* are particularly important in summative assessment.

For assessment to be *reliable*, conditions have to be maximized to ensure that any repeats of the assessment would provide the same outcome, i.e. performance has been assessed accurately. Multiple-choice items, done under examination conditions and with responses scored by optical scanning, are often claimed to be a reliable form of assessment. Threats to reliability can come from variability in examiners' judgements and variability in pupils' performance. Whilst steps can be taken to minimize the former through, for example, checking procedures and second marking, the problem of variability in pupils' performance is less easily addressed. Pupils' performance may well vary from day to day, yet the nature of most summative assessment is that it takes place on a very limited number of occasions. Little work has been done to explore the variation in performance from day to day. Even when tested on the same aspects of content, an individual pupil's performance can vary from question to question, depending on the style, context and language used. One illustration of this is provided by Murphy (1982), who demonstrated that boys' performance on the same subject matter was better than that of girls where multiple-choice tests were used in assessment, whilst the reverse was true for free response questions.

For assessment to be *valid*, it has to provide an appropriate measure of what it intends to assess. The notion of validity has received considerable attention in the literature, and a variety of different types of validity described. Those most frequently mentioned are *content validity* and *construct validity*. Taking multiple-choice questions as an example, one could ask several questions about their validity. Did they test areas of the curriculum specified in, for example, the examination syllabus? If not, there are problems with *content validity*. What inferences are being drawn about pupils' abilities in science from the results? Multiple-choice questions rely heavily on pupils' abilities to recall information, and most science courses would claim to develop a much broader range of abilities. If the results of a multiple-choice test were used as the basis for drawing inferences about a range of abilities, there would be problems with the *construct validity* of the test. Thus multiple-choice tests, though meeting a number of criteria for reliability, may not be particularly valid, and this is one of the reasons why they have fallen out of favour.

With the increasing prominence being given to assessment, attention has also been given to a further form of validity, *face validity*. Assessment tasks are seen as having face validity if they match normal classroom tasks. Developing assessment tasks with face validity is seen as an important way of reducing 'assessment backwash' whereby a particular style of assessment forces teachers to teach in ways which may have undesirable effects on classroom practice.

Norm and criterion referencing as a means of making comparisons

One purpose of assessment is to make comparisons, and two approaches are normally adopted to generate data for this purpose: norm referencing and criterion referencing. *Norm referencing* involves putting pupils' marks into a distribution graph and assigning particular percentages to each grade, such as the top 10 per cent of pupils getting the highest grade. Thus the grade awarded to an individual pupil depends in part on the performance of other pupils. Norm referencing assumes that the marks will follow the same general pattern each time assessment is undertaken. There are a number of potential problems associated with the validity of norm referencing. First, the sample used to generate the norm has to be both sufficiently large and sufficiently representative of the population as a whole to make comparisons valid. Second, changes to the educational experiences pupils receive may well affect the norm. An alternative is to use *criterion referencing*, where pupils' performance is judged against their ability to meet particular criteria (e.g. able to write simple word equations or distinguish between series and parallel circuits). Criterion referencing has become more popular in recent years. In part, this is because it is seen as more attractive than norm referencing in that assessment of an individual pupil's performance is independent of the performance of other pupils. However, the main reason for the increase in popularity of criterion referencing is that, unlike norm referencing, it provides data which enables the monitoring of changes in standards of performance over time.

Two points are worth making about norm and criterion referencing. First, they are related, rather than different, forms of assessment, as criteria are often developed with reference to norms. For example, if assessment is to be used for the purposes of making comparisons, little useful information is gained from a test which is non-discriminating (i.e. at the extremes all pupils met all, or none, of the criteria). Therefore some reference to the likely performance of pupils as a whole is normally used in identifying appropriate criteria. Second, despite its attractions and increase in popularity, criterion referencing is not unproblematic: as tasks become more complex and demanding, it becomes increasingly difficult to specify criteria with precision. The danger here is that the curriculum becomes one which involves, in the words of Gitomer and Duschl (1998: 807), 'partitioning concepts, investigative processes and reasoning into discrete measurement categories which provide only limited information . . . '. In other words, the curriculum is reduced to those aspects which can be most easily specified and assessed. The assessment of investigative skills described in Chapter 4 provides one illustration of problems

---

Box 10.2: Key research findings

- A curriculum dominated by an assessment model used for the purposes of accountability results in 'curriculum backwash': teaching becomes led by preparation for assessment.
- The use of criterion referencing may help pupils appreciate the standards for which they are aiming, but may also have the effect of reducing a curriculum to those aspects which can most easily be specified and therefore assessed.
- Teachers are able to make reliable and valid assessments of their pupils for the purposes of summative assessment.
- Assessment models which re-interpret formative data for summative purposes are likely to yield invalid data.
- There is evidence to suggest that pupils' performance in tests improves when feedback on their work no longer includes grades, but takes the form of constructive written comments.
- The validity of 'league tables' of the performance of schools in national tests has been questioned, leading to the incorporation of measures of 'value-added' to show the contribution a school makes to the improvement in pupils' performance.
- A variety of factors make the undertaking and interpretation of international surveys of performance problematic.
- Although comparatively little formative assessment is used in science lessons, there is evidence to indicate that the use of such assessment raises standards.
- Teachers who have made use of a range of formative assessment strategies in their lessons report benefits in terms of pupils' learning and motivation.
- Incorporating formative assessment strategies into teaching requires significant changes to current practice.

---

caused by attempting to reduce complex tasks into a series of discrete criteria.

Having considered general issues relating to assessment, the next two sections look in turn at research and areas of debate in each of the two main areas, summative assessment and formative assessment. Box 10.2 summarizes the key research findings.

Research and areas of debate in summative assessment

This section considers issues to do with summative assessment, looking in particular at:

- the role of teachers in summative assessment;
- data from national tests and surveys;
- data from international surveys;
- problems associated with summative assessment.

Discussion of some of these assessment issues may also be found in Chapter 5, which looks at the use of context-based questions in examinations, and in Chapter 9, which examines gender differences in performance.

The role of the teacher in summative assessment

One area where there has been considerable discussion and debate is that of the teacher's role in contributing to summative assessment, particularly when such assessment forms part of national tests and examinations. The assessment model developed for the National Curriculum in England and Wales provides an interesting case study which highlights a number of tensions. As originally conceived, the assessment system was to consist of two components, teacher assessment and national tests, called Standard Assessment Tasks (SATs). Teacher assessment was intended to be a continuous, comprehensive assessment of pupils made by teachers through a variety of informal and formal methods, ranging from conversations to short tests. At designated key points (at ages 7, 11 and 14), teachers were asked to give pupils a mark on a ten-point scale. The SATs were centrally produced tests, also administered at ages 7, 11 and 14, to indicate levels of attainment on the same ten-point scale. A key issue when teacher assessment forms a component of national summative assessment is the reliability of the assessment, and an important feature of the National Curriculum assessment model therefore involved moderation between the teacher assessment and the SAT marks to provide a check on the reliability of teachers' assessments.

The assessment model described above clearly incorporates both formative and summative assessment. The task group which developed the model (DES/WO, 1988) felt it would work, provided the formative element formed the foundation of the system. In the words of the task group: 'It is possible to build up a comprehensive picture of the overall achievements of a pupil by aggregating, in a structured way, the separate results of a set of assessments designed to serve a formative purpose' (section V, paragraph 25). The problems experienced by teachers in working with such a model are well documented (see, for example, Daugherty, 1995). Initially, teachers certainly felt uncomfortable with the dual roles of 'friend' and 'judge', and unsure as to what data should be used as a basis for reporting on the ten-point scale. For example, a survey by Swain (1995) showed that most science teachers (88 per cent) saw end-of-module tests as the most important and reliable basis for grading, with far less use being made of written work and homework.

Opinions differ as to the success of the model. Many judged it to be a failure, principally because it expected teachers to undertake two tasks which were seen as incompatible: to use assessment to support teaching and learning whilst at the same time provide information for accountability. However, the real difficulty lay in trying to make information initially gathered for one purpose serve another. As Gipps and Stobart (1993) comment: 'Assessment information collected formatively by teachers, when summarised, can be unreliable, and is unsuitable for the purposes of accountability or quality control. Its use for this latter purpose severely impairs its formative role' (p. 98). Wiliam and Black (1996) expand on this point by distinguishing between two different processes in assessment, elicitation (gathering evidence) and interpretation (making decisions and judgements based on the evidence). For Wiliam and Black, the problems encountered with the National Curriculum assessment model arose from the reinterpretation of formative evidence for summative purposes in order to report to external agencies. In their words: 'The question is not, therefore, can assessment serve both functions, but the extent to which serving one has an adverse affect on its ability to serve the other.' (p. 544).

Two years after its introduction, the National Curriculum assessment model was altered so that teacher involvement was significantly reduced and the summative assessment of most areas achieved through written national tests. In science, teachers' contribution to summative assessment was restricted to assessment of practical work. Though teachers are still required to produce their own assessment of pupils' grades, these are now done *after* the results of the national tests have been published, and the latter are not adjusted in the light of teacher assessments. Such a strategy would certainly seem to imply that there are questions about the reliability of teachers' assessments. Those involved in developing the original model felt that reducing teachers' involvement in assessment after only two years had given teachers insufficient time to adapt to the new system and showed a lack of respect for teachers' professionalism.

The issues raised by the development and implementation of the assessment model for the National Curriculum in England and Wales are by no means unique. Many other countries (for example, Australia, Canada, New Zealand and the USA) have been developing national or state assessment models, some which appear to have been less problematic than that in England and Wales. For example, a much more positive picture of the reliability of teachers' contribution to summative assessment may be found in the changes made to the assessment system in Queensland, Australia (Butler, 1995). Here, external examinations have been replaced completely by teacher assessment. The unproblematic introduction of this system is attributed to teacher involvement at each stage in the initial development of the assessment system and to teachers playing a major role in the review panels which now monitor certification of pupil achievement.

National tests and surveys

National tests and examinations gather data of a particular kind and provide one, rather limited, picture of performance. The use of such data to generate 'league tables' has been the focus of considerable controversy. In an article entitled 'Drawing outrageous conclusions from national assessment results: where will it all end?', Murphy (1997) raises a number of concerns about the assumptions underlying the comparisons made on the basis of league tables. For example, they assume that schools start with pupils of similar ability, that performance is independent of the social context of the area served by the school and that the knowledge and skills tested in a range of subjects can be easily compared. Such assumptions are clearly open to question, with, for example, Gibson and Asthana (1998) arguing that uncontextualized performance statistics have little validity. One outcome of this and other criticism has been a move towards producing additional data on performance which incorporates measures of 'value added' – performance are measured relative to baseline data to provide an indication of the improvement a school has made in pupils' performance (see, for example, DfEE, 1995; Jesson, 1997).

Educational research has also contributed to building up national pictures of performance, of which the studies undertaken by the Assessment of Performance Unit (APU) in the UK and the National Assessment of Educational Progress (NAEP) in the USA in the 1970s and 1980s provide two examples. (The work of the APU on the assessment of practical abilities in science was discussed in Chapter 4, and further details of the NEAP work may be found in Gipps and Murphy, 1994.) When the APU was established in 1975, it was charged with providing an indicator of educational standards and how they changed over time. This was to be achieved through annual rounds of surveys looking at performance in five areas: design technology, language, modern languages, maths and science. This did not prove an easy task due to problems over valid ways of making comparisons. The curriculum and teaching techniques change with time, thus tests become dated – but changing the tests makes valid comparisons difficult. Thus, ultimately, the APU was unable to provide data on changes in standards but, by the time it was disbanded in the late 1980s, it had produced an extensive and detailed database on pupils' levels of performance in a range of subjects.

In addition to the data gathered in the APU surveys, the work raised a number of issues about assessment. Black (1990) suggested that that three key messages emerged from the work. First, valid assessment of a pupil's abilities can only be achieved through a wide range of assessment methods. Second, assessment based on short tests was unreliable. Finally, he argued that, with appropriate support and training, teachers could make more reliable assessment than those provided by external testing. These are clearly issues that will continue to be debated.

One final study worthy of mention in the context of national pictures gained through summative assessment is that of Fitz-Gibbon and Vincent (1994). They set out to explore the comparability of grading standards in A level (18+) examinations in England and Wales. Using a variety of comparative indicators, including looking at the performance of pupils taking particular pairs of subjects, the study established that lower grades were awarded in some subjects than others, with physics and chemistry being the subjects in which pupils were most likely to achieve lower grades. For example, a pupil taking sociology and chemistry was likely to achieve well over one grade higher in sociology than chemistry. One interpretation placed on these findings – and certainly one which received attention in the media – was that physical science subjects were 'more difficult' than others because it was harder to achieve a particular grade in physical sciences than in many other subjects. However, this conclusion has been criticized, with Newton (1997) suggesting that there are serious questions over the validity of the data in terms of providing a measure of comparability of subjects. Certainly the data appear to point more to an issue to do with grading standards rather than providing evidence of the inherent difficulty of physical science subjects.

International surveys

A number of international surveys of performance has been undertaken in the last thirty years. Three groups have been involved in these studies: the IEA (International Association for the Evaluation of Educational Achievement), the IEAP (International Assessment of Educational Progress) and the OECD (Organization for Economic Co-operation and Development).

The IEA has undertaken three major international science surveys in the last three decades, with the most recent being the Third International Mathematics and Science Study (TIMSS), which ran from 1995–7. Data were gathered from three cohorts: age 11+, age 14+ and pupils in the final year of secondary schooling. One measure of the increasing interest in the data from such studies comes from the number of participating countries: the figures rose from twenty in the first study to fifty in TIMSS. The two IEAP studies, one in 1988 and the second in 1990, gathered data from pupils aged 9+ and 13+.

The TIMSS survey showed that pupils in Pacific Rim countries (Singapore, South Korea and Japan) performed best in the science and maths tests. A subsequent study (Reynolds and Farrell, 1996) to identify key differences in classroom practice between these countries and European countries suggested that countries where pupils had performed best made extensive use of 'whole-class interactive instruction', used specialist teachers in primary schools, made frequent use of tests in core subjects and took steps to ensure pupils stayed within a fairly narrow range of achievement by providing extra tuition after school or not letting pupils progress into the next class at the end of the year. Such findings are clearly of interest, though have to be considered against the cultural context and features of teaching which are seen as important in different countries. For example, there is incompatibility between some of the features of teaching described above and the aims of formative assessment.

The findings of the international studies mentioned above have been reported in detail in a range of publications (e.g. IEAP 1: Keys and Foxman, 1989, LaPointe *et al.*, 1989; IEAP 2: LaPointe *et al.*, 1992, Foxman, 1992; IEA 1: Comber and Keeves, 1973; IEA 2: IEA, 1988; TIMSS: TIMSS, 1996, TIMSS, 1997, TIMSS, 1998, Shorrocks-Taylor *et al.*, 1998).

The most recent international survey began in 1999 and is being undertaken by OECD/PISA (Organization for Economic Co-operation and Development/Programme for International Student Assessment), or the 'PISA' study, described in detail in Harlen (2001). One strand of this study involves gathering data on scientific literacy at three-year intervals. The first survey took place in 2000, and involved 32 countries. The findings are reported in OECD/PISA (2001). The PISA study differs from previous studies in that it plans to assess the abilities and skills needed by future citizens, rather than focusing on a common core of concepts taught in a number of countries. Box 10.3 presents the findings from the first PISA survey of scientific literacy.

From the point of view of research in science education, international studies bring very sharply into focus many of the issues to do with assessment, particularly in terms of the concepts and skills to be assessed, the way in which data should be gathered, and the validity of the data for the purposes of making comparisons. Several factors make for additional difficulties in international comparisons,

> **Box 10.3: An example of a large-scale study on assessment**
> OECD/PISA (2001) – the first of a series of international surveys
>
> *Aim*
> To explore aspects of 15-year-old students' scientific literacy.
>
> *Research question*
> What understandings do 15-year-old students have of a range of scientific processes, concepts, applications and situations which they may need to draw on in adult life?
>
> *Research strategy and techniques*
> The research took the form of a large-scale survey of 265 000 students in 32 countries. Data were gathered through the use of pencil-and-paper, contextualized questions. The questions explored students' capacity to use scientific knowledge, identify what is involved in scientific investigations, relate data to claims and conclusions and communicate these aspects of science. The tasks varied in aspects such as the complexity of science concepts, the amount of data provided and the chain of reasoning required. Supplementary data were gathered from pupils and teachers in order to help identify factors which might affect performance.
>
> *Main findings*
> The mean scores of a number of countries were very similar, and variation around the mean introduced a degree of possible imprecision into final rankings. Pupils in South Korea and Japan obtained the highest scores. Other countries with scores which were statistically significantly above the average for all countries were Finland, the United Kingdom, Canada, New Zealand, Australia, Austria, Ireland, Sweden and the Czech Republic.

including the age at which pupils begin school, the curriculum they have experienced by the time the assessment takes place, classroom practices used by teachers, home experiences to support learning, pupils' attitudes and the value placed on education in society.

Because international comparisons involve large-scale surveys, they have generally made use of multiple-choice items to facilitate coding and analysis. These have been supplemented by a range of additional data gathered from teachers, pupils and other sources to provide background and context against which interpretations might be made. Unsurprisingly, the use of multiple-choice items has been criticized (e.g. Black, 1990) for its narrowness and lack of validity. The PISA study, though still making some use of multiple-choice items, also asks open-ended questions. The questions are also set in context, an approach which has raised questions about the nature of appropriate contexts for different countries, and possible difficulties with the increased reading demands placed on pupils by the use of contextualizing information. Despite these problems, in a climate which attaches ever increasing importance to monitoring standards and to accountability, it seems likely that interest in international comparisons will remain strong.

Is there evidence to suggest that summative assessment raises standards?

The importance attached to monitoring and raising standards has been a particular feature of the last decade. 'Standards' is a word which is often used in educational contexts, most usually in relation to pupils' performance in tests, which may then be used as indicators of standards of teaching. The justification for the attention being paid to standards has arisen from a general perception that standards are falling, and steps need to be taken to reverse this situation. Put bluntly, improving standards is seen as making the education system accountable to those who provide the financial support, many of whom are tax-paying parents.

Some studies have indicated that more frequent testing improves performance. For example, Bangert-Drowns *et al.* (1991) reviewed forty studies on the use of classroom testing with a view to establishing the optimum frequency for using tests. Their meta-analysis (i.e. analysis of the analyses reported in the studies) showed that pupils' marks generally improved if tests were administered more frequently – though only up to a certain frequency before performance started to decline, and that several short tests had a more positive effect on performance than fewer longer tests. However, it is important to note that the studies only reported on the effects of more frequent testing, not on any other effects on teaching resulting from the increased use of tests. Black (1993) also reports on the findings of a number of studies which indicated that pupils' learning was improved in a variety of contexts through the use of written questions.

Problems with summative assessment

It is clear from the discussion above that, despite its extensive use, summative assessment has its limitations and problems. Drawing on the findings of a number of studies, Black (1993: 52) identified a number of problems associated with summative assessment:

- science is reduced to learning of isolated facts and skills;
- the cognitive level of classroom work is lowered;
- pupils have to work at too great a pace for effective learning;
- in particular, ground being 'covered' by a race through the textbook;
- much teaching time is devoted to direct test preparation;
- pupils' questioning is inhibited;
- learning follows testing in focusing on aspects that are easy to test;
- laboratory work stops unless tests include laboratory tests;
- creative, innovative methods and topical content are dropped;
- teachers' autonomy is constrained and their methods revert to a uniform style;
- teachers are led to violate their own standards of good teaching.

These problems have resulted in an increasing interest in the possibilities offered to teachers and their pupils by formative assessment.

Research and areas of debate in formative assessment

Whilst the results of national and international comparisons based on summative assessment have gained an increasingly high profile in the last decade or so, much of the writing on assessment has been concerned with the role of formative assessment and the way in which it might improve teaching and learning. This section considers the nature and purpose of formative assessment, and research evidence into the use and effects of formative assessment, including effects on standards.

The nature and purpose of formative assessment

The central feature of formative assessment is that it involves gathering information which is used in the short term to modify teaching and learning. In a widely cited paper called *Inside the Black Box: Raising Standards through Classroom Assessment*, Black and Wiliam (1998a) summarize assessment as:

> ... all those activities undertaken by teachers, *and by their students in assessing themselves*, which provide information to be used as feedback to modify the teaching and learning activities in which they are engaged. *Such assessment becomes 'formative assessment' when the evidence is actually used to adapt the teaching work to meet the needs.* (p. 2; italics in original)

Here it is interesting to note that emphasis is being given to the role pupils, as well as teachers, might play in formative assessment.

Sources of information which can contribute to formative assessment include: pupils' class work, pupils' homework exercises, dialogue with pupils during lessons, informal tests set during teaching and end-of-topic tests. Some of this information may be generated by pupils engaging in self- or peer assessment of their own work

Formative assessment clearly has a diagnostic component, and may sometimes be referred to as 'diagnostic assessment', though this latter term is often used in science education to describe techniques employed to gather information on pupils' ideas and understanding in topics where they are known to have difficulty, that is as a first step in constructivist teaching (see Chapter 2).

Research evidence into the use and effects of formative assessment

Black and Wiliam (1998b) have undertaken an extensive review of research studies on formative assessment. (Black and Wiliam's *Inside the Black Box*, 1998a, summarizes the key findings from the review.) Two areas explored in the review were the extent to which formative assessment was being used in teaching, and its effects on standards. The review revealed that relatively little formative assessment was being routinely undertaken in teaching. For example, a survey of 100 secondary schools in England (Daws and Singh, 1996) indicated that the principal method of teacher assessment in science lessons was end-of-topic tests, with fewer than a quarter of teachers drawing on dialogue with pupils, a key element of formative assessment, to assess pupils' understanding. Similar findings were reported from a number of other countries, including Australia, England, Scotland, and the USA (Black, 1993; Black and Wiliam, 1998b).

Formative assessment and standards

Despite the lack of use in practice, Black and Wiliam (1998a; 1998b) concluded that there was evidence in the studies they reviewed to suggest that formative assessment does raise standards of performance, particularly for lower-attaining pupils. Some of the studies reviewed (e.g. Butler, 1988) demonstrated that pupils' performance in tests improved when feedback on their work no longer included grades, but took the form of constructive written comments. Additional benefits in the form of improved pupil self-esteem and motivation were also reported. The review also enabled them to identify a number of difficulties associated with introducing effective formative assessment into classroom practice. These include encouragement of rote learning through teachers' use of tests, lack of discussion between teachers over the nature and purpose of questions used in assessment, over-emphasizing marks and grades at the expense of giving advice, and use of approaches which involve norm rather than criterion referencing with a consequent demotivating effect on lower attaining pupils.

Using formative assessment in the classroom

Bell (2000) argues that one of the problems with formative assessment arises from the lack of research into the process of what goes on in classrooms where formative assessment is being used. Drawing on observation data gathered in a study undertaken with teachers and pupils in upper secondary science lessons in New Zealand (Bell and Cowie, 1999), Bell distinguishes between planned and interactive formative assessment. The former, as its name suggests, relates to assessment activities the teacher planned to include in their lessons, whilst the latter emerged from unplanned teacher–pupil interactions. She goes on to identify a number of essential features of formative assessment, including the need for planning, the importance of acting on information elicited from pupils, the need to develop a learning partnership between teachers and pupils, and the key role of language in helping teachers and pupils describe and negotiate meanings. Another typology of formative assessment has been developed on the basis of research in primary classrooms (Tunstall and Gipps, 1996; Stobart and Gipps, 1997). Essential features of this typology include the need for positive feedback related specifically to criteria, and clear guidance on goals or ways of improving the work.

It is clear from the literature that the incorporation of formative assessment strategies into teaching requires more than just 'tinkering' with current practice. Drawing on evidence from three small-scale case studies, Daws and Singh (1999) suggest that the successful practice of formative assessment requires:

> ... fostering collaborative, democratic discussion that critically appraises the process of learning and assessment, helping pupils monitor their learning against clearly-specified learning objectives, supporting pupils in taking some responsibility for managing their learning ... (p. 78)

A comparatively recent development in formative assessment is the use of pupil self- or peer assessment. Such assessment can take a variety of forms, such as pupil sheets incorporating 'can do' statements, pupils marking informal tests and pupils designing questions to test understanding. A number of small-scale studies on the use of such strategies in science lessons have reported benefits to both pupils and teachers arising from such strategies (e.g. Fairbrother *et al.*, 1995; Daws and Singh, 1999; Black and Harrison, 2001). Benefits cited include pupils gradually gaining a better perception of what makes a good question to test understanding after developing and trying out questions of their own, improving pupils' clarity of explanations, both verbal and written, and improvements in performance on end-of-topic tests. Box 10.4 describes a small-scale study on pupil self-assessment in science.

Box 10.4: An example of a small-scale study on assessment (Wall, 2002)

Aim
To explore the effects of pupil self- and peer assessment in science lessons with a view to improving their learning skills.

Research question
How can teachers use formative assessment to support pupils in setting effective short-term targets for improvement in their work?

Research strategy and techniques
The research took the form of a case study of practice in one school. Self-assessment pro-formae were developed and used with a group of pupils in Year 7 and in Year 8. In addition to the data gathered from these sheets, follow-up interviews were undertaken. Further evidence also came from a questionnaire completed by pupils on the use of the self-assessment sheets.

Main findings
Most pupils found it difficult to set effective short-term targets for improvement. The targets set tended to be vague and not reflect the pupils' subject weaknesses.

The use of self-assessment sheets proved popular with pupils as it provided the opportunity to highlight strengths and weaknesses and provided more specific areas for pupils to set targets.

In addition, the use of learning objectives, written in 'pupil speak', proved a popular and effective method of assisting revision.

Whilst the appeal of formative assessment is undeniable, and those teachers who have taken steps to include it in their teaching certainly feel there are benefits, it is certainly the case that formative assessment makes considerable demands on time – time for planning how it should be incorporated into lessons as well as time in lessons to make use of formative assessment strategies. Black and Harrison (2001) observed that it took six months for the teachers involved in their study in six schools to move from isolated attempts at using formative assessment in their lessons to developing more formal policies on the use of formative assessment. Nonetheless, all the teachers felt that time spent on developing and using formative assessment strategies was worthwhile in terms of the benefits to both themselves and pupils.

Conclusions: where next for assessment?

This chapter began by saying that assessment plays an important and necessary part in teaching. Research has helped identify some implications for practice, and these are summarized in Box 10.5. However, what has also emerged from the discussion and research findings is a somewhat complex picture. There are clearly tensions between, on the one hand, using a system of summative assessment which is driven by the need for accountability and, on the other, using formative assessment to assist with teaching and learning. The

---

Box 10.5: Implications for practice

- Whilst teachers clearly have to conform to the external summative assessment system which is in place, care should be taken to ensure as far as possible that pupils' learning is not adversely affected by assessment-driven teaching, with good practice being curtailed in order to prepare for summative assessment.
- Teachers need to be provided with training and time to help develop skills associated with formative assessment, and to plan strategies for its incorporation into their teaching.
- Feedback to pupils on their work should make less use of grades and concentrate on providing pupils with comments on what they have achieved, directing them to next steps and giving pointers for possible improvement.

former inevitably leads to a style of teaching which is incompatible with the latter. What seems desirable is an assessment system which draws on a range of methods to yield sufficient reliable and valid data to enable standards to be monitored whilst, at the same time, providing appropriate measures of pupils' understanding to provide them with feedback which assists them with their learning. Inevitably such a system will involve an element of compromise between the limited but comparatively easily processed and reliable data generated by summative assessment and the potentially detailed and helpful information but resource-intensive information yielded by formative assessment.

The research evidence suggests that a valid system of reporting the results of national tests and examinations needs to go beyond presenting raw scores to provide contextualizing information to enable judgements to be reached about 'value added'. The research evidence also indicates that, with appropriate training, teachers can use their professional judgement to produce reliable and valid data which can contribute to summative assessment. Perhaps the main message from research about international comparisons is that they are always going to be problematic, given the many different factors which can influence performance, coupled with the need to collect data from very large samples.

The literature on assessment is currently heavily promoting the use of formative assessment strategies in science teaching. Certainly the evidence which exists at present suggests that the potential benefits, in terms of both improved pupil performance and motivation, are considerable. Educational research will clearly have an important role to play in exploring in more detail the contribution formative assessment might make to improving science teaching.

Box 10.6: First stops for further reading

A book aimed at teachers and providing an accessible overview of many aspects of assessment is:
Black, P. (1998) *Testing: Friend or Foe?: Theory and Practice of Assessment and Testing.* London: Falmer Press.

One of the comparatively few recent papers on research on summative assessment is:

Swain, J. (2000). Summative assessment. In M. Monk and J. Osborne (eds) *Good Practice in Science Teaching: What Research has to Say*. Buckingham: Open University Press.

A widely cited and concise overview of research on formative assessment is in the booklet:
Black, P. and Wiliam, D. (1998) *Inside the Black Box: Raising Standards through Classroom Assessment*. London: King's College.

A useful discussion of specific strategies employed in science lessons may be found in:
Daws, N. and Singh, B. (1999) Formative assessment strategies in secondary science. *School Science Review*, 80 (293), 71–8.

A book describing a number of small-scale innovations involving formative assessment in science teaching is:
Fairbrother, B., Black, P. and Gill, P. (1995) *Teachers Assessing Pupils: Lessons from the Science Classroom*. Hatfield: Association for Science Education.

A book which reviews assessment issues, particularly those raised by the assessment models associated with the National Curriculum in England and Wales is:
Stobart, G. and Gipps, C. (1997) *Assessment: A Teachers' Guide to the Issues* (3rd edn). London: Hodder Stoughton.

Endpiece

Each chapter in this book has reviewed a key area in science education through exploring answers to a number of key questions, and their implications for classroom practice. This final section considers briefly some of the more general messages about research in science education which have emerged from the review.

Research in science education has certainly changed in the last twenty years. Apart from the dramatic increase in the volume of literature, areas of work are expanding to incorporate ideas and theories from other disciplines. For example, work on constructivism has shifted from its initial focus on children's understanding of scientific ideas to explore the effects of social features on learning environments. In the area of language and science, strong links are being made with Vygotsky's theories on the role of language in the development of thinking processes. This is very different to the earlier focus on difficulties posed by particular words and phrases in science lessons. Attitude research now has a much stronger link with psychological theory, and current writing on gender and science is drawing on feminist perspectives. Such moves are positive in that they are contributing to the provision of a firmer theoretical basis for research in science education. However, they pose something of a challenge for those engaging in research as they have added to the ever-expanding field of literature relevant to a particular area.

There is certainly evidence of a number of benefits arising from research in science education. It has been successful in documenting and illuminating problems, such as in pupils' misunderstandings of key science ideas, or the reasons why so many pupils, particularly girls, seem alienated by science. Research has also helped establish how changes in policy or in the curriculum have an impact on classroom practice, such as in implementing new assessment strategies and in exploring the effects of the use of context-based approaches. Research has also drawn attention to issues which may otherwise have not been noticed, such as the reading levels and gender imbalance in science text books of two decades ago. Addressing these issues provide examples of where research has led very obviously to improvements in practice. Research findings have also influenced practice such as in using pupils' existing ideas and contexts relevant to their lives as starting points to develop scientific ideas and understanding. This is particularly the case where these ideas have been built into curriculum materials. However, research findings do not always point to easy solutions. For example, whilst much is known about the reasons why young people seem to become increasingly alienated by science during secondary school, it has proved much harder to identify action which has any significant and lasting effect. Similarly, despite a wealth of evidence on the difficulties pupils encounter with many ideas in science, only limited inroads have been made into identifying teaching strategies to help overcome these difficulties.

Research in science education (and other areas of educational research) has so far proved to be better at identifying and illuminating problems than at pointing to possible solutions. The current debate and discussion about the objectives of educational research and the most appropriate strategies for gathering data, together with moves to link research more closely to curriculum development and evaluation, may well lead to clearer guidance emerging for certain areas of policy and practice, though the complex nature of educational contexts means that there will always be limits on the extent to which research can provide solutions.

The aspirations of research in science education are well summed up by Richard Whitfield in his presidential address to the Association of Science Education (ASE) in the UK:

> Above all, however, one might hope that . . . we would begin to perceive more consciously that our curriculum, work schemes and laboratory courses are essentially *hypotheses* designed to

achieve valued outcomes, and that as such they must be inherently open to modification in the light of *both* research evidence *and* professional experience. (1979: 428)

Although these words were spoken well over two decades ago, they illustrate very clearly that research in science education is a collaborative activity and one which, in seeking answers to some questions, will inevitably give rise to more.

Appendix 1: Features of Educational Research

Research in education draws on the approaches and techniques developed in the social sciences. One helpful way of thinking about reports of educational research studies is to consider five particular principal features of the research. These are summarized below, together with their associated aspects.

Feature of educational research	Associated aspects
Research strategy	• action research • case study • ethnography • experiment • survey
Research technique	• document study • focus groups • interview • observation • questionnaire
Type of data	• quantitative • qualitative
Type of researcher	• professional • practitioner researcher
Scale of study	• large scale • small scale

Many factors influence the choice of approach and techniques in a research study, and the prime consideration in making decisions should be the question(s) the research is addressing. Certain strategies are more commonly associated with large- or small-scale studies and employ particular techniques which, in turn, yield particular types of data. Each strategy and technique has advantages and disadvantages, and any research study needs to take steps to minimize the effects of the latter.

Research strategies

Action research

Action research is an approach which has become increasingly popular with small-scale research in educational settings as it is about finding practical solutions to practical problems. A central feature of action research is that the researcher is involved in the research process. Much practitioner research therefore takes the form of action research. A typical action research study would have three main stages: identifying a problem, identifying and implementing a course of action, and evaluating the success of the action. Action research is often described as a cyclical process, as evaluation may well lead to further action.

Case study

Case studies have become very widely used in social research, and are very popular in small-scale research undertaken by practitioner researchers. They focus on one aspect of a particular situation and use a range of research techniques to explore the situation in depth with a view to identifying the various processes at work in the situation. A criticism of case studies concerns the extent to which their findings can be generalized – features which exert a strong influence in one context may not be present in another. However, case studies are normally judged by their 'relatability', rather than by their generalizability – a good case study will be reported in such way that the members of a similar group will be able to identify with the problems and issues being reported, and draw on these to see ways of solving similar problems in their own situation.

Ethnography

Ethnography has its origins in the work of anthropologists studying aspects of a particular group in depth. It involves the researcher becoming a member of the group being studied in order to share their experiences and try to understand why members of the group act in particular ways. As with case studies, there are problems with the reliability of ethnographic studies. Whilst there are some examples of researchers joining staff in a school, the nature of much educational research, with its focus on pupils, makes ethnographic research difficult in educational contexts.

Experiments

Experiments are conducted to discover new relationships or to test out theories. The key feature of experiments is that they involve identifying and isolating individual aspects of a situation (variables), making changes and observing the effects in detail. Two factors have made experiments comparatively rare in educational contests. First, controlling variables often presents problems in educational settings. Second, conducting experiments in educational settings raises ethical issues. Changes to curriculum provision are made in the hope that they will lead to improvements, and experiments therefore involve depriving one group of something which it is hoped will be beneficial, though this outcome is by no means certain and cannot be judged in advance. Recently, however, there have been calls to make more use of experiments in educational research (see Chapter 1). One of the best-known recent examples of an educational experiment is the work done for the Cognitive Acceleration through Science (CASE) project (see Chapter 3).

Survey

Surveys aim to collect data from a representative sample group with a view to presenting the findings as being applicable to a much larger group. Surveys tend to be associated with large-scale studies and make use of questionnaires in order to gather data, which is often quantitative in nature. The major advantage of a survey lies in the breadth and inclusive nature of the data collected. Surveys are less good at yielding explanations for events. Surveys are often employed when one aim of the research is to be able to make comparisons between different groups. Examples of surveys in science education include those of the Assessment of Performance Unit (APU) (see Chapters 4 and 10) and international studies of performance such as the Third International Mathematics and Science Study (TIMSS) and the PISA study (see Chapter 10).

Research techniques

Document study

As its name implies, this involves a detailed study of documents relevant to a study. Such documents might include policy statements and accounts of innovation.

Focus groups

Focus groups are comparatively new in educational research. They are used to gather views and opinions by giving participants a topic or a series of questions to discuss. The researcher's main role in the discussion is simply to listen. One reason for the increasing popularity of focus groups is that, like interviews, they can be used to explore topics in depth, but, unlike interviews, they can gather a relatively large amount of data in a short time. One example of the use of focus groups in science education research is the study undertaken by Osborne and Collins (2001) on pupils' and parents' views of the role and value of the science curriculum (see Chapter 8).

Interviews

Interviews are a very popular technique in educational research as they enable research questions to be explored in depth by going beyond factual matters to seek views and explanations. They are often used in conjunction with questionnaires, either to identify aspects to be explored in a questionnaire, or to probe the responses on questionnaires in more depth.

Observation

Observation is used in educational research to gather data on actual practice. Like questionnaires, observation generates factual information rather than explanations.

Questionnaires

Questionnaires are also a very popular technique in educational research as they provide a cost-effective means of gathering a wide range of fairly straightforward, factual information. Questionnaires are usually better at answering questions about 'what' and 'how' rather than 'why'.

One related technique which has been widely used in science education research involves *diagnostic questions*. Diagnostic questions normally have two parts. In the first part, respondents are required to answer a factual question and, in the second part, to explain their reasoning. Diagnostic questions, followed up by interviews to probe understanding further, formed the backbone of the work undertaken for the Children's Learning in Science Project (CLISP) (see Chapter 2).

Types of research data

Data gathered in a research study are generally classified as either *quantitative* (makes use of numbers) or *qualitative* (makes use of words in the form of descriptions).

Quantitative data can be analysed by statistical techniques if drawn from a wide sample. Such techniques allow researchers to establish the extent to which their findings are statistically significant, or not down to mere chance. There are two risks associated with quantitative data. The first is that studies which rely heavily on such data run the risk of missing out on the in-depth insights gained from qualitative data. The second risk lies in the solid and reliable 'feel' that can come from numbers – but it is important to note that numbers are only as good as the measures used to obtain them.

The terms qualitative and quantitative have come to be associated with particular 'traditions' in educational research, each with differing commitments to the ways in which it is appropriate to investigate educational contexts. These are the *positivist* tradition and the *interpretative* tradition. The positivist tradition holds that research in the social sciences should draw on the approaches of the natural sciences and seek to establish general 'laws' about educational matters. Positivist research therefore tends to be characterized by experiments which involve the careful formulation and testing of hypotheses, and the gathering of quantitative data. The interpretative approach, however, argues against the search for general laws and emphasizes the need to understand situations and actions. The approaches and techniques of interpretative research normally rely on gathering qualitative data.

Two key ideas about research data, whether quantitative or qualitative, are *reliability* and *validity*. Data are said to be *reliable* if repeating the technique gives the same result again. Undertaking trials of research instruments is an important step in ensuring reliability. Data are said to be *valid* if they measure what they claim to be measuring.

Types of researcher

Until comparatively recently, educational research was most usually undertaken by 'professional' researchers – people who work in higher education institutions and for whom undertaking research is a part of their job, or in groups set up specifically to undertake research, such as the National Foundation for Educational Research (NFER) in the UK. However, the last fifteen years or so has seen the growth of the 'practitioner researcher'. A practitioner researcher – a teacher in educational contexts – is simultaneously working in a particular field and researching an aspect of practice.

Scale of study

The terms large-scale and small-scale are used loosely to describe the size of a study. A *small-scale study* is likely to be one undertaken by a single researcher, and involve collecting from a limited number of sources, such as a teacher collecting data in their own school as part of a higher degree research study. The term *large-scale study* tends to be associated with projects which may well require a number of researchers, have external funding and involve the collection of data from a large number of people in a range of locations. Examples of large-scale studies in science education include the Procedural and Conceptual Knowledge in Science (PACKS) project (see Chapter 4).

Further reading

The following provide accessible introductions to research methods in education:

Bell, J. (1999) *Doing Your Research Project: A Guide for First-Time Researchers in Education and Social Science*, 3rd edition. Buckingham: Open University Press.

Blaxter, L., Hughes, C. and Tight, M. (1996) *How to Research*. Buckingham: Open University Press.

Denscombe, M. (1998) *The Good Research Guide*. Buckingham: Open University Press.

Appendix 2: Theories and Ideas about Learning

All the chapters in this book make reference to the theories and ideas about learning. This appendix provides more information about the most influential 'big names' and the ideas which have had a particular impact on science education. These big names have tended to operate in the field of *cognitive psychology*: they are interested in the thinking processes associated with learning. It is impossible to do justice in just a few short paragraphs to the many decades of work undertaken by each of these people, and details of further reading may be found at the end of this appendix. For ease of reference here, names are listed alphabetically.

David Ausubel

David Ausubel, an American psychologist working in the 1950s and 1960s, proposed a theory of learning which dealt with what he called 'meaningful verbal learning' and how such learning might be brought about. According to Ausubel, an object has meaning to a learner when it can be related to an idea already present in the mind. Thus learning involves relating new ideas to existing ones. Ausubel's work led him to criticize the discovery approaches advocated by Jerome Bruner (see below) on the grounds that they were time-consuming and there was little research evidence to support the claim that they led to superior learning. Indeed, Ausubel's work contrasts with that of Bruner at a fundamental level: Ausubel sees effective learning arising from presenting learners with organized information (and hence leads him to support expository teaching), whereas Bruner sees effective learning as taking place when the learner develops the organizational framework.

Ausubel's work has been most influential in science education in the work done on constructivism (see Chapter 2).

Jerome Bruner

Jerome Bruner, an American psychologist, used work he began in the 1940s to develop theories about learning which emphasized the ways in which people attempt to makes sense of information. His work led him to propose that a central element of learning was allowing learners themselves to establish patterns and make connections between items of information, or to engage in *discovery learning*. Bruner's work contrasts with that of Jean Piaget (see below) in that Bruner believed that any subject could be taught to any child in some honest form. Critics of Bruner have argued that children need to have reached a certain stage of intellectual maturity to be able to deal with some concepts. Bruner's work has also been criticized by David Ausubel (see above) for its lack of basis in research.

Bruner's ideas about discovery learning were very influential in the design of materials in the science curriculum development projects of the 1960s and 1970s, particularly the early Nuffield projects.

George Kelly

The work of the American psychologist, George Kelly, undertaken in the 1940s and 1950s, has had an increasing impact on educational research. Kelly began work as a school psychologist dealing with problem children. His work in this area led him to conclude that the ways in which individuals perceive their environment, and the people, objects and events in that environment, have a crucial impact on leaning and behaviour. Kelly developed this idea into his theory of personal constructs. Kelly likened people's behaviour to that of scientists, seeking to make sense of and therefore predict events. One product of Kelly's work was the development of the repertory grid technique to analyse behaviour, first in the area of psychiatric counselling and, more recently, in educational settings.

The most significant impact of Kelly's work in science education has been its contribution to the theoretical underpinning of constructivism (see Chapter 2).

Jean Piaget

Jean Piaget's work is the most influential child development theory of the twentieth century and the one which has had most impact on education. Piaget was a Swiss biologist who, in the 1920s, began observing young children as they developed. He used these observations as a basis for proposing a four-stage theory of intellectual development, a key element of which is that a child is unable to grasp particular concepts until a particular stage has been attained. This work led to Piaget being seen as a developmental psychologist.

The four stages Piaget identified are summarized below:

- In the *sensori-motor phase* (birth to about age 2), children learn from information which they gather directly through their senses and physical experiences.
- In the *pre-operational stage* (from about age 2–7), children reason directly from what they perceive, though their reasoning may not always be logical.
- In the *concrete operational stage* (from about age 7–11), thinking becomes characterized by logic and does not require real objects to be to hand. The characteristic of thinking which most significantly marks the transition to this stage is the ability to conserve – to see that quantities such as mass and volume remain constant in operations.
- In the *formal operational stage* (from about age 11 onwards), children become capable of abstract thought and are able to grasp ideas such as those involved in the control of variables and ratio and proportion.

It is also worth noting that one element of Piaget's theory deals with children's thinking in the context of their moral development.

Central to Piaget's stage theory are two key processes in learning:

assimilation (interpreting new learning experiences within existing frameworks) and *accommodation* (modifying existing thinking to take account of new learning experiences). Piaget saw *equilibration*, or maintaining a balance between these two processes, as a key element of learning. Too much assimilation results in no new learning, but too much accommodation causes confusion in thinking. Although Piaget's work has been criticized on the grounds of small sample size, absence of adequate controls and underestimating children's abilities in the earlier stages of development, attempts at replicating his studies in a number of countries have provided evidence which supports the notion of a sequence of intellectual stages through which children pass. There are, however, question-marks over the age at which children attain particular stages. In particular, there is strong evidence to suggest that many children do not attain the formal operational stage until the age of 14, with some not demonstrating formal operational thinking at the age of 16. However, there is also some evidence that cognitive development can, in certain circumstances, be accelerated. Both these pieces of evidence have important messages for school science curricula.

Science education researchers have drawn on Piaget's work to suggest that one of the reasons why many upper secondary age pupils struggle with science ideas is that they have not yet attained a sufficient stage of intellectual development to be able to grasp a particular idea. Piaget's theory also underpins the Cognitive Acceleration through Science Education (CASE) work (see Chapter 3).

Lev Vygotsky

Although Vygotsky's work became increasingly influential in the latter part of the twentieth century, it is worth noting that he was a contemporary of Piaget who worked in the former Soviet Union in the 1920s and 1930s. However, his work did not become well known in other countries until much later.

Vygotsky's work embraced a number of areas and emphasized the roles of culture and language in the development of thinking processes. One of Vygotsky's strong interests was in maximizing intellectual development. This led him to propose that children learn best if placed in an environment which required thinking slightly in advance of their current developmental level, that is requiring children to function in their zone of proximal development (ZPD).

In science education, Vygotsky's ideas have had a particular impact on work on the role of language in science teaching (see Chapter 7) and have also been linked retrospectively to the Cognitive Acceleration through Science Education (CASE) work (see Chapter 3).

Further reading

Wood, D. (1998) *How Children Think and Learn* 2nd edition. Oxford: Blackwell.

Bibliography

Abraham, M. (1998) The learning cycle approach as a strategy for instruction in science. In B. Fraser and K. Tobin (eds) *International Handbook of Science Education*, Part 1, 513–24.

Adamczyk, P., Wilson, M. and Williams, D. (1994) Concept mapping: a multi-level and multi-purpose tool. *School Science Review*, 76 (275), 116–25.

Adams, S. (1991) All in the mind. *School Science Review*, 72 (260), 95–103.

Adey, P. (1987a) Science develops logical thinking – doesn't it? Part 1. Abstract thinking and school science. *School Science Review*, 68 (245), 622–34.

Adey, P. (1987b) Science develops logical thinking – doesn't it? Part 1l. The CASE for science. *School Science Review*, 68 (246), 17–27.

Adey, P. (1988) Cognitive acceleration: review and prospects. *International Journal of Science Education*, 10 (2), 121–34.

Adey, P. (1989) Cognitive acceleration through science education. In S. McLure and P. Davies (eds) *Learning to Think: Thinking to Learn*. Oxford: Pergamon Press.

Adey, P. (2000) Science teaching and the development of intelligence. In M. Monk and J. Osborne (eds) *Good Practice in Science Teaching: What Research has to Say*. Buckingham: Open University Press.

Adey, P. and Shayer, M. (1993) An exploration of long-term far-transfer effects following an extended intervention programme in the high-school science curriculum. *Cognition and Instruction*, 2, (1), 190–220.

Adey, P. and Shayer, M. (1994) *Really Raising Standards: Cognitive Intervention and Academic Achievement*. London: Routledge.

Adey, P., Shayer, M. and Yates, C. (1989) *Thinking Science: The Curriculum Materials of the CASE Project*. London: Nelson.

Ahmed, A. and Pollitt, A. (2000) Observing context in action. Paper presented at the IAEA Conference, Jerusalem, May 2000.

Aikenhead, G. (1994) What is STS teaching? In J. Solomon and G. Aikenhead (eds) *STS Education: International Perspectives on Reform*. New York: Teachers

College Press.

Aikenhead, G. and Ryan, A. (1992) The development of a new instrument: views on Science–Technology–Society (VOSTS). *Science Education*, 76 (4), 477–91.

Alton-Lee, A. Nuthall, G. and Patrick, J. (1993) Reframing classroom research: a lesson from the private world of children. *Harvard Educational Review*, 63 (1), 50–84.

American Association for the Advancement of Science (AAAS) (1967) *Science – A Process Approach (SAPA)*. Washington, DC: AAAS.

American Chemical Society (ACS) (1988) *ChemCom: Chemistry in the Community*. Dubuque, Iowa: Kendall-Hunt.

American Chemical Society (ACS) (1994) *Chemistry in Context*. Dubuque, Iowa: Kendall-Hunt.

Andersson, B. (1986) Pupils' explanations of some aspects of chemical reactions. *Science Education*, 70, 549–63.

Archer, A. and Lloyd, B. (1982) *Sex and Gender*. London: Penguin.

Arnot, M., Gray, J., James, M., Rudduck, J. and Duveen, G. (1998) *Recent Research on Gender and Educational Performance*. London: The Stationery Office.

Assessment of Performance Unit (APU) (1983–5) *Science Reports for Teachers. 1: Science at Age 11. 3: Science at Age 13. 5: Science at Age 15*. London: DES/ Welsh Office (DENI).

Assessment of Performance Unit (APU) (1984 onwards) *Science Reports for Teachers. Numbers 1–11*. London: DE Science.

Assessment of Performance Unit (APU) (1988a) *Science at Age 11: A Review of APU Survey Findings 1980–84*. London: HMSO.

Assessment of Performance Unit (APU) (1988b) *Science at Age 15: A Review of APU Survey Findings 1980–84*. London: HMSO.

Assessment of Performance Unit (APU) (1989a) *National Assessment: The APU Science Approach*. London: HMSO.

Assessment of Performance Unit (APU) (1989b) *Science at Age 13: A Review of APU Survey Findings 1980–84*. London: HMSO.

Association for Science Education (ASE) (1978) *Science for Less Academically Motivated Pupils (the 'LAMP' Project)*. Hatfield: ASE.

Association for Science Education (ASE) (1981) *Education through Science: Policy Statement*. Hatfield: ASE.

Association for Science Education (ASE) (1986) *Science and Technology in Society (SATIS)*. Hatfield: ASE.

Atkinson, P. and Delamont, S. (1976) Mock-ups and cock-ups – the stage management of guided discovery instruction. In M. Hammersley and P. Woods (eds) *The Process of Schooling*. London: Routledge and Kegan Paul.

Ausubel, D. (1968) *Educational Psychology: A Cognitive View*. New York: Holt, Rinehart and Winston.

Bangert-Drowns, R., Kulik, C., Kulik, J. and Morgan, M. (1991) Effects of frequent classroom testing. *Journal of Educational Research*, 85, 89–99.

Banks, P. (1997) Students' understanding of chemical equilibrium. Unpublished MA thesis, University of York.

Barber, M. (2000) A comparison of NEAB and Salters A-level Chemistry: student views and achievements. Unpublished MA thesis, University of York.

Barker, V. and Millar, R. (2000) Students' reasoning about basic chemical thermodynamics and chemical bonding: what changes occur during a context-based post-16 chemistry course? *International Journal of Science Education*, 22 (11), 1171–200.

Barnes, D. (1976) *From Communication to Curriculum*. Harmondsworth: Penguin.

Barnes, D., Britton, J. and Rosen, H. (1969) *Language, the Learner and the School*. Harmondsworth: Penguin.

Barton, R. (1997a) How do computers affect graphical interpretation? *School Science Review*, 79 (287), 55–60.

Barton, R. (1997b) Does data-logging change the nature of children's thinking in experimental work in science? In B. Somekh and N. Davies (eds) *Using Information Technology Effectively in Teaching and Learning*. London: Routledge.

Barton, R. (1998) IT in practical work: assessing and increasing the value-added. In J. Wellington (ed.) *Practical Work in Science: Which Way Now?* London: Routledge.

Beatty, J. and Woolnough, B. (1982a) Why do practical work in 11–13 science? *School Science Review*, 63 (225), 768–70.

Beatty, J. and Woolnough, B. (1982b) Practical work in 11–13 science: the context, type and aims of current practice. *British Educational Research Journal*, 8 (1), 23–31.

Bell, B. (2000) Formative assessment and science education: a model and theorising. In R. Millar, J. Leach and J. Osborne (eds) *Improving Science Education: The Contribution of Research*. Buckingham: Open University Press.

Bell, B. and Cowie, B. (1999) Researching formative assessment. In J. Loughran (ed.) *Researching Teaching: Methodologies and Practices for Understanding Pedagogy*. London: Falmer Press.

Bell, J. (1997) Sex differences in performance in Double Award science GCSE. Paper presented at the British Educational Research Association Annual Conference, 11–14 September 1997, University of York.

Bell, J. (1999) *Doing Your Research Project: A Guide for First-Time Researchers in Education and Social Science*, 3rd edition, Buckingham: Open University Press.

Bennett, J. (2001) Science with attitude: the perennial problem of pupils' responses to science. *School Science Review*, 82 (300), 59–70.

Bennett, J. and Holman, J. (2002) Context-based approaches to the teaching of chemistry: what are they and what are their effects? In J. Gilbert (ed.) *Chemical Education Research-based Practice*. Dordrecht: Kluwer Academic Publishers.

Bentley, D. and Watts, M. (1986) Courting the positive virtues: a case for feminist science. *European Journal of Science Education*, 8 (1), 121–34.

Bentley, D. and Watts, M. (1992) *Communicating in School Science*. London: Falmer Press

Black, P. (1990) APU science – the past and the future. *School Science Review*, 72 (258), 13–28.

Black, P. (1993) Formative and summative assessment by teachers. *Studies in Science Education*, 12, 49–97.

Black, P. (1998) *Testing: Friend or Foe?: Theory and Practice of Assessment and Testing*. London: Falmer Press.

Black, P. and Harrison, C. (2001) Self- and peer-assessment and taking responsibility: the science student's role in formative assessment. *School Science Review*, 83 (302), 43–9.

Black, P. and Solomon, J. (1987) Can pupils use taught analogies for electric current? *School Science Review*, 69 (247), 249–54.

Black, P. and Wiliam, D. (1998a) *Inside the Black Box: Raising Standards through Classroom Assessment*. London: King's College.

Black, P. and Wiliam, D. (1998b) Assessment and classroom learning. *Assessment in Education*, 5 (1), 7–75.

Blaxter, L., Hughes, C. and Tight, M. (1996) *How to Research*. Buckingham: Open University Press.

Bloom, B., Hastings, J. and Maduas, G. (eds) (1971) *Handbook on the Formative and Summative Evaluation of Student Learning*. New York: McGraw Hill.

Borgford, C. (1995) The Salters Science materials: a study of teachers' use and areas of focus. Unpublished DPhil thesis, University of York.

Brasell, H. (1985) The effect of real-time lab graphing on learning graphing representation of distance and time. *Journal of Research in Science Teaching*, 24 (4), 223–28.

Breakwell, G. and Robertson, T. (2001) The gender gap in science attitudes, parental and peer influences: changes between 1987–88 and 1997–98. *Public Understanding of Science*, 10 (1), 72–82.

British Educational Communications and Technology agency (BECTa) (2001a) *Primary Schools of the Future: Achieving Today*. Coventry: BECTa.

British Educational Communications and Technology agency (BECTa) (2001b) *The Secondary School of the Future*. Coventry: BECTa.

Britton, J. (1970) *Language and Learning*. Harmondsworth: Penguin.

Britton, J., Burgess, T., Martin, N., McLeod, A. and Rosen, H. (1975) *The Development of Writing Abilities (11–18)*. London: Macmillan.

Brook, A. and Driver, R. (1984) *Aspects of Secondary Students' Understanding of Energy: Summary Report*. University of Leeds: Children's Learning in Science Project.

Brown, A. (1992) Design experiments: theoretical and methodological challenges in creating complex interventions in classroom settings. *The Journal of the Learning Sciences* 2(2), 141–78.

Brown, G. and Desforges, C. (1979) *Piaget's Theory: A Psychological Critique*. London: Routledge Kegan Paul.

Brown, S., Collins, A. and Duguid, P. (1989) Situated cognition and the culture of learning. *Educational Researcher*, 18 (1), 32–41.

Bryce, T., Mecalfe, J., MacGregor, J., Weston, R. and Robertson, I. (1983) *Techniques for the Assessment of Practical Skills (TAPS) in Science. Teachers' Guide*. London: Heinemann.

Bulman, L. (1985) *Teaching Language and Study Skills in Secondary Science*. London: Heinemann Educational Books.

Burton, W., Holman, J., Pilling, G. and Waddington, D. (1994) *Salters Advanced Chemistry*. Oxford: Heinemann.

Butler, J. (1995) Teachers judging standards in senior science subjects: fifteen years of the Queensland experience. *Studies in Science Education*, 26, 135–57.

Butler, R. (1988) Enhancing and undermining intrinsic motivation: the effects of task-involving and ego-involving evaluation on interest and performance. *British Journal of Educational Psychology*, 58, 1–14.

Bybee, R. (ed.) (1985) *Science–Technology–Society. 1985 NSTA Yearbook*. Washington, DC: National Science Teachers Association.

Byrne, M., Johnstone, A. and Pope, A. (1994) Reasoning in science: a language problem revealed? *School Science Review*, 75 (272), 103–7.

Campbell, B., Hogarth, S. and Lubben, F. (2000a) Contextualising the physics curriculum: learners' perceptions of interest and helpfulness. Paper presented at the Annual Conference of the British Educational research Association (BERA), Cardiff, September 2000.

Campbell, B., Lubben, F. and Dlamini, Z. (2000b) Learning science through contexts: helping pupils make sense of everyday situations. *International Journal of Science Education*, 22 (3) 239–52.

Campbell, R., Lazonby, J., Millar, R., Nicolson, P., Ramsden, J. and Waddington, D. (1994) Science: the Salters approach: a case study of the process of large scale curriculum development. *Science Education*, 78 (5), 415–47.

Carey, S. (1985) *Conceptual Change in Childhood*. Cambridge, MA: MIT Press.

Carmichael, P., Driver, R., Holding, B., Phillips, I., Twigger, D. and Watts, M. (1990) *Research on Students' Conceptions in Science: A Bibliography*. University of Leeds: Children's Learning in Science Research Group.

Carson, S. (1997) The use of spreadsheets in science – an overview. *School Science Review*, 79 (287), 69–80.

Cassels, J. and Johnstone, A. (1985) *Words that Matter in Science*. London: Royal Society of Chemistry.

Cathcart, W. (1990) Effects of LOGO instruction on cognitive style. *Journal of Educational Computing Research*, 6 (2), 231–42.

Chambers, D. (1983) Stereotypic images of the scientist: the draw-a-scientist test. *Science Education*, 67 (2), 255–65.

Champagne, A., Klopfer, L., Desena, A. and Squires, B. (1981) Structural representations of students' knowledge before and after science instruction. *Journal of Research in Science Teaching*, 18 (2), 97–111.

Chemical Industry Education Centre (CIEC) (1992) *Farming Tales*. York: University of York.

Chemical Industry Education Centre (CIEC) (1996) *Room for Improvement*. York: University of York.

Cheng, Y., Payne, J. and Witherspoon, S. (1995) *Science and Mathematics in Full-time Education after 16: England and Wales Youth Cohort Study*. Sheffield: Department for Education and Employment.

Children's Learning in Science Project (CLISP) (1984, 1985) *Full Reports and Summary Reports on Energy, Plant Nutrition, Elementary Ideas in Chemistry*.

University of Leeds: Children's Learning in Science Project.

Clackson, S. and Wright, D. (1992) An appraisal of practical work in science education. *School Science Review*, 74 (266), 39–42.

Claxton, G. (1993) Mini-theories: a preliminary model for learning in science. In P. Black and A. Lucas (eds) *Children's Informal Ideas in Science*. London: Routledge.

Collins, A. (1993) Towards a design science of education. In E. Scanlon and T. O'Shea (eds) *New Directions in Educational Technology*. New York: Springer Verlag.

Collins, J., Hammond, M. and Wellington, J. (1997) *Teaching and Learning with Multimedia*. London: Routledge.

Comber, L. and Keeves, J. (1973) *Science Education in Nineteen Countries: An Empirical Study*. London: John Wiley.

Coolican, H. (1995) *Introduction to Research Methods and Statistics in Psychology*. Bath: Hodder & Stoughton.

Cosgrove, M. and Osborne, R. (1985) Lesson frameworks for changing children's ideas. In R. Osborne and P. Freyberg (eds) *Learning in Science*. Auckland: Heinemann.

Cox, M. (2000) Information and communications technologies: their role and value for science education. In M. Monk and J. Osborne (eds) *Good Practice in Science Teaching: What Research has to Say*. Buckingham: Open University Press.

Craig, J. and Ayers, D. (1988) Does primary science affect girls' and boys' interest in secondary science? *School Science Review*, 69 (3), 417–26.

Crossman, M. (1987) Teachers' interactions with girls and boys in science lessons. In A. Kelly (ed.) *Science for Girls?* Buckingham: Open University Press.

Dale, R. (1974) *Mixed or Single-sex Schools?* London: Routledge and Kegan Paul.

Daugherty, R. (1995) *National Curriculum Assessment: A Review of Policy 1987–94*. London: Falmer Press.

Davies, F. and Greene, T. (1984) *Reading for Learning in the Sciences*. Edinburgh: Oliver Boyd.

Dawes, C. (1996) How does teaching in single-sex groups affect the way pupils view science? Unpublished MA thesis, University of York.

Daws, N. and Singh, B. (1996) Formative assessment: to what extent is its potential to enhance pupils' science being realised? *School Science Review*, 77 (281), 93–100.

Daws, N. and Singh, B. (1999) Formative assessment strategies in secondary science. *School Science Review*, 80 (293), 71–8.

Dawson, C. (2000) Upper primary boys' and girls' interests in science: have they changed since 1980? *International Journal of Science Education*, 22 (6), 557–70.

Denscombe, M. (1998) *The Good Research Guide*. Buckingham: Open University Press.

Department for Education and Employment (DfEE) (1987) *Statistical Bulletin 3/97*. London: HMSO.

Department for Education and Employment (DfEE) (1995) *Value Added in Education*. London: DfEE.

Department for Education and Employment/Welsh Office (DfEE/WO) (1995) *Science in the National Curriculum.* London: QCA.

Department for Education and Employment (DfEE) (1998) *Survey of Information and Communications Technology in Schools, Statistical Bulletin No. 11/98.* London: The Stationery Office.

Department for Education and Skills (DfES) (2001) *Statistical Bulletin 36/ 2001.* London: The Stationery Office.

Department of Education and Science (DES) (1968) *Enquiry into the Flow of Candidates in Science and Technology into Higher Education* (the Dainton Report). London: HMSO.

Department of Education and Science (DES) (1975) *A Language for Life* (the Bullock Report). London: HMSO.

Department of Education and Science (DES) (1975) *Curricular Differences for Boys and Girls. Education Survey 21.* London: HMSO.

Department of Education and Science (DES) (1979) *Aspects of Secondary Education: A Survey by HMI.* London: HMSO.

Department of Education and Science (DES) (1985) *Science 5–16: A Statement of Policy.* London: HMSO.

Department of Education and Science/Welsh Office (DES/WO) (1988) *National Curriculum Task Group on Assessment and Testing (TGAT).* London: DES/WO.

Department of Trade and Industry (DTI) (1997) *Breaking the Mould: An Assessment of Successful Strategies for Attracting Girls into Science, Engineering and Technology.* London: DTI.

diSessa, A. (1988) Knowledge in pieces. In D. Gentler and A. Stevens (eds) *Mental Models.* Hillsdale, NJ: Erlbaum.

diSessa, A. and Sherin, B. (1998) What changes in conceptual change? *International Journal of Science Education,* 20 (10), 1155–91.

Ditchfield, C. and Scott, L. (1987) *Better Science: For Both Girls and Boys.* Oxford: Heinemann/ASE.

Dlamini, B., Lubben, F. and Campbell, B. (1994) Teacher growth through curriculum renewal: an African experience. In M. Glencross (ed.) *Proceedings of the Second Annual Meeting of the Southern African Association for Research in Mathematics and Science Education (SAARMSE).* Westville, South Africa: University of Durban.

Donaldson, M. (1978) *Children's Minds.* London: Fontana.

Donnelly, J., Squires, A., Jenkins, E., Laws, P. and Welford, G. (1996) *Investigations by Order.* Nafferton: Studies in Education Ltd.

Driver, R. (1975) The name of the game. *School Science Review,* 56 (197), 800–4.

Driver, R. (1983) *The Pupil as Scientist?* Buckingham: Open University Press.

Driver, R. (1985) Beyond appearances: the conservation of matter. In R. Driver, E. Guesne and A. Tiberghien (eds) *Children's Ideas in Science.* Buckingham: Open University Press.

Driver, R. and Bell, B. (1986) Students' thinking and the learning of science: a constructivist view. *School Science Review,* 67 (240), 443–56.

Driver, R. and Erickson, G. (1983) Theories-in-action: some theoretical and empirical issues in the study of students' conceptual frameworks in science. *Studies in Science Education,* 10, 37–60.

Driver, R. and Oldham, V. (1986) A constructivist approach to curriculum development. *Studies in Science Education*, 13, 105–22.

Driver, R., Guesne, E. and Tiberghien, A. (eds) (1985) *Children's Ideas in Science*. Buckingham: Open University Press.

Driver, R., Squires, A., Rushworth, P. and Wood-Robinson, V. (eds) (1994a) *Making Sense of Secondary Science: Research into Children's Ideas*. London: Routledge.

Driver, R., Asoko, H., Leach, J., Mortimer, E. and Scott, P. (1994b) Constructing scientific knowledge in the classroom. *Educational Researcher*, 23 (7), 5–12.

Dutch Physics Curriculum Development Project (Projekt Leerpakketontwikkeling Natuurkunde (PLON)). (1988) Utrecht: Rijksuniversteit Utrecht, Vagroep Natuurkunde-Didactiek.

Edwards, J. and Power, C. (1990) Role of laboratory work in a national junior secondary science project: Australian science education project (ASEP). In E. Hegarty-Hazel (ed.) *The Student Laboratory and the Science Curriculum*. London: Routledge.

Eggleston, J., Galton, M. and Jones, M. (1976) *Processes and Products of Science Teaching*. London: Macmillan.

Eijkelhof, H. and Kortland, K. (1988) Broadening the aims of physics education. In P. Fensham (ed.) *Development and Dilemmas in Science Education*. New York: Falmer Press.

Elwood, J. and Comber, C. (1996) Gender differences in examinations at 18+: final report. London: University of London Institute for Education.

Engel-Clough, E., Driver, R. and Wood-Robinson, C. (1987) How do children's scientific ideas change over time? *School Science Review*, 69 (247), 255–67.

Fairbrother, B., Black, P. and Gill, P. (1995) *Teachers Assessing Pupils: Lessons from the Science Classroom*. Hatfield: Association for Science Education.

Fairbrother, R. (1991) Principles of practical assessment. In B. Woolnough (ed.) *Practical Science*. Buckingham: Open University Press.

Fensham, P. (1988) Approaches to the teaching of STS in science education. *International Journal of Science Education*, 10 (4), 346–56.

Fensham, P., Garrard, J. and West, L. (1981) The use of cognitive mapping in teaching and learning strategies. *Research in Science Education*, 11, 121–9.

Fitz-Gibbon, C. and Vincent, L. (1994) *Candidates' Performance in Public Examinations in Mathematics and Science. A Report for the Schools Curriculum and Assessment Authority (SCAA)*. Newcastle: University of Newcastle upon Tyne.

Foulds, K., Gott, R. and Feasey, R. (1992) *Investigative Work in Science*. Durham: University of Durham.

Foxman, D. (1992) *Learning Mathematics and Science: The Second IEAP in England*. Windsor: National Foundation for Educational Research (NFER).

Fuerstein, R., Rand, Y., Hoffman, M. and Miller, M. (1980) *Instrumental Enrichment: An Intervention Programme for Cognitive Modifiability*. Baltimore: University Park Press.

Gardner, P. (1972) *Words in Science*. Melbourne: Australian Science Education Project.

Gardner, P. (1974) Language difficulties of science students. *Australian Science Teachers' Journal*, 20 (1), 63–76.

Gardner, P. (1975) Attitudes to science: a review. *Studies in Science Education*, 2, 1–41.

Gardner, P. (1977) Logical connectives in science – a summary of the findings. *Research in Science Education*, 7, 9–24.

Gardner, P. and Gauld, C. (1990) Labwork and students' attitudes. In E. Hegarty-Hazel (ed.) *The Student Laboratory and the Science Curriculum*. London: Routledge.

Garrett, R. and Roberts, I. (1982) Demonstration versus small group practical work in science education: a critical review of studies since 1900. *Studies in Science Education*, 9, 109–46.

Gauld, C. and Hukins, A. (1980) Scientific attitudes: a review. *Studies in Science Education*, 7, 129–61.

Gee, B. and Clackson, S. (1992) The origin of practical work in the English school science curriculum. *School Science Review*, 73 (265), 79–83.

George, J. and Lubben, F. (2002) Facilitating teachers' professional growth through their involvement in creating context-based materials in science. *International Journal of Educational Development*, 22(6), 657–70.

Gibson, A. and Asthana, S. (1998) Schools, pupils, and examination results: contextualising school performance. *British Educational Research Journal*, 24 (3), 269–82.

Gilbert, J. (2001) Science and its 'other': looking underneath 'woman' and 'science' for new directions in research on gender and science education. *Gender and Education*, 13 (3), 291–305.

Gilbert, J., Osborne, R. and Fensham, P. (1982) Children's science and its consequences for teaching. *Science Education*, 66 (4), 623–33.

Gilbert, J., Watts, M. and Osborne, R. (1985) Eliciting student views using an interview-about-instances technique. In L. West and L. Pines (eds) *Cognitive Structure and Conceptual Change*. London: Academic Press.

Gipps, C. and Murphy, P. (1994) *A Fair Test?: Assessment, Achievement and Equity*. Buckingham: Open University Press.

Gipps, C. and Stobart, G. (1993) *Assessment: A Teachers' Guide to the Issues*, 2nd edition. London: Hodder, Stoughton.

Gitomer, D. and Duschl, R. (1998) Emerging issues and practices in science assessment. In B. Fraser and K. Tobin (eds) *International Handbook of Science Education*, Part 2, 791–810.

Glynn, S., Duit, R. and Thiele, R. (1995) Teaching science with analogies: a strategy for constructing knowledge. In S. Glynn and R. Duit (eds) *Learning Science in Schools: Research Reforming Practice*. Hillsdale, NJ: Lawrence Erlbaum.

Goldstein, G. (1997) *Information Technology in English Schools: A Commentary on Inspection Findings 1995–1996*. London: The Stationery Office.

Gorard, S., Rees, G. and Salisbury, J. (2001) Investigating the patterns of differentiated attainment of boys and girls at school. *British Educational Research Journal*, 27 (2), 125–39.

Gott, R. and Duggan, S. (1995) *Investigative Work in the Science Curriculum*. Buckingham: Open University Press.

Guesne, E. (1985) Light. In R. Driver, E. Guesne and A. Tiberghien (eds) *Children's Ideas in Science*. Buckingham: Open University Press.

Gunstone, R. (1991) Reconstructing theory from practical experience. In B. Woolnough (ed.) *Practical Science*. Buckingham: Open University Press.

Hadden, R. and Johnstone, A. (1983) Secondary school pupils' attitudes to science: the year of erosion. *European Journal of Science Education*, 5 (3), 309–18.

Halliday, M. and Martin, J. (1993) (eds) *Writing Science: Literacy and Discursive Power*. Pittsburgh, PA: University of Pittsburgh Press.

Hand, B., Prain, V., Lawrence, C. and Yore, L. (1999) A writing in science framework designed to enhance science literacy. *International Journal of Science Education*, 21 (10), 1021–35.

Harding, J. (1979) Sex differences in performance in examinations at 16+. *Physics Education*, 14 (5), 280–4.

Harding, J. (1981) Sex differences in science examinations. In A. Kelly (ed.) *The Missing Half*. Manchester: Manchester University Press.

Harding, J. (1983) *Switched Off: The Science Education of Girls*. York: Longman.

Harding, J. (1986) *Perspectives on Gender and Science*. London: Falmer Press.

Harding, J. (1996) Science in a masculine straight-jacket. In L. Parker, L. Rennie and B. Fraser (eds) *Gender, Science and Mathematics: Shortening the Shadow*. Dordrecht: Kluwer Academic Publishers.

Harding, J. and Sutoris, M. (1987) An object-relations account of the differential involvement of girls in science and technology. In A. Kelly (ed.) *Science for Girls?* Buckingham: Open University Press.

Harding, S. (1991) *Whose Science? Whose Knowledge? Thinking from Women's Lives*. New York: Cornell University Press.

Hargreaves, D. (1996) *Teaching as a Research-based Profession: Possibilities and Prospects. Teacher Training Agency Annual Lecture*. London: Teacher Training Agency (TTA).

Hargreaves, D. (1999) Revitalising educational research: lessons from the past and proposals for the future. *Cambridge Journal of Education*, 29 (2), 239–49.

Harlen, W. (1999) *Effective Teaching of Science: A Review of Research*. Edinburgh: Scottish Council for Research in Education.

Harlen, W. (2001) The assessment of scientific literacy in the OECD/PISA project. *Studies in Science Education*, 36, 79–104.

Harris, B. (1994) The future curriculum with IT: implications for science education. *School Science Review*, 76 (275), 15–25.

Hartley, J. (1994) Multimedia views of science education. *Studies in Science Education*, 23, 75–87.

Havard, N. (1996) Students' attitudes to studying A-level sciences. *Public Understanding of Science*, 5 (4), 321–30.

Head, J. (1980) A model to link personality characteristics to a preference for science. *European Journal of Science Education*, 2 (3), 295–300.

Head, J. (1985) *The Personal Response to Science.* Cambridge: Cambridge University Press.

Head, J. (1996) Gender identity and cognitive style. In P. Murphy and C. Gipps (eds) *Equity in the Classroom: Towards Effective Pedagogy for Girls and Boys.* Buckingham: Open University Press.

Head, J. (1999) *Understanding the Boys: Issues of Behaviour and Achievement.* London: Falmer Press.

Head, J. and Ramsden, J. (1990) Gender, psychological type and science. *International Journal of Science Education*, 12 (1), 115–21.

Head, J. and Shayer, M. (1980) Loevinger's ego development measures: a new research tool? *British Educational Research Journal*, 6 (1), 21–7.

Hegarty-Hazel, E. (ed.) (1990) *The Student Laboratory and the Science Curriculum.* London: Routledge.

Henderson, J. and Wellington J. (1998) Lowering the language barrier. *School Science Review*, 79 (288), 35–46.

Hendley, D., Parkinson, J., Stables, H. and Tanner, H. (1995) Gender differences in pupil attitudes to the National Curriculum foundation subjects of English, mathematics, science and technology in Key Stage 3 in South Wales. *Educational Studies*, 21 (1), 85–97.

Henerson, M., Lyons Morris, L. and Taylor Fitz-Gibbon, C. (1987) *How to Measure Attitudes.* New York: Sage.

Hennesey, S., Twigger, D., Driver, R., O'Shea, T., O'Malley, C., Byard, M., Draper, S., Hartley, R., Mohamed, R. and Scanlon, E. (1995) A classroom intervention using computer augmented curriculum for mechanics. *International Journal of Science Education*, 17 (2), 189–206.

Heywood, F. and Miller, K. (2001) Boxed in or coming out?: on the treatment of science, technology and gender in educational research. *Gender and Education*, 13 (3), 237–42.

Hildebrand, G. (1996) Redefining achievement. In P. Murphy and C. Gipps (eds) *Equity in the Classroom: Towards Effective Pedagogy for Girls and Boys.* Buckingham: Open University Press.

Hillage, L., Pearson, R., Anderson, A. and Tamkin, P. (1998) *Excellence in Research on Schools.* Brighton: Institute for Employment Studies.

Hodson, D. (1990) A critical look: at practical work in school science. *School Science Review*, 71 (256), 33–40.

Hodson, D. (1992) Redefining and reorienting practical work in school science. *School Science Review*, 73 (264), 65–78.

Hodson, D. (1993) Re-thinking the old ways: towards a more critical approach to practical work in school science. *Studies in Science Education*, 22, 85–142.

Hodson, D. (1998) Is this really what scientists do?: Seeking a more authentic science in and beyond the school laboratory. In J. Wellington (ed.) *Practical Work in Science: Which Way Now?* London: Routledge.

Hodson, D. and Hodson, J. (1998) From constructivism to social constructivism: a Vygotskian perspective on teaching and learning in science. *School Science Review*, 79 (289), 33–41.

Hofstein, A., Aikenhead, G. and Riquarts, K. (1988) Discussions over STS at the Fourth IOSTE Symposium. *International Journal of Science Education*, 10 (4), 357–66.

Howe, C. (1999) *Gender and Classroom Interaction: A Research Review*. Edinburgh: Scottish Council for Research in Science Education.

Hunt, A. and Millar, R. (eds) (2000) *AS Science for Public Understanding*. Oxford: Heinemann Educational.

Hyde, J. (1981) How large are cognitive gender differences? *American Psychologist*, 36 (8), 892–901.

IEA (1988) *Science Achievement in Seventeen Countries*. Oxford: Pergamon.

Ingle, R. and Shayer, M. (1971) Conceptual demands in Nuffield 'O' level chemistry. *Education in Chemistry*, 8, 182–3.

Inhelder, B. and Piaget, J. (1958) *The Growth of Logical Thinking from Childhood to Adolescence*. New York: Basic Books.

Institute of Electrical Engineers (IEE) (1994) *Views of Science amongst Students, Teachers and Parents*. London: Institute of Electrical Engineers.

Jackson, C. (2002a) Can single-sex classes in co-educational schools enhance the learning experiences of girls and/or boys?: an exploration of pupils' perceptions. *British Educational Research Journal*, 28 (1), 37–48.

Jackson, C. (2002b) 'Laddishness' as a self-worth protection strategy. *Gender and Education*, 14 (1), 2002.

Jackson, R. and Bazley, M. (1997) Science education and the Internet – cutting through the hype. *School Science Review*, 79 (287), 41–4.

Jenkins, E. (1995) When is a policy not a policy?: School-based assessment of practical work at 16+. *International Journal of Science Education*, 17 (5), 555–63.

Jenkins, E. (1998) The schooling of laboratory science. In J. Wellington (ed.) *Practical Work in Science: Which Way Now?* London: Routledge.

Jenkins, E. (2000a) Research in science education: time for a health check? *Studies in Science Education*, 35, 1–26.

Jenkins, E. (2000b) Constructivism in school science education: powerful model or the most dangerous intellectual tendency? *Science and Education*, 9, 599–610.

Jenkins, E. (2001) Research in science education in Europe: retrospect and prospect. In H. Behrendt, H. Dahncke, R. Duit, W. Gräber, M. Komorek, A. Kross and P. Reiska (eds) *Research in Science Education – Past, Present and Future*. Dordrecht: Kluwer Academic Publishers.

Jesson, D. (1997) *Value Added Measures of School GCSE Performance*. London: Department for Education and Employment (DfEE).

Johnson, R. (1979) Readability. *School Science Review*, 60 (212), 562–8.

Johnson, S. (1987) Gender differences in science: parallels in interest, experience and performance. *International Journal of Science Education*, 9 (4), 467–81.

Johnson, S. and Murphy, P. (1986) Girls and physics. *APU Occasional Paper No. 4*. London: HMSO.

Jones, C. (2000) The role of language in the teaching and learning of science. In M. Monk and J. Osborne (eds) *Good Practice in Science Teaching: What Research has to Say*. Buckingham: Open University Press.

Jones, M. and Gott, R. (1998) Cognitive acceleration through science education: alternative perspectives. *International Journal of Science Education*, 20 (7), 755–68.

Jörg, T. and Wubbels, Th. (1987) Physics a problem for girls or girls a problem for physics? *International Journal of Science Education*, 9 (2), 297–308.

Kearsey, J. and Turner, S. (1999) Evaluating textbooks: the role of genre analysis. *Research in Science and Technological Education*, 17 (1), 35–43.

Keeves, J. (1992) *Learning Science in a Changing World: The Contribution of IEA Research to a World Perspective*. Amsterdam: International Association for the Evaluation of Educational Achievement (IEA).

Keiler, L. and Woolnough, B. (2002) Practical work in school science: the dominance of assessment. *School Science Review*, 83 (304), 83–8.

Keith, A. (1997) CASE in question: an evaluation of the problems associated with an innovation. Unpublished MA thesis, University of York.

Keller, E. and Longino, H. (eds) (1996) *Feminism and Science*. Oxford: Oxford University Press.

Kelly, A. (1978) *Girls and Science: An International Study of Sex Differences in School Science Achievement*. Stockholm: Almqvist and Wiskell.

Kelly, A. (1981) *The Missing Half: Girls and Science Education*. Manchester: Manchester University Press.

Kelly, A. (1985) The construction of masculine science. *British Journal of Sociology of Education*, 6 (2), 133–54.

Kelly, A. (1986) The development of children's attitudes to science. *European Journal of Science Education*, 8 (4), 399–412.

Kelly, A. (1987) *Science for Girls?* Buckingham: Open University Press.

Kelly, G. (1955) *The Psychology of Personal Constructs*. New York: Norton.

Kelly, G. (1971) Ontological acceleration. In B. Maher (ed.) *The Selected Papers of George Kelly*. London: Wiley.

Kempa, R. and Dias, M. (1990a) Students' motivational traits and preferences for different instructional modes in science education. Part 1: Students' motivational traits. *International Journal of Science Education*, 12 (2), 195–203.

Kempa, R. and Dias, M. (1990b) Students' motivational traits and preferences for different instructional modes in science education. Part 2. *International Journal of Science Education*, 12 (2), 205–16.

Kenway, J. and Gough, A. (1998) Gender and science education: a review 'with attitude'. *Studies in Science Education*, 31, 1–29.

Kerr, J. (1963) *Practical Work in School Science*. Leicester: Leicester University Press.

Key, M. (1998) Student perceptions of chemical industry: influences of course syllabi, teachers, firsthand experience. Unpublished DPhil thesis, University of York.

Keys, C. (1999) Revitalising instruction in scientific genres: connecting knowledge production with writing to learn in science. *Science Education*, 83 (2), 115–30.

Keys, W. and Foxman, D. (1989) *A World of Differences: A United Kingdom Perspective on an International Assessment of Mathematics and Science*. Windsor: National Foundation for Educational Research (NFER).

Keys, W., Harris, S. and Fernandes, C. (1996) *Third International Mathematics and Science Study. First National Report, Part 1.* Windsor: National Foundation for Educational Research (NFER).

King's College/University of Liverpool (1992) *Primary SPACE Project Research Reports.* Liverpool: Liverpool University Press.

Klaassen, C. and Lijnse, P. (1996) Interpreting students' and teachers' discourse in science classes: an underestimated problem? *Journal of Research in Science Teaching*, 33 (2), 115–34.

Knutton, S. (1983) Chemistry textbooks – are they readable? *Education in Chemistry*, 20 (3), 100–5.

Koballa, T. (1984) Designing a Likert-type scale to assess attitude towards energy conservation. *Journal of Research in Science Teaching*, 20 (7), 709–23.

Koufetta-Menicou, C. and Scaife, J. (2000) Teachers' questions – types and significance in science education. *School Science Review*, 81 (296), 79–84.

Kreinberg, N. and Lewis, S. (1996) The politics and practice of equity: experiences from both sides of the pacific. In L. Parker, L. Rennie and B. Fraser (eds) *Gender, Science and Mathematics: Shortening the Shadow.* Dordrecht: Kluwer Academic Publishers.

Kress, G., Jewitt, C., Ogborn, J. and Tsatsarelis, C. (2001) *Multimodal Teaching and Learning: The Rhetorics of the Science Classroom.* London: Continuum.

Krynowski, B. (1988) Problems in assessing students attitude in science education: a partial solution. *Science Education*, 72 (4) 575–84.

Kyriacou, C. (1998) *Essential Teaching Skills*, 2nd edition. Cheltenham: Stanley Thornes.

LaPointe, A., Mead, N. and Askew, J. (1992) *Learning Science: The Second International Assessment of Educational Progress.* Princeton, NJ: Educational Testing Service.

LaPointe, A., Mead, N. and Phillips, G. (1989) *A World of Differences: An International Assessment of Mathematics and Science.* Princeton, NJ: Educational Testing Service.

Lave, J. and Wenger, E. (1991) *Situated Learning: Legitimate Peripheral Participation.* Cambridge, MA: Cambridge University Press.

Lazonby, J., Nicolson, P. and Waddington, D. (1992) Teaching and learning the Salters way. *Journal of Chemical Education*, 69 (11), 899–902.

Leach, J. and Paulsen, A. (eds) (1999) *Practical Work in Science Education: Recent Research Studies.* Copenhagen: Roskilde University Press.

Leach, J. and Scott, P. (1995) The demands of learning science concepts: issues of theory and practice. *School Science Review*, 76 (277), 47–51.

Leach, J. and Scott, P. (2000) Children's thinking, learning, teaching and constructivism. In M. Monk and J. Osborne (eds) *Good Practice in Science Teaching: What Research has to Say.* Buckingham: Open University Press.

Leas, M. and Pachler, N. (1999) *Learning to Teach Using ICT in the Secondary School.* London: Routledge.

Leaver, J. (1999) The CITRUS project: perceptions of web-based industrial chemistry teaching resources and of implementing on-line questionnaires. Unpublished MA thesis, University of York.

Lefrançois, G. (1968) A treatment hierarchy for the acceleration of conservation of substance. *Canadian Journal of Psychology*, 22, 277–84.

Lemke, J. (1990) *Talking Science*. New York: Ablex Publishing Corporation.

Leo, E. and Galloway, D. (1995) Conceptual links between cognitive acceleration through science education and motivational style: a critique of Shayer and Adey. *International Journal of Science Education*, 18 (1), 35–49.

Lewis, J. (1981) *Science in Society*. London: Heinemann Educational Books.

Linn, M. and Hyde, J. (1989) Gender, mathematics and science. *Educational Researcher*, 18, 17–27.

Lock, R. (1988) A history of practical work in school science and its assessment, 1860–1986. *School Science Review*, 69 (250), 115–19.

Loevinger, J. (1976) *Ego Development: Conceptions and Theories*. New York: Jossey Bass.

Long, R. (1991) Readability for science: some factors which may affect students' understanding of worksheets etc. *School Science Review*, 73 (262), 21–33.

Lubben, F., and Millar, R. (1996) Children's ideas about the reliability of experimental data. *International Journal of Science Education*, 18 (8), 955–68.

Lubben, F. Campbell, B. and Dlamini, B. (1996) Contextualising science teaching in Swaziland: some student reactions. *International Journal of Science Education*, 18 (3), 311–20.

Maccoby, E. and Jacklin, C. (1975) *The Psychology of Sex Differences*. London: Wiley.

Mali, G. and Howe, A. (1979) Development of Earth and gravity concepts amongst Nepali children. *Science Education*, 63 (5), 685–91.

Manthorpe, C. (1982) Men's science or women's science or science?: some issues relating to the study of girls' science education. *Studies in Science Education*, 9, 65–80.

Markham, K., Mintzes, J. and Jones, M. (1994) The concept map as a research and evaluation tool: evidence of validity. *Journal of Research in Science Teaching*, 31 (1), 91–101.

Martin, J. (1993) Literacy in science: learning to handle text as technology. In M. Halliday and J. Martin (eds) *Writing Science: Literacy and Discursive Power*. Pittsburgh, PA: University of Pittsburgh Press.

Matthews, B. (1996) Drawing scientists. *Gender and Education*, 8 (2), 231–43.

Matthews, M. (1994) *Science Teaching. The Role of History and Philosophy of Science*. London: Routledge.

Mayoh, K. and Knutton, S. (1997) Using out-of-school experiences in science lessons: reality or rhetoric? *International Journal of Science Education*, 19 (7), 849–67.

McClelland, J. (1984) Alternative frameworks: interpretation of evidence. *European Journal of Science Education*, 6 (1), 1–6.

McCloskey, M. (1983) Naïve theories of motion, In D. Gentner and A. Stevens (eds) *Mental Models*. Hillsdale, NJ: Lawrence Erlbaum Associates.

McEwen, A., Knipe, D. and Gallagher, T. (1997) The impact of single-sex and co-educational schooling on participation and achievement in science: a 10-

year perspective. *Research in Science and Technological Education*, 15 (2), 223–33.

McKinsey and Co. (1997) *The Future of Information Technology in UK Schools.* London: McKinsey and Co.

Mehan, H. (1979) *Learning Lessons: Social Organisation in the Classroom.* Cambridge, MA: Harvard University Press.

Merzyn, G. (1987) The language of school science. *International Journal of Science Education*, 9 (4), 483–9.

Meyerson, M., Ford, M., Jones, W. and Ward, M. (1991) Science vocabulary knowledge of third and fifth grade students. *Science Education*, 10 (5), 419–28.

Millar, R. (1998) Rhetoric and reality: what practical work in science is *really* for. In J. Wellington (ed.) *Practical Work in Science: Which Way Now?* London: Routledge.

Millar, R. (1989a) Constructive criticisms. *International Journal of Science Education*, 11 (5), 587–96.

Millar, R. (1989b) What is 'scientific method' and can it be taught? In J. Wellington (ed.) *Skills and Processes in Science Education.* London: Routledge.

Millar, R. and Driver, R. (1987) Beyond processes. *Studies in Science Education*, 14, 33–62.

Millar, R. and Lubben, F. (1996) Knowledge and action: students' understanding of the knowledge and procedures of scientific enquiry. In G. Welford, J. Osborne and P. Scott (eds) *Science Education in Europe: Proceedings of the first conference of the European Science Education Research Association (ESERA).* London: Falmer.

Millar, R. and Osborne, J. (eds) (1998) *Beyond 2000: Science Education for the Future.* London: King's College.

Millar, R., Le Maréchal, J.-F. and Tiberghien, A. (1999) 'Mapping' the domain: varieties of practical work. In J. Leach and A. Paulsen (eds) *Practical Work in Science Education: Recent Research Studies.* Copenhagen: Roskilde University Press.

Millar, R., Leach, J. and Osborne, J. (2000) *Improving Science Education: The Contribution of Research.* Buckingham: Open University Press.

Millar, R., Gott, R., Lubben, F. and Duggan, S. (1994) Investigating in the school science laboratory: conceptual and procedural knowledge and their influence on performance. *Research Papers in Education*, 9 (2), 207–48.

Mokros, J. and Tinker, R. (1987) The impact of microcomputer-based labs on pupils' abilities to interpret graphs. *Journal of Research in Science Teaching*, 24 (4), 369–83.

Mortimer, E. and Scott, P. (2000) Analysing discourse in science classrooms. In R. Millar, J. Leach and J. Osborne (eds) *Improving Science Education: The Contribution of Research.* Buckingham: Open University Press.

Mortimore, P. (2000) Does educational research matter? *British Educational Research Journal*, 26 (1), 3–24.

Munby, H. (1990) Attitude: invited commentary. *Science Education*, 74 (3), 377–81.

Murphy, P. (1991) Gender differences in pupils' reactions to practical work. In B. Woolnough (ed.) *Practical Science.* Buckingham: Open University Press.

Murphy, P. (1993) Assessment and gender. In J. Bourne (ed.) *Thinking through Primary Practice.* London: Routledge.

Murphy, P. (1996) Assessment practices and gender in science. In L. Parker, L. Rennie and B. Fraser (eds) *Gender, Science and Mathematics: Shortening the Shadow.* Dordrecht: Kluwer Academic Publishers.

Murphy, P. (1999) Supporting collaborative learning: a gender dimension. In P. Murphy (ed.) *Learners, Learning and Assessment.* London: Paul Chapman and the Open University.

Murphy, P. (2000) Are gender differences in achievement avoidable? In J. Sears and P. Sorensen (eds) *Issues in Science Teaching.* London: RoutledgeFalmer.

Murphy, P. and Gipps, C. (1996) (eds) *Equity in the Classroom: Towards Effective Pedagogy for Girls and Boys.* Buckingham: Open University Press.

Murphy, R. (1982) Sex difference is objective test performance. *British Journal of Educational Psychology,* 52, 213–19.

Murphy, R. (1997) Drawing outrageous conclusions from assessment results: where will it all end? *British Journal of Curriculum and Assessment,* 7 (2), 32–4.

Nagy, P. and Griffiths, A. (1982) Limitations of recent research relating Piaget's theory to adolescent thought. *Review of Educational Research,* 52, 513–56.

Nakhleh, M. and Krajcik, J. (1993) A protocol analysis of the influence of technology on students' actions, verbal commentary and thought processes during the performance of acid-base titrations. *Journal of Research in Science Teaching,* 30 (9), 1149–68.

National Council for Educational Technology (NCET) (1994) *Information Technology Works! Stimulate to Educate.* Coventry: NCET.

Naylor, S. and Keogh, B. (2000) *Concept Cartoons in Science Education.* Crewe: Millgate House Publishers.

Newton, L. (1997) Graph talk: some observations and reflections on students' data-logging. *School Science Review,* 79 (287), 49–54.

Newton, L. (2000) Data-logging in practical science: research and reality. *International Journal of Science Education,* 22 (12), 1247–59.

Newton, L. and Rogers, L. (2001) ICT for teaching science – some prospects from research. In L. Newton and L. Rogers. *Teaching Science with ICT.* London: Continuum.

Newton, P. (1997) Measuring comparability of standards between subjects; why our statistical techniques do not make the grade. *British Educational Research Journal,* 23 (4), 433–49.

Newton, P., Driver, R. and Osborne, J. (1999) The place of argumentation in the pedagogy of school science. *International Journal of Science Education,* 21 (5), 553–76.

Noss, R. and Pachler, N. (1999) The challenge of new technologies; doing old things in a new way, or doing new things? In P. Mortimore (ed.) *Understanding Pedagogy and its Impact on Learning.* London: Sage.

Novak, J. (1978) An alternative to Piagetian psychology for science and mathematics education. *Studies in Science Education,* 5, 1–30.

Novick, S. and Nussbaum, J. (1978) Junior high school pupils' understanding of the particulate nature of matter: an interview study. *Science Education*, 62 (3), 273–81.

Nuffield Foundation (1966a) *Chemistry*. London: Longman.

Nuffield Foundation (1966b) *Physics*. London: Longman.

Nuffield Foundation (1972) *Science 5–13*. London: Longman.

Nuffield Foundation (1980) *Nuffield Science 13–16*. York: Longman.

Nussbaum, J. (1979) Children's conception of the earth as a cosmic body: a cross age study. *Science Education*, 63 (1), 83–93.

Nussbaum, J. and Novick. S. (1982) Alternative frameworks, conceptual conflict and accommodation. *Instructional Science*, 11, 183–200.

O'Shea, T., Scanlon, E., Byard, M., Draper, S., Driver, R., Hennessey, S., Harteley, R., O'Malley, C., Mallen, C., Mohammed, G. and Twigger, D. (1993) Twenty-nine children, five computers and a teacher. In D. Edwards, E. Scanlon and R. West (eds) *Teaching, Learning and Assessment in Science Education*. Buckingham: Open University Press.

O'Toole, M. (1996) Science, schools, children and books: exploring the classroom interface between science and language. *Studies in Science Education*, 28, 113–43.

Oakley, A. (2000) *Experiments in Knowing*. Cambridge: Polity Press.

Office for Standards in Education (Ofsted) (1998) *Recent Research on Gender and Educational Performance*. London: The Stationery Office.

Office of Science and Technology and the Wellcome Trust (2000) *Science and the Public: A Review of Science Communication and Public Attitudes to Science in Britain*. London: Office of Science and Technology and the Wellcome Trust.

Ogborn, J. (1990) A future for modelling in science education. *Journal of Computer Assisted Learning*, 6, 103–12.

Ogborn, J. (1997) Constructivist metaphors of learning science. *Science and Education*, 6, 121–33.

Ogborn, J., Kress, G., Martins, I. and McGillicuddy, K. (1996) *Explaining Science in the Classroom*. Buckingham: Open University Press.

Oppenheim, A. (1992) *Questionnaire Design, Interviewing and Attitude Measurement*. London: Pinter.

Organization for Economic Co-operation and Development/Programme for International Student Assessment (OECD/PISA) (2001) *Measuring Student Knowledge and Skills: The PISA 2000 Assessment of Reading, Mathematical and Scientific Literacy*. OECD/PISA.

Ormerod, M. (1973) Social and subject factors in attitude to science. *School Science Review*, 54 (189), 645–60.

Ormerod, M. and Duckworth, D. (1975) *Pupils' Attitudes to Science: A Review of Research*. London: NFER.

Osborne, J. (1996) Beyond constructivism. *Science Education*, 80 (1), 53–82.

Osborne, J. (1997) Practical alternatives. *School Science Review*, 78 (285), 61–6.

Osborne, J. and Collins, S. (2001) Pupils' views of the role and value of the science curriculum. *International Journal of Science Education*, 23 (5), 441–67.

Osborne, J., Driver, R. and Simon, S. (1998) Attitudes to science: issues and concerns. *School Science Review*, 79 (288), 27–33.

Osborne, J., Erduran, S., Simon, S. and Monk, M. (2001) Enhancing the quality of argument in school science. *School Science Review*, 82 (301), 63–70.

Osborne, R. and Freyberg, P. (eds) (1985) *Learning in Science: The Implications of Children's Science.* Auckland: Heinemann.

Osborne, R. and Gilbert, J. (1980) A technique for exploring students' views of the world. *Physics Education*, 15, 376–9.

Osborne, R. and Wittrock, M. (1985) The generative learning model and its implications for science education. *Studies in Science Education*, 12, 59–87.

Papert, S. (1980) *Mindstorms: Children, Computers and Powerful Ideas.* New York: Basic Books.

Parker, L., Rennie, L. and Fraser, B. (eds) (1996) *Gender, Science and Mathematics: Shortening the Shadow.* Dordrecht: Kluwer Academic Publishers.

Parvin, J. (1999) *Children Challenging Industry: The Research Report. A Study of the Effects of Industry-based Science Activities on the Views of Primary School Children and their Teachers of Industry and Science.* York: University of York.

Pea, R., Kurland, M. and Hawkins, J. (1986) LOGO and the development of thinking skills. In K. Sheingold (ed.) *Mirrors of the Mind.* New Jersey: Ablex.

Pfundt, H. and Duit, R. (2000) *Bibliography. Students' Alternative Frameworks and Science Education*, 5th edition. University of Kiel: IPN.

Piaget, J. (1932) *The Moral Judgement of the Child.* London: Routledge and Kegan Paul.

Piaget, J. (1961) The genetic approach to the psychology of thought. *Journal of Educational Psychology*, 52, 275–81.

Piburn, M. and Baker, D. (1993) If I were the teacher: qualitative study of attitude towards science. *Science Education*, 77 (4), 393–406.

Pickersgill, S. and Lock, R. (1991) Student understanding of selected non-technical words in science. *Research in Science and Technological Education*, 9 (1), 71–9.

Pilling, G. (1999) Private communication.

Pilling, G. (2002) Private communication.

Poole, P. (2000) Information and communications technology in science education: a long gestation. In J. Sears and P. Sorensen (eds) *Issues in Science Teaching.* London: RoutledgeFalmer.

Popper, K. (1959) *The Logic of Scientific Discovery.* London: Hutchinson.

Posner, G., Strike, K., Hewson, P. and Gertzog, W. (1982) Accommodation of a scientific conception: towards a theory of conceptual change. *Science Education*, 66 (2), 211–27.

Powney, J. (1996) *Gender and Attainment: A Review.* Edinburgh: Scottish Council for Research in Education.

Prain, V. and Hand, B. (1995) Writing for learning in science. In B. Hand and V. Prain (eds) *Teaching and Learning in Science.* Sydney: Harcourt Brace.

Qualter, A. (1993) I would like to know more about that: a study of the interest shown by girls and boys in scientific topics. *International Journal of Science Education*, 15 (3), 307–17.

Raghaven, K. and Glaser, R. (1995) Model-based analysis and reasoning in science: the MARS curriculum. *Science Education*, 79 (1), 37–61.

Ramsden, J. (1990) All quiet on the gender front? *School Science Review*, 72 (259), 49–55.

Ramsden, J. (1992) If it's enjoyable is it science? *School Science Review*, 73 (265), 65–71.

Ramsden, J. (1994) Context and activity-based science: some teachers' views of the effects on pupils. *School Science Review*, 75 (272), 7–14.

Ramsden, J. (1997) How does a context-based approach influence understanding of key chemical ideas at 16+? *International Journal of Science Education*, 19 (6), 697–710.

Ramsden, J. (1998) Mission impossible: can anything be done about attitudes to science? *International Journal of Science Education*, 20 (2), 125–37.

Reid, D. and Hodson, D. (1987) *Science for All: Teaching Science in the Secondary School*. London: Cassell.

Rennie, L., Parker, L. and Kahle, J. (1996) Informing teaching and research in science education through equity initiatives. In L. Parker, L. Rennie and B. Fraser (eds) *Gender, Science and Mathematics: Shortening the Shadow*. Dordrecht: Kluwer Academic Publishers.

Reynolds, D. and Farrell, S. (1996) *Worlds Apart?: A Review on International Surveys of Educational Achievement Involving England*. London: HMSO.

Rodrigues, S. (1997) The role of IT in secondary school science: an illustrative review. *School Science Review*, 79 (287), 35–40.

Rodrigues, S. and Thompson, I. (2001) Cohesion on science lesson discourse: clarity, relevance and sufficient information. *International Journal of Science Education*, 23 (9), 929–40.

Rogers, L. and Newton, N. (2001) Integrated learning systems – an 'open' approach. *International Journal of Science Education*, 23 (4), 405–22.

Rogers, L. and Wild, P. (1996) Data-logging: effects on practical science. *Journal of Computer Assisted Learning*, 12 (3), 130–45.

Rollnick, M (2000) Current issues and perspectives on second language learning of science. *Studies in Science Education*, 35, 93–122.

Rowell, P. (1997) The promises and practices of writing. *Studies in Science Education*, 30, 19–56.

Roychoudhury, A., Tippins, D. and Nichols, S. (1995) Gender-inclusive science teaching: a feminist-constructivist approach. *Journal of Research in Science Teaching*, 32 (9), 897–924.

Scaife, J. and Wellington, J. (1993) *Information Technology in Science and Technology Education*. Buckingham: Open University Press.

Schibeci, R. (1984) Attitudes to science: an update. *Studies in Science Education*, 11, 26–59.

Schools Examination and Assessment Council (SEAC) (1991) *Assessment Matters. Numbers 1–8*. London: SEAC.

Science Curriculum Improvement Study (SCIS) (1970) *Science Curriculum Improvement Study*. Chicago: Rand McNally.

Scott, P. (1987) *A Constructivist View of Learning and Teaching in Science*. University of Leeds: CLIS Research Group.

Scott, P. (1998) Teacher talk and meaning making in science classrooms: a Vygotskian analysis and review. *Studies in Science Education*, 32, 45–80.

Screen, P. (1986) *Warwick Process Science*. Southampton: Ashford Press.

Secondary Science Curriculum Review (SSCR) (1987) *Better Science: Making it Happen*. London: ASE/Heinemann.

Shapiro, B. (1998) Reading the furniture: the semiotic interpretations of science learning environments. In B. Fraser and K. Tobin (eds) *International Handbook of Science Education*, 609–22.

Shayer, M. (1972) Conceptual demands in the Nuffield 'O' level physics course. *School Science Review*, 54, (186), 26–34.

Shayer, M. (1974) Conceptual demands in the Nuffield 'O' level biology course. *School Science Review*, 56 (195), 381–8.

Shayer, M. (1979) Has Piaget's construct of formal operational thinking any utility? *British Journal of Educational Psychology*, 49, 265–76.

Shayer, M. (1987) Neo-Piagetian theories and educational practice. *International Journal of Psychology*, 22 (5–6), 751–77.

Shayer, M. (1999) Cognitive acceleration through science education II: its effects and scope. *International Journal of Science Education*, 21 (8), 883–902.

Shayer, M. and Adey, P. (1981) *Towards a Science of Science Teaching*. London: Heinemann.

Shayer, M. and Beasley, F. (1987) Does instrumental enrichment work? *British Educational Research Journal*, 13 (2), 101–19.

Shayer, M. and Wharry, D. (1974) Piaget in the classroom, Part 1: testing a whole class at the same time. *School Science Review*, 55 (192), 447–58.

Shayer, M. and Wylam, H. (1978) The distribution of Piagetian stages of thinking in British middle and secondary school children II: 14–16 year olds and sex differentials. *British Journal of Educational Psychology*, 48, 62–70.

Sheeran, Y. and Barnes, D. (1991) *School Writing: Discovering the Ground Rules*. Buckingham: Open University Press.

Shipstone, D. (1985) Electricity in simple circuits. In R. Driver, E. Guesne and A. Tiberghien (eds) *Children's Ideas in Science*. Buckingham: Open University Press.

Shipstone, D., Rhoneck, C., Jung, W., Karrqvist, C., Dupin, J., Joshua, S. and Licht, P. (1989) A study of students' understanding of electricity in five European countries. *International Journal of Science Education*, 10 (3), 303–16.

Shorrocks-Taylor, D., Jenkins, E., Curry, J., Swinnerton, B., Laws, P., Hargreaves, M. and Nelson, N. (1998) *An Investigation of the Performance of English Pupils in the Third International Mathematics and Science Study (TIMSS)*. Leeds: Leeds University Press.

Simon, S. (2000) Students' attitudes towards science. In M. Monk and J. Osborne (eds) *Good Practice in Science Teaching: What Research has to Say*. Buckingham: Open University Press.

Sinclair, J. and Coulthard, M. (1975) *Towards an Analysis of Discourse*. Oxford: Oxford University Press.

Sjøberg, S. (2000) Interesting all children in 'science for all'. In R. Millar, J. Leach and J. Osborne (eds) *Improving Science Education: The Contribution of Research*. Buckingham: Open University Press.

Slater, B. and Thompson, J. (1984) How useful are readability formulae? *Education in Chemistry*, 21, 92–4.

Smail, B. (1984) *Girl-friendly Science: Avoiding Sex Bias in the Curriculum*. York: Longman.

Smail, B. (2000) Has the mountain moved? In K. Myers (ed.) *What Ever Happened to Equal oppurtunities in Schools?: Gender Equality Initiatives in Education*. Buckingham, Open University Press.

Smail, B. and Kelly, A. (1984) Sex differences in science and technology among 11-year-old schoolchildren: II-affective. *Research in Science and Technological Education*, 2 (2), 87–106.

Smedslund, J. (1961) The acquisition of conservation of substance and weight in children I. Introduction. *Scandinavian Journal of Psychology*, 2, 11–20.

Smith, J. (1994) Are students' attitudes to science indicative of their general attitude to school and is there a gender bias in such attitudes? Unpublished MA thesis, University of York.

Smithers, A. and Collings, J. (1981) Girls studying science in the sixth form. In A. Kelly (ed.) *The Missing Half*. Manchester: Manchester University Press.

Solomon, J. (1983) Learning about energy: how pupils think in two domains. *European Journal of Science Education*, 5 (1), 49–59.

Solomon, J. (1992) The classroom discussion of science-based social issues presented on television: knowledge, attitudes and values. *International Journal of Science Education*, 14 (4), 431–44.

Solomon, J. (1993) *Teaching Science, Technology and Society*. Buckingham: Open University Press.

Solomon, J. (1994) The rise and fall of constructivism. *Studies in Science Education*, 23, 1–19.

Solomon. J., Duveen, J., Scott, J. and McCarthy, S. (1992) Teaching about the nature of science through history: action research in the classroom. *Journal of Research in Science Teaching*, 29 (4), 409–21.

Somekh, B. and Davies, N. (1997) Using Information Technology Effectively in Teaching and Learning. London: Routledge.

Spear, M. (1987) Teachers' views on the importance of science to boys and girls. In A. Kelly (ed.) *Science for Girls?* Buckingham: Open University Press.

Staples, R. and Heselden, R. (2001) Science teaching and literacy, part 1: writing. *School Science Review*, 83 (303) 37–46.

Stobart, G. and Gipps, C. (1997) *Assessment: A Teachers' Guide to the Issues*, 3rd edition. London: Hodder & Stoughton.

Supported Learning in Physics Project (SLIP) (1997) *Eight Units for Advanced Level*. Buckingham: Open University Press.

Sutman, F. and Bruce, M. (1992) Chemistry in the Community – ChemCom: a five-year evaluation. *Journal of Chemical Education*, 69 (7), 564–7.

Sutton, C. (1989) Writing and reading in science: the hidden messages. In R.

Millar (ed.) *Doing Science: Images of Science in Science Education*. London: Falmer Press.

Sutton, C. (1992) *Words, Science and Learning*. Buckingham: Open University Press.

Sutton, C. (1996) Beliefs about science and beliefs about language. *International Journal of Science Education*, 18 (1), 1–18.

Swain, J. (1995) Survey on National Curriculum statutory assessment in science. In B. Fairbrother, P. Black and P. Gill (eds) *Teachers Assessing Pupils: Lessons from Science Classrooms*. Hatfield: Association for Science Education.

Swain, J. (2000) Summative assessment in M. Monk and J. Osbourne (eds) *Good Practice in Science Teaching: What Research has to Say*. Buckingham: Open University Press.

Swain, J., Monk, M. and Johnson, S. (1998) A comparative historical review of attitudes to the aims of practical work in science education in England: 1962, 1979 and 1997. Unpublished research paper, King's College London.

Tal, R., Dori, Y., Keiny, S. and Zoller, U. (2001) Assessing conceptual change of teachers involved in STES education and curriculum development – the STEMS project approach. *International Journal of Science Education*, 23 (3), 247–62.

Thiele, R. and Treagust, D. (1991) Using analogies in secondary chemistry teaching. *Australian Science Teachers' Journal*, 37 (1), 10–14.

Third International Mathematics and Science Study (TIMSS) (1996) *Science Achievement in Middle School Years*. Boston, MA: TIMSS International Study Centre.

Third International Mathematics and Science Study (TIMSS) (1997) *Science Achievement in Primary School Years*. Boston, MA: TIMSS International Study Center.

Third International Mathematics and Science Study (TIMSS) (1998) *Mathematics and Science Achievement in the Final Year of Secondary School*. Boston, MA: TIMSS International Study Centre.

Thomas, G. and Durant, J. (1987) Why should we promote the public understanding of science? In M. Shortland (ed.) *Scientific Literacy Papers*. Oxford: University of Oxford Department of External Studies.

Thomson, J. (ed.) (1976) *Practical Work in Sixth Form Science*. Oxford: Department of Educational Studies, University of Oxford.

Thompson, J. (1918) *Report of the Committee to Enquire into the Position of Natural Sciences in the Educational System of Great Britain* (The Thomson Report). London: HMSO.

Tompkins, S. (2000) An investigation of children's understanding of experimental evidence at Key Stage 2. Unpublished MA thesis, University of York.

Tooley, J. and Darbey, D. (1998) *Educational Research: A Critique. A Survey of Published Educational Research*. London: Office for Standards in Education (Ofsted).

Toulmin, S. (1958) *The Use of Argument*. Cambridge: Cambridge University Press.

Tunstall, P. and Gipps, C. (1996) Teacher feedback to young children in formative assessment: a typology. *British Educational Research Journal*, 22 (4), 389–404.

Underwood, J. and Brown, J. (eds) (1997) *Integrated Learning Systems: Potential into Practice.* Oxford: National Council for Educational Technology (NCET)/Heinemann.

University of York Science Education Group (UYSEG) (1984–8) *Chemistry: The Salters Approach: 16 Unit Guides.* York/London: UYSEG/Heinemann Educational.

University of York Science Education Group (UYSEG) (1990–2) *Science: The Salters Approach: 22 Unit Guides for Key Stage 4.* York/Oxford: UYSEG/Heinemann Educational.

University of York Science Education Group (UYSEG) (1992–4) *Science Focus.* Oxford: Heinemann Educational.

University of York Science Education Group (UYSEG) (2000) *Salters Horners Advanced Physics.* Oxford: Heinemann Educational.

University of York Science Education Group (UYSEG) (2001) *QCA Key Stage 4 Curriculum Models Project. A Report to the Qualifications and Curriculum Authority for England and Wales.* York: University of York.

University of York Science Education Group (UYSEG)/The Nuffield Foundation (2002) *Salters Nuffield Advanced Biology (SNAB) Trial Materials.* York: UYSEG/London: The Nuffield Foundation.

Unsworth, L. (2001) Evaluating the language of different types of explanations in junior high school science texts. *International Journal of Science Education*, 23 (6), 585–609.

Valentine, P. (1996) Difficulties in learning science for second language learners. Unpublished MA thesis, University of York.

van Berkel, B. (2000) *Salters Chemistry: A Curriculum Analysis of its Process of Development.* Utrecht: University of Utrecht.

Van Praagh, G. (1973) *H. E. Armstrong and Science Education.* London: John Murray.

Viennot, L. (2001) *Reasoning in Physics: The Part of Common Sense.* Dordrecht: Kluwer Academic Publishers.

von Glasersfeld, E. (1995) *Radical Constructivism.* London: Falmer.

Vygotsky, L. (1962) *Thought and Language.* Cambridge, MA: Massachusetts Institute of Technology.

Vygotsky, L. (1978) *Mind in Society.* London: Phaidon.

Walford, G. (1980) Sex bias in physics textbooks. *School Science Review*, 62 (219), 220–5.

Wall, A. (2002) Using formative assessment to support pupils in setting effective short-term targets. *Education in Science*, 197, 18–19; and also at: www.dfee.gov.uk/bprs/index.cfm

Walton, A. (1986) Women scientists: are they really different?: an exploration of the significance of attitudes. In J. Harding (ed.) *Perspectives on Gender and Science.* London: Falmer Press.

Wason, P. and Johnson-Laird, P. (1972) *Psychology of Reasoning: Structure and Content.* London: Batsford.

Watson, R. (1997) ASE–Kings Science Investigations in School (AKSIS)

project: Investigations at KS2 and KS3. *Education in Science*, 171, 22–3.

Watson, R. (2000) The role of practical work. In M. Monk and J. Osborne (eds) *Good Practice in Science Teaching: What Research has to Say*. Buckingham: Open University Press.

Watson, R. and Fairbrother, R. (1993) Open-ended work in science (OPENS) project: managing investigations in the laboratory. *School Science Review*, 75 (271), 31–8.

Watson, R., Goldsworthy, A. and Wood-Robinson, V. (1998) Getting AKSIS to investigations. *Education in Science*, 177, 20–1.

Watson, R., Goldsworthy, A. and Wood-Robinson, V. (1999) What is not fair with investigations? *School Science Review*, 80 (292), 101–6.

Watson, R., Prieto, T. and Dillon, J. (1995) The effect of practical work on students' understanding of combustion. *Journal of Research in Science Teaching*, 32 (5), 487–502.

Watts, M. (1983) A study of schoolchildren's alterative frameworks of the concept of force. *European Journal of Science Education*, 5 (2), 217–30.

Watts, M., Gould, G. and Alsop, S. (1997) Questions of understanding: categorising pupils' questions in science. *School Science Review*, 79 (286), 57–63.

Weinburgh, M. (1995) Gender differences in student attitudes toward science: a metaanalysis of the literature from 1970 to 1991. *Journal of Research in Science Teaching*, 32 (4), 387–98.

Weiner, G., Arnot, M. and David, M. (1997) Is the future female?: female success, male disadvantage and changing gender patterns in education. In A. Halsey, H. Lauder, P. Brown and A. Stuart Wells (eds) *Education, Economy, Culture and Society*. Oxford: Oxford University Press.

Weinreich-Haste, H. (1986) Brother sun, sister moon: does rationality overcome a dualistic world view? In J. Harding (ed.) *Perspectives on Gender and Science*. London: Falmer Press.

Wellington, J. (1981) 'What's supposed to happen, sir?' – some problems with discovery learning. *School Science Review*, 63 (222), 167–73.

Wellington, J. (1983) A taxonomy of scientific words. *School Science Review*, 64 (229), 767–73.

Wellington, J. (1989) Skills and processes in science education: an introduction. In J. Wellington (ed.) *Skills and Processes in Science Education*. London: Routledge.

Wellington, J. (ed.) (1998) *Practical Work in Science: Which Way Now?* London: Routledge.

Wellington, J. (1999) Integrating multimedia into science teaching: barriers and benefits. *School Science Review*, 81 (295), 49–54.

Wellington, J. (2001) School textbooks and reading in science. *School Science Review*, 82 (300), 71–81.

Wellington, J. and Osborne, J. (2001) *Language and Literacy in Science Education*. Buckingham: Open University Press.

White, R. and Gunstone, R. (1992) *Probing Understanding*. London: Falmer Press.

Whitelegg, E. and Parry, M. (1999) Real-life contexts for learning physics:

meanings, issues and practice. *Physics Education*, 34 (2), 68–72.

Whitfield, R. (1979) Educational research and science teaching. *School Science Review*, 60 (212), 411–30.

Whyte, J. (1986) *Girls into Science and Technology*. London: Routledge.

Wiliam, D. and Black, P. (1996) Meanings and consequences: a basis for distinguishing formative and summative components of assessment. *British Educational Research Journal*, 22 (5), 537–48.

Wilson, J. (1999) Using words about thinking: content analyses of chemistry teachers' classroom talk. *International Journal of Science Education*, 21 (10), 1067–84.

Wood, D. (1998) *How Children Think and Learn*, 2nd edition. Oxford: Blackwell.

Wood-Robinson, C. (1991) Young people's ideas about plants. *Studies in Science Education*, 19, 119–35.

Woodward, C. and Woodward, N. (1998) Girls and science: does a core curriculum in primary school give cause for optimism? *Gender and Education*, 10 (4), 387–400.

Woolnough, B. (1990) *An Enquiry into the Attitude of Sixth-formers towards Choice of Science and Technology Education in Higher Education*. Oxford: Oxford University Department of Educational Studies.

Woolnough, B. (ed.) (1991) *Practical Science*. Buckingham: Open University Press.

Woolnough, B. (1994) *Effective Science Teaching*. Buckingham: Open University Press.

Woolnough, B. and Allsop, T. (1985) *Practical Work in Science*. Cambridge: Cambridge University Press.

Wray, D. and Lewis, M. (1997) *Extending Literacy: Children Reading and Writing Non-fiction*. London: Routledge.

Wray, J. (ed.) (1987) *Science in Process*. London: Heinemann.

Yager, R. and Casteel, J. (1968) The University of Iowa science and culture project. *School Science and Mathematics*, 67 (5), 412–16.

Yager, R., Englen, H. and Snider, B. (1969) Effect of laboratory and demonstration methods upon the outcomes of instruction in secondary biology. *Journal of Research in Science Teaching*, 6, 76–86.

Index

Page numbers in **bold** refer to whole chapters.
Page numbers in *italics* refer to boxed summaries.